TERRITORIAL POWER DOMAINS, SOUTHEAST ASIA, AND CHINA
The Geo-Strategy of an Overarching Massif

The aim of the **Strategic and Defence Studies Centre**, which was set up in the Research School of Pacific Studies in The Australian National University, is to advance the study of strategic problems, particularly those relating to the general region of the Indian and Pacific Oceans and Southeast Asia. Participation in the Centre's activities is not limited to members of the University, but includes other interested professional and Parliamentary groups. Research includes not only military, but political, economic, scientific and technological aspects. Strategy, for the purpose of the Centre, is defined in the broadest sense of embracing not only the control and application of military force, but also the peaceful settlement of disputes which could cause violence. This is the only academic body in Australia which specialises in these studies.

The **Institute of Southeast Asian Studies** was established as an autonomous organization in May 1968. It is a regional research centre for scholars and other specialists concerned with modern Southeast Asia. The Institute's research interest is focused on the many-faceted problems of development and modernization, and political and social change in Southeast Asia.

The Institute is governed by a twenty-two-member Board of Trustees on which are represented the National University of Singapore, appointees from the government, as well as representatives from a broad range of professional and civic organizations and groups. A ten-man Executive Committee oversees day-to-day operations; it is chaired by the Director, the Institute's chief academic and administrative officer.

The responsibility for facts and opinions expressed in this publication rests exclusively with the author and his interpretations do not necessarily reflect the views or the policy of the Institute, the Centre, or their supporters.

TERRITORIAL POWER DOMAINS, SOUTHEAST ASIA, AND CHINA
The Geo-Strategy of an Overarching Massif

Lim Joo-Jock

Published by the

**Regional Strategic Studies Programme
Institute of Southeast Asian Studies, Singapore**

and the

**Strategic and Defence Studies Centre
Australian National University**

Published by
Institute of Southeast Asian Studies
Heng Mui Keng Terrace
Pasir Panjang
Singapore 0511

UA
830
.L56
1984

All rights reserved. No part of this publication may be reproduced, stored in a retrieval system, or transmitted in any form or by any means, electronic, mechanical, photocopying, recording or otherwise, without the prior permission of the Institute of Southeast Asian Studies.

© 1984 Institute of Southeast Asian Studies

ISBN 9971-902-85-0 (hard cover)

ISBN 9971-902-89-3 (soft cover)

Contents

	Page
Introduction	xi
Chapter One THE MOUNTAINS, WARFARE, AND THE MINORITIES	1
Chapter Two INTERACTION BETWEEN LOWLANDER AND HIGHLANDER	23
Chapter Three INTERSTATE BOUNDARIES AND THE FRONTIERS	51
Chapter Four BOUNDARIES AS SYMBOLS IN INTERNATIONAL RELATIONS	67
Chapter Five POWER AND ITS TERRITORIAL BASIS	85
Chapter Six TERRITORIAL POWER, POWER ISOBARS, AND CORE AND PERIPHERAL DOMAINS	101
Chapter Seven DEVELOPMENTAL AND STRATEGIC ISSUES IN THE FRAME OF CORE AND PERIPHERAL DOMAINS	124
Chapter Eight OPIUM IN THE HIGHLAND ECONOMY, PERIPHERALITY, AND POLITICAL CONSOLIDATION	138

Chapter Nine
GEO-POWER, NATIONAL POWER, AND REGIONAL STABILITY 167

Chapter Ten
THE POST-1975 POWER SITUATION IN "INDOCHINA" 187

Conclusion: Southeast Asia and China 207

Bibliography 215

Index 230

Preface

If the rulers of Nanchao — that long vanished kingdom — had published a map of what they saw as the world around them, they would have left for posterity a depiction of a rugged corner of Asia, not as a rejected backwater which it has been for centuries, but as a centrepiece around which momentous events revolved. It is this perceived centrality of the mountains north of Southeast Asia which is basic to the theme of this book.

This is an attempt to rectify, in a small way, the relative neglect of a little-known region between China and Southeast Asia. Here kingdoms have risen and fallen and here civilizations have sprung, flourished, matured, and decayed. It is a region normally poor, and now made poorer in many parts by the ravages of war. Much has taken place within its confines and this book will try to show that it is worthy of study as a regional entity *per se*.

The pale silhouettes of the mountains looming north of places like Chiengmai or Taunggyi and stretching in desolate tangles northwards into China have exerted a fascination on many. The flavour of the place is uniquely compelling. Much of this comes from the inhabitants and their culture. To hear, for example, some plaintive, even soporific, snatches of a Tai or Shan tune, and to feel the wild exuberance of a H'mong song shouted from the mountain tops is perhaps one way of knowing the region's pulse. Many years ago, I first heard such a hillman's song, not in the fresh, cloud-swept uplands, but in a grimy back street of Kuala Lumpur, where an old, blind and half-starved Hakka Chinese, in the hope of a few cents, sang interminable songs of human hope and despair in tunes which the Hakka refer to as "mountain song". Ever since then that faraway heap of mountains and its people have not ceased to draw my attention.

The mountain region is poor and grossly underdeveloped and has always been subject to more powerful forces, such that the interests of the inhabitants have been for long subordinated to those of outsiders. This book will try to demonstrate the crucial role which this area, and its often rejected peoples, can play in the power equilibrium of a far wider region, and to amplify on the hypothesis that many of the kinds of policies evident especially since the end of World War II may in fact be self-defeating.

"A man in authority who oppresses poor people is like a driving rain that destroys the crops."
(*The Book of Proverbs*, Chapter 28, Verse 3.)

★ ★ ★

A wide variety of sources have been relied upon. Data gathered has covered many fields of study. In the analysis that follows I have chosen, with some hesitation, to deal with the wide-ranging nature of the data, on a sectional basis, with each section given an appropriate subtitle. In this I would ask for the reader's indulgence, for it is realized that such a layout may give a staccato effect and can lack the smooth flow of a continuous narrative.

As for nomenclature, in order to relieve monotony, I have felt free to use many terms and names interchangeably. Thus Beijing, the PRC, and China mean the same thing, as does Miao and H'mong and so on. Tai is generally used for the Tai-speakers of the upland valleys often outside Thailand, while Thai is used for the lowland dwellers of the Kingdom of Thailand. Usually Cambodia is used for the country and Khmer for the people. The metric system is adhered to as far as possible.

It remains for me to acknowledge, and to give thanks, to my teacher and counsellor, Yahweh Yireh Rabboni, without whose constant and unfailing help this book would not have seen the light of day. To my family, Gueh Ee, Mei-Yi and Ken and our unity, I owe much. The Strategic and Defence Studies Centre, Research School of Pacific Studies, Australian National University generously extended me a visiting fellowship in 1983, during five months of which I was given every possible help to complete the manuscript. I am also grateful to the

Preface

City Uniting Church for the warmth of fellowship during that frosty yet strangely sunlit, tree-scented, and curiously colourful winter in Canberra.

LIM JOO-JOCK

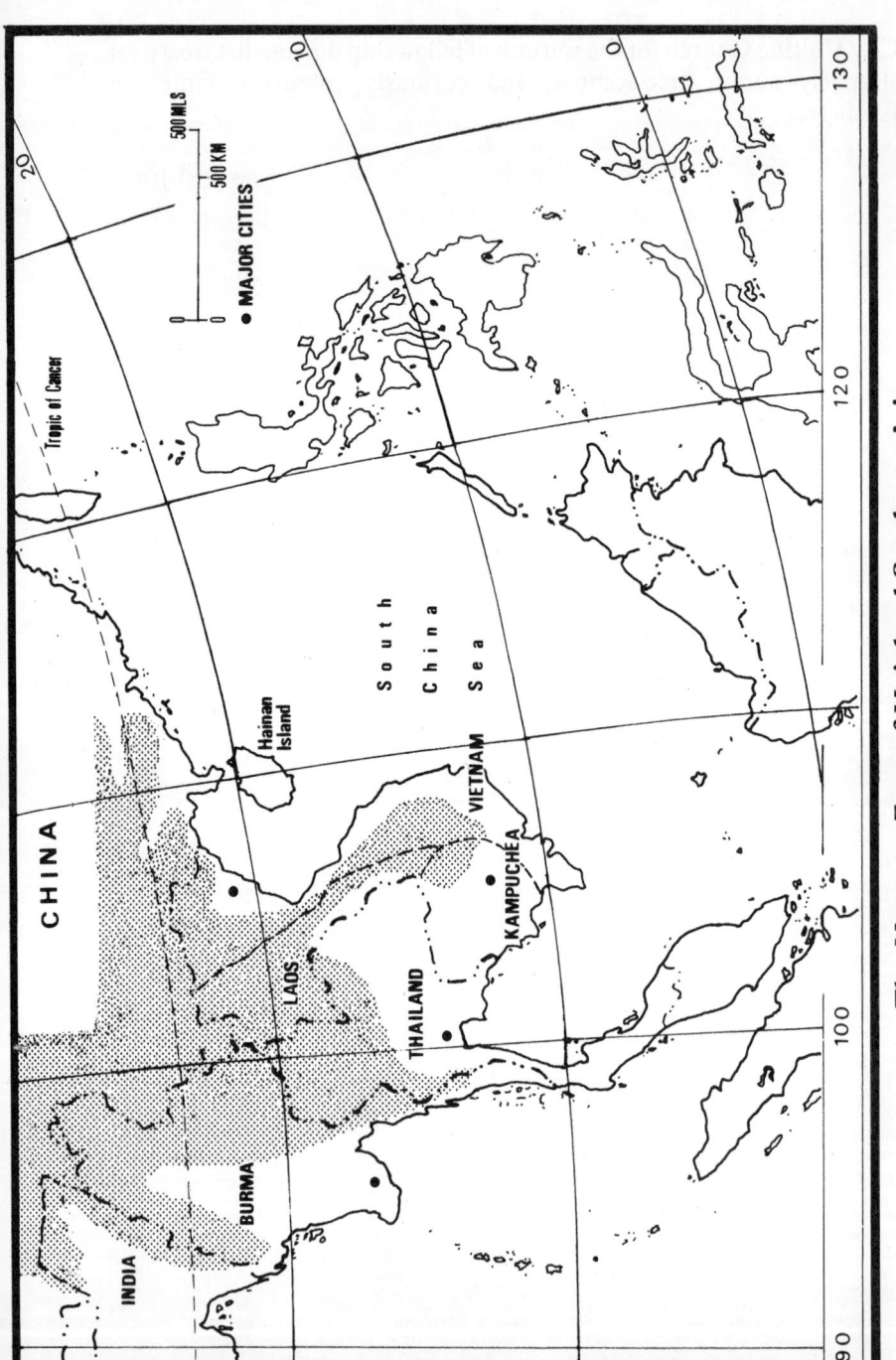

The Montane Zone of Mainland Southeast Asia

Introduction

This study deals with the general topic of China and mainland Southeast Asia and the territorial power relationships that are involved. It does not purport, however, to cover all aspects of the bilateral and multilateral relationships that exist between China and the various states of mainland Southeast Asia. Attention is given to the qualitative manifestations of territorial power as they occur in the region.

The subject is viewed largely within a geo-strategic frame. The term "geo-strategy", as given here, is used in a regional frame "wherein the sum of geographic factors interact to influence or to give advantage to one adversary or intervene to modify strategic planning as well as political and military venture" (Lim Joo-Jock, *Geo-Strategy and the South China Sea Basin* [Singapore, 1979], p. 4). While this present study does focus to a considerable extent on geo-political relationships and the role of the "traditional" factors of geo-politics — size and location of territory; shape of territory; transportation; possession of coastlines and access to the sea; population; agricultural, industrial, and human resources — it does not do so to the exclusion of other factors such as the economic, the socio-cultural, the ethnic, the military, and the attitudes and opinions which help shape a nation's policies.

Within this framework, the study is thus an attempt at a cross-disciplinary approach to the analysis of strategic problems. There is some emphasis on the analytical tools which are normally, though not exclusively, associated with the systematic study of issues in a geo-political setting. With this orientation, the approach itself is an attempt to view as a single entity the large stretch of mountainous territory between northeastern India and the Tonkin highlands on the one hand and the area between China and its southern neighbours, referred to in this study as the southern lowland states, on the other. This seemingly amorphous zone, divided as it is between six states — India, Burma, Thailand, Laos, Cambodia (to a limited extent), Vietnam, and China — does not appear to have been studied as a strategic region before. Put in another way, six states have a share in this massif. Here their territories are in contact and their interests meet in conflict or co-operation. There is a need to study this zone of physical convergence.

Even in nomenclature it has been found to be elusive. The term "Indochina", which is all the land between India and China, is a rough approximation; however, the more precise term "the mountainous northern zone of Indochina" is rather clumsy. Kipling in his famous poem "On the Road to Mandalay" refers to Burma, and presumably to the whole of Indochina, as Outer China. Bernatzik in his monograph on *The Akha and the Miao* refers to the whole region, as have British writers before him, as Further India. The difficulty is seen when E.R. Leach, in his penetrating anthropological study, *The Frontiers of 'Burma'*, first published in 1960, proposed the term "Burma" to cover the entire zone, in the mountains of which, as distinct from the lowlands, he saw a certain unity with its special pecularities of political organization, culture, ethnicity, and economic activity. As a corollary to this unity which he saw Leach pointed to the sharp differentiation in culture and social organization existing between mountain and plain. In this present study, the term "montane mainland southeast Asia" is most often used. Though not the most concise or elegant of terms, it has at least the advantage of greater precision than the other definitions.

Studies of the area (with exceptions such as Leach's) have largely been confined to one country or one set of countries as defined by their international boundaries. Examples are Herold Wiens' 1954 work *China's March to the Tropics* and George V.H. Moseley III's study *Consolidation of the South China Frontier*, published in 1973. These two studies are, as indicated by their titles, confined to China. Studies from the southern or the Southeast Asian angle are similarly framed within the confines of single countries or groups of countries. This includes earlier historical works such as G.E. Harvey's book on the history of Burma. However, because Burma's boundary was then ill-defined and a source of contention between the British and the Chinese, Harvey's study did include the Chinese-administered tracts adjoining Burma. Herein lies the essence of the matter. The very nature of the country, as explained in this present study, hinders any reliance on boundaries, or rather the spatial units within these boundaries, as an exclusive basis for interpretation. While this study does not go so far as to reject the existence or the function and usefulness of international boundaries, it pays, what is here thought to be much-needed attention to the elements of homo-

Introduction　　　　　　　　　　　　　　　　　　　　　　　　xiii

geneity of the montane region as a whole. Due cognizance is given not only to the way the boundaries divide this region, but also to the units or parts of the region enclosed by boundaries. Evidence is presented to show, in both the historical and modern contexts, the limited nature of the dividing function of the boundaries in terms of the interplay of power relationships in the region. The basic unit of analysis in this study is therefore the geographically-defined montane region of mainland Southeast Asia as a whole.

The study begins with a brief review of the relationship between terrain and warfare, and proceeds to examine the linkage between mountain dwellers, who are minorities in the states they inhabit, and the conduct of warfare. It then goes on in the second chapter to study the main outlines of the relationships that exist, and have existed, between plainsmen and highlanders. These majority–minority relations are viewed in the light of the political and strategic issues facing the region. The next two chapters deal with the condition and the strategic significance of international boundaries in the region.

This is followed by a discussion on the territorial bases of power and the concept of spatial power domains, with the implications of separation, in terms of power, of the core from the periphery. Some examples of the application of this perception of differentiation to contemporary strategic problems are given. It should be noted that the use of the concept of core and periphery is not connected with what can be termed the dependency schools of thought which place emphasis on the relationship of dependence of the periphery on the centre. Here the focus is instead on the varying degrees of power which are available to a state with large tracts of territory of differing strategic characteristics, and which are manifested in the core–periphery dichotomy.

The differing attitudes and policies to the highlands, the highland inhabitants, and their resources are analysed, with emphasis on the various methods by which states increase their power through control of the highland areas. The widely differing reactions of states to the strategic environment of the highlands are discussed. The next chapter proceeds to examine the applications of various forms of power in the light of aggregate national power and the maintenance of stability in the region. The post-1975 power situation in mainland Southeast Asia is discussed in this connection.

The study concludes with a summary of the thrust of the argument and indicates the need to view definitions of regionality in flexible terms. It also stresses the uniqueness of the strategic environment of the montane zone of mainland Southeast Asia, and this is, to a large degree, a study of power. More specifically, it is, in part at least, a study of the territorial foundations of power. Here an attempt has been made to examine and, where possible and relevant, to apply the concepts developed by sociologists, political scientists, political geographers, and those concerned with the study of international affairs and power relationships. The concepts and perceptions advanced by Karl Deutsch and E.R. Leach have proved basic and seminal to this essay. The works and theories of Jean Gottman, C.P. Fitzgerald, Owen Lattimore, and Robert Sack, and the research of Robert Solomon, John T. McAlister, Jr., and Moseley, among others, have been used and have proved invaluable in this attempt at refining a geo-strategic concept of the territorial variations of power. The works of many other scholars and writers on the region have also been used and are duly acknowledged in the course of the study. The concepts put forward by geographers, have been fundamental to the approach used. Generally, this study comprises an effort to unify, in the context of Southeast Asia, the various concepts, notably Deutsch's power domain theory, with the work of those like Gottmann who have studied the implications of the differentiation between core and periphery. This has been done in order to relate the strategic function of land space more directly to the issues of the genesis of power and its exercise in international relations.

While much attention is given to the regionality *per se* of montane mainland Southeast Asia and its strategic role in the wider region around it, it is not the sole purpose of this book to examine the strategic issues of the region thus defined, as an end in itself, and to go no further. Having proposed a method of analysing the territorial bases of power and its variations, the study goes on in a modest way to apply this to the contemporary situation of the late 1970s and the early 1980s, especially in the framework of the power relationships existing between states of the region. In the course of this, it also examines the validity of the analytical separation of regionally "internal", and "external" factors in the understanding of the strategic affairs of Southeast Asia.

This study offers a framework for analysis, which it is hoped will be enduring, rather than ephemeral. In this connection, while contemporary data is used wherever possible as illustrative material, the purpose of the book is not a chronological compilation of current events. What it does try to give is a conceptual frame within which the multifarious elements and issues of the strategic situation of the region can be usefully ordered, and thus be more easily comprehended. If this is achieved, even in a very limited way, then it is felt that perhaps there has been some purpose in the effort expended in writing this book.

CHAPTER *1*

The Mountains, Warfare, and the Minorities

This chapter deals with the relationships existing between terrain and the conduct of war, and the role of minorities and "ethnicity"[1] in military and political affairs.

Geo-Strategy and Montane Southeast Asia

The main theme devolves around the place of the highlands in the strategic environment of the region. The highland zone in question stretches from Assam in northeastern India through northern and northeastern Burma, comprising the partly Shan-populated areas bordering on China and Thailand, and sweeping again through northern and north-northeastern Thailand and Laos to the uplands of northern Vietnam. From the northern highlands of Vietnam the belt stretches through the Annamite chain southwards to the rugged dissected plateaux and ridges of the Vietnamese south, named during the Vietnam War as the "Central Highlands" of South Vietnam. This southward extension of the montane belt is paralleled in the western portion of the region by the mainly Chin-inhabited Arakan Yoma of Burma, the Karen-inhabited highlands which stretch southwards from the main body of the high region under study and which lie between Burma and Thailand, as well as the mountains rimming the Cambodian basin. All these southward extensions can be considered outliers of the main montane belt of mainland Southeast Asia. Its northern limits stretch well into southern and southwestern China and include large tracts of Sichuan and Guangdong provinces, as well as all, or nearly all of Yunnan, Guizhou, and Guangxi. This mountain zone is approximately 1300 to 1500 km. from east to west and at its broadest is about 950 km. from north to south, that is if the southward protruding

1

extensions are excluded. Although referred to as a massif, it is in fact topographically a southeasterly extension of the Tibetan and west Sichuan ranges. Most of it lies in China.

This study will attempt to show that this montane belt *per se* has distinctive strategic features which have to be considered in any study of the interrelated areas of geopolitics, strategic affairs, and international relations of the region. The analysis is from the viewpoint of the place of the highlands in the aggregate of regional affairs, rather than from the perspective of any one of the countries concerned.

Topography and Military Affairs

The role of geography and terrain in the flux of relations between states has been recognized as being crucial at various times in history. Examples abound: Britain's geopolitical advantage springing from her offshore location in Western Europe stood her in good stead in the era of competitive maritime expansion by European states; the vastness and location of China and Russia were important, if not crucial in their resistance to Japanese and German invaders, respectively, in World War II. Narrowing down the geographical factor to the issue of terrain alone, suffice it to give two examples here: the Hellenic defence of Thermopylae and the maintenance of their freedom by the Swiss in their mountain-locked cantons, both of which are well-known.

There are equally valid examples which show human endeavour overcoming natural obstacles. These are Hannibal's Alpine crossing, the trans-Himalayan invasion and devastation by the Qing of the "Gurkha"-inhabited southern slopes, the 1962 People's Republic of China (PRC) mountain campaign against the Indian Army, the episode of Mao's Long March, and the North Vietnamese movement along the Ho Chi Minh Trail.

While geographical factors, like terrain, climate, and vegetation, do not necessarily determine the course or outcome of conflict and war, the influences they exercise on warfare is often considerable and are neglected only at considerable risk. This may appear trite, but there is sufficient evidence to indicate that lessons learned in wars in difficult geographical environments have been ignored and the same mistakes repeated in later campaigns. The British and the Dutch in their Kandyan campaigns were impeded and suffered losses because of their unsuitable clothing, weaponry, and other equipment.[2] The inability or refusal to adapt infantry equipment including uniforms, headgear, and footwear to special conditions was a mistake repeated again by the

British and the Australian forces in the Japanese invasion of Malaya in 1941–42.

Terrain and Power

The early unification of China, under Ch'in Shih-huangti, the First Emperor of the Ch'in, has been recognized as being partly due at least to the geopolitical advantages of location within a mountain-ringed upland area, accessible only through one, easily defended pass. This has been alluded to in commentaries on the history of early China.

In a motley collection of small states at the time of Confucius in the sixth century B.C., China was, in the period of the Three Kingdoms, composed of a number of autonomous states "engaged in a constant struggle for expansion or survival. The number of these states eventually narrowed to half a dozen, among which the most powerful were Ch'i in the northeast, Ch'u in the south and Ch'in in the west. This last, with its capital in the so-called area within the Pass, near present-day Sian in Shansi, continued to grow in size and power until, under the leadership of the famous Ch'in Shih-huangti, or First Emperor of the Ch'in, it succeeded in 221 B.C. in conquering the other states and uniting China under one rule."[3] Easily defensible terrain added to the power of the Ch'in state.

Topography and the Vietnam War

Much more recently, the Vietnam Wars lasting approximately three decades up until 1975 witnessed the tactical use of terrain to the fullest advantage of the side which better understood its relevance to modern warfare. The advantages of use of high ground were amply demonstrated many times in Vietnam. The most dramatic instance of this was the Vietminh victory at the battle of Dien Bien Phu, where the defenders of strongly fortified and defended low-lying positions were forced into surrender by adversaries ensconced on heights commanding the plain of Dien Bien Phu. It has been said that the French commander, General Henri Navarre, had not known of a principle from a classic Chinese military manual which runs as follows, "Never fight on terrain which looks like a tortoise turned upside down. Never camp there for long."[4] The French had miscalculated the role of terrain at Dien Bien Phu whereas the Vietminh had put it to tactical use, thereby bringing about the turning point of the first Indochina War.

Nor did the French planners, relying on what they thought to be their superior fire-power and preoccupied with building and holding an airstrip for re-supply, seem to recall Machiavelli's advice to military commanders to take advantage of heights and to avoid locations dominated by higher ground. "[T]he most important point is not to gather your army on a plain situated at the foot of a mountain which the enemy might be able to occupy unimpeded; for with his artillery he would crush you from the neighbouring heights ... ceaselessly ... embarrassed by your own troops, you would find it impossible to harm him."[5] This condition was clearly discernible in the defence of the besieged French garrison in Dien Bien Phu, when the airstrip came under Vietminh artillery fire from the surrounding heights.

Terrain and Other Factors in Geo-Strategy

What had been neglected at Dien Bien Phu had been evident to the British in their colonial wars of the nineteenth century. The importance of maximizing the tactical use of terrain was reiterated by the injunction to control any heights overlooking the line of movement or the bivouacking of troops.

"Hill-men moreover always retire to the high ground when the troops advance against villages or show disposition for a fight. As a result, what is technically known as 'crowning the heights', is at almost all times an essential part of any operation in hill warfare...."[6] The British colonial experience of the peculiarities of irregular warfare in hilly or mountainous terrain was extensive enough for the proposal to be put forward that hill warfare by itself be considered a separate subject in military studies.[7]

In view of the evidence from the past on the important, if not crucial, role of topography in war, it is not surprising that the early 1980s saw a resurgence, for example, in the U.S. Army, in the analysis of terrain as a factor in warfare, and "the recognition of terrain as a potential multiplier of combat power...."[8] As with the Ch'in State of China, the influence of terrain on the alignment and nature of routes is important. In fact, it has been asserted that "... [w]ars are largely battles for routes...."[9] Especially for large conventional armies, the mountains of mainland Southeast Asia, like any extensive mountainous area, pose added hazards when dependence on logistical re-supply is vital to continued operations.

In this study, however, the geographical element in the geopolitical and strategic situation includes not only the factors of topography or terrain and position, but also such factors as population, cultural differences, and resources. This would comply with the wider definitions of geography embracing ethno-geography and the consideration of natural resources. The eclectic approach adopted by some political geographers should be noted, as it is relevant to many areas of strategic study and analysis. For example, it has been said that: "The political geographer, concerned as he is primarily with place and space relations, cannot ignore the human realities which give uniqueness to the many Asian societies and conditions their politics. Some review of the historical and social factors is therefore necessary for the disentangling of the more important interlaced patterns."[10] Of the human realities that have influenced, possibly even conditioned, much of the politics of mainland Southeast Asia, there is perhaps none more outstanding than the reality of the existence of the minorities in the mountains.

Strategic Importance of the Mountain Minorities

The use of the term "minority" in both popular writing and scholarly studies denotes ethnic or tribal groups who are minorities in the total population. In the post-war period many of these such groups in the various states that comprise mainland Southeast Asia have taken up arms against their respective governments.

Ethnically- or minority-based insurgencies have been a constant feature of mainland Southeast Asia since the colonial withdrawal. It would be useful, therefore, to begin by first examining some features of the montane belt and its inhabitants which are closely related to insurgency and conflict in the mountains. The durability of some of these insurgencies would indicate the need to understand them in the context of the environment in which they operate.

Furthermore, the role of the minorities in large-scale conflict between conventional armies can be of considerable importance. Of the Nagas, it has been stated that during World War II ". . . the British succeeded in enlisting their cooperation against the Japanese. Without this help from the Nagas, Kohima would have fallen into Japanese hands, and the way into the plains of Assam would have been thrown open."[11] The place in warfare of minorities inhabiting inhospitable regions deserves attention and will now be looked into in some detail.

The Long March and the Minorities

Mao Zedong has often been quoted as saying men are more important than arms. People are also as important as topography. The existence of friendly, and helpful, groups living in remote areas of difficult terrain is a factor decidedly in favour of any insurgency operating against the central authorities of the states which occupy mainland Southeast Asia. The undoubtedly localized power of the insurgent group is enhanced by having access to, if not control, of the assets of the indigenous ethnic group. Thus a mountain minority could provide manpower for porterage and even riflemen. It could also be a source of food supply. These sources may not be either large or continuous, yet they can be critical, for though small in amount, deliveries of food supplied at crucial moments could ensure the survival of roving insurgent units.

The provision of guides embodies both the physical as well as the intangible resources of such groups. The guide himself represents the physical resources of manpower, but probably more crucial both in this instance and in the overall context of military movements in contested areas is the guide's knowledge of the local terrain and routes. The skills of mountain minorities are especially useful in insurgent warfare. Denial of such resources would hamper military operations to groups external to the area. This was what happened to the Red Army when Mao Zedong undertook that part of his Long March across the rugged country of Yunnan and Sichuan. A brief recapitulation of these events would be useful in setting the background to the theme of this study.

Passage of the Red Army in flight from the forces of the Guomindang through the mountains of Guizhou and Yunnan were facilitated by overtures of friendship towards the Miao (or H'mong) and the Shan. The Luoluos of Yunnan, who had strong antipathies to the Chinese, were armed with flintlocks and other weapons, and thus would have proved to be formidable enemies to Chinese armies moving slowly with their baggage trains through the mountainous Luoluo homeland.

To overcome this hostility, however, Liu Bocheng in Yunnan sealed an alliance with one of the Luoluo tribes by following their customs and drinking rooster's blood and swearing brotherhood with the chief.[12]

In the course of the Long March, a formidable barrier existed in the densely forested and steep mountain ranges of Sichuan parallelling the course of the Yangzijiang as the river sweeps in a broad arc southwards in the area just east of the Tibetan borderlands. This mountainous obstacle had to be surmounted before the vital crossing of the river Dadu. The negotiations for a joint alliance and uncontested passage through the Luoluo-inhabited mountains observed two principles in addition to the required observance of Luoluo rituals. These two principles were embodied in the negotiations which were held in the Luoluo tongue, and a pronouncement by the Chinese communist policy of autonomy for all national minorities. Not only was the march through the area uncontested, but some Luoluo even joined the ranks of the up to then almost entirely Han-manned Red Army. The Red Army was guided by Luoluos safely across the mountains to emerge out of the forest and to take the Dadu river crossing largely by surprise.

By contrast, further on in the high marshy grasslands in the plateau on the Tibet-Sichuan borderlands, an example of minority hostility took a dramatic turn in the form of heavy casualties suffered by the Red Army. This episode is vividly described by Edgar Snow.[13]

The terrain that had to be crossed in the final phase of the Long March "led through wild country inhabited by the independent Mantzu tribesmen, and the nomadic Hsifan, a warring people of eastern Tibet, passing through . . . the Reds for the first time faced a populace united in its hostility to them, and their suffering on this part of the trek exceeded anything in the past. They had money, but could not buy food. They had guns, but their enemies were invisible."[14]

In addition to having to cross the rushing headwaters of several major rivers and traversing upland grass-covered marshes where men sank out of sight, their difficulties were compounded by the disappearance of all sources of food. In this variant of the "scorched earth" tactics, the tribesmen drove their cattle and poultry to the higher elevations, stripped their villages bare, carrying off in their retreat all available food. No guides were to be had and there were constant sniping and ambushes by the hostile tribesmen. Deprived of food by hostile minority action, the Red troops even had to eat their horses and then went on to consume their leather shoes and belts. Many troops died from eating poisonous plants.

The final stages of the forced march to cross the grassy upland bogs began with a force of about 30,000.[15] The difficulties were of such magnitude that only 7,000 or 8,000 men emerged from the ordeal.[16] Had the Mantzu and Hsifan been friendly, or even neutral, such heavy losses need not have been incurred.

It would be all too easy to dwell on the heroics and the organizational skills which were undoubtedly important and enabled the Red Army to survive the Long March. This is often the case with accounts of the March and the tendency is to overlook the wider strategic factors which were mainly topographical and ethno-geographical. The upland bogs, a morass where men disappeared into the mud, were a formidable obstacle. But just as important, if not more so, was the fact that some of the non-Han minorities living in the upland marshes of Sichuan proved hostile to all Chinese, and were unconvinced that the Red Army was any different from other Chinese. This is an example of widespread highlander hostility to lowlanders who are regarded as intruders and exploiters. In the course of the Long March, it was this attitude of the mountain people, and not the activities of the Guomindang, which was important. The determination of the highlanders not to co-operate with the intruders was in military terms close to decisive in the attempted elimination of the Red Army.

The morale and will of the Red Army and its leadership proved decisive in the end. But with a less determined army the terrain and the hostility of the inhabitants would have aborted the Long March. This was in fact the conclusion which the Guomindang commanders reached.

The example of the Long March shows most of the strategic elements encountered in minority-inhabited highlands. Most of these exist in the montane zone of Southeast Asia abutting as it does upon the highlands of South and Southwest China. However, in mainland Southeast Asia these elements, both in terms of the inhospitality of the terrain and the ferocity as of the Mantzu and Hsifan minority resistance, are more muted than in China. Nevertheless the co-operation forthcoming from minorities is important to all governments which have dealings with the highlands.

Although the Long March is probably an extreme case, involving an army in flight, this kind of experience would no doubt have left an indelible mark in the minds of the leaders of the Red Army and later the leadership of the People's Republic of China (PRC) as to the strategic importance of the hitherto neglected minorities living in their mountainous southern and southwestern borderlands.

The experience of Mao Zedong and his followers during the Long March, it can be argued, impressed on them the importance of a supportive attitude on the part of the minorities, particularly the mountain minorities of South and Southwest China. The communist policy of reconciliation to cultural minorities had been explained to the leaders of the various groups whose territory had been traversed by the Red Army. Apart from any possible question of gratitude, the formation of the PRC saw the implementation of the promised autonomy, in varying degrees, for the more sizeable minority groups dwelling in the mountains.

Minorities and the Strategic Affairs of Laos and Cambodia

Experience in countries other than China gives further support to the importance of the attitude of the inhabitants of mountain areas in warfare, especially in guerrilla wars of survival. It should be noted again that in the highlands of what would be termed the lowland or southern states of mainland Southeast Asia, the terrain does not approach the ruggedness seen in Sichuan. Nevertheless, the mountains and their inhabitants are important in the current strategic environment.

In Cambodia, for example, Sihanouk has stressed that Pol Pot's survival during his resistance against Lon Nol and later the Khmer Rouge resistance against Vietnam's occupation, relied heavily on the support of about 150,000 members of the highland minorities living in and scattered around the guerrilla sanctuary areas of the uplands rimming the central Cambodian plain.

> The majority of the mountaineers support Pol Pot because during his fighting against Sihanouk, Pol Pot stayed with them in the mountains for quite a long time. The sanctuaries of Pol Pot and of the Vietnamese, who helped Pol Pot in the beginning, were in Ratanakiri, Mondolkiri and in the mountain regions, like in the Cardamon mountains.[17]

The Vietnamese in their efforts to subdue Khmer Rouge resistance, and with their previous experience in Cambodia during the wars against Lon Nol and the United States, have also realized the value of these groups and, accordingly, compete with Khmer Rouge for the allegiance of the hill folk. "In the Northeastern Provinces of Cambodia, i.e., in Stung Treng, Mondolkiri, Ratanakiri and Kratie, the Vietnamese and Heng Samrin have one part of the mountaineers on their side and the Pol Potians the other."[18] In the Khmer Rouge strongholds near the Thai border, that is, in the provinces of Pursat, Battambang, and Koh Kong, partly or wholly forested and mountainous, "Pol Pot alone has contact with the small tribes, the minorities. . . ."[19] This situation incorporating linkages between mountain minorities and resistance forces is a re-enaction of a theme consistent with armed dissidence in Southeast Asia.

In Laos, the Pathet Lao relied on the mountain dwelling groups for the bulk of their manpower. It was in the mountains, too, that the Pathet Lao mainly operated during the Indochina War. It has been observed that "[I]n large measure the Laotian Communist movement appears to be based not on the ethnic Laotian lowlanders but on many of the minorities of Laos — Thai, Meo and Malayo-Polynesian (i.e., *Kha* Lao for slave) peoples".[20] The United States competed successfully with the Pathet Lao for the allegiance of the Miao (or H'mong) of Laos.

Minorities in the Franco-Vietminh War

The Vietnamese too have experienced the help of mountain people in their struggle against the French. The importance, strategically and tactically, to military operations in rugged country inhabited by cultural groups co-operating with one or the other of the protagonists was demonstrated forcibly in the 1950s during the Vietminh war against France. One of the most dramatic demonstrations of the strategic importance of the ethnic minorities in mountain warfare occurred in mountains rimming the northern edge of the Red River Delta during the first Indochina War.

The cultural group referred to as the Tho live in rough mountain terrain between the Tonkin delta and Vietnam's boundary with the PRC. The Tho are also referred to as Tay, a Sino-Vietnamese term for "soil", used sometimes to refer to anyone living in remote areas. Vietnamese sources place the current Tho population at around 800,000. The Tho are the most Vietnamized of the hills peoples.[21] The Tho territory was located favourably in strategic terms of the Vietnamese resistance against the returning French colonial power. During the Vietminh phase of the Indochina wars it was not only important as a close-to-the-border sanctuary but its possession also meant control of a re-supply route from China to the plains of North Vietnam. It had a decided advantage over other defended highland areas because it was within a short distance from the urban areas of the Tonkin delta with its densely populated rice-growing plains, yet it was at the same time contiguous to the China border. The Tho were largely on the side of the Vietminh and Tho manpower was an important and integral part of the Vietminh field forces. This was to be proved in the battle of Route Coloniale 4, in which the French moved into the mountains in order to disrupt the link, through Tho country, bringing supplies from China to the Vietminh.

French attempts to block this important supply link were severely crushed in 1950 when the Vietminh wiped out a six to ten thousand-man French force during the famous "Battle of R.C.4".[22] Route Coloniale 4 was one of the very few all-weather roads traversing the Tho country. In a narrow sense, this battle was crucial for it showed the French the dangers of moving armour-supported infantry into the mountains. It meant that the Vietminh border sanctuaries and the vital route to China would not again be seriously contested. The support by the Tho for the Vietminh ensured the French defeat in the Battle of R.C.4.

The Tho had provided most of the men (about 20,000) for two of the six Vietminh divisions fielded in 1954. This was about a third of the Vietminh forces committed to the Battle of R.C.4. These 20,000 men constituted about five per cent of the total Tho population at that time.[23] In terms of the proportion to the total adult male population of the Tho the figure would have been very high.

Furthermore, as an indication of Tho support for the Vietminh and their own capabilities, three Thos rose to the rank of general in the Vietminh armed forces. After proclamation by Ho Chi Minh of independence in 1945, one of these three, Chu Van Tan, became Minister of Defence.[24] The contribution in manpower and military skill came from an estimated total Tho population of about only 400,000 in the 1950s.[25] This is an indication that in areas of difficult terrain, small numbers of an ethnic group can be of telling significance.

In times of conflict, the strategic significance of the minorities is often out of proportion to their small population. Given the requisite leadership, organization, and ideology or commitment, their military capacity can far outweigh the power suggested by their numbers and poverty. If the Tho had been pro-French, the outcome might have been radically different.

Indeed, the French successfully used the policy of ethnic differentiation in order to subdue the Vietnamese through the manipulation of ethnic differences. The French aim was achieved through gaining the allegiance of the highlanders, thus using the ethnic minorities and the territories they occupied as hostile communal barriers. In this manner the French colonial government was able to isolate the lowland Vietnamese from Chinese assistance in the earlier stages of anti-colonial resistance.[26] It has been noted by French sources, that the policy had been successful. This was attested to by the fact that the H'mongs had captured rebellious and anti-French Vietnamese and handed them over to the French. The Tai, Yao, H'mong, Nung, and Tho of the mountains effectively blocked anti-French Vietnamese from southern China, otherwise a source of aid and a refuge.[27]

When the French-inspired interdiction of supplies from China ceased, the balance shifted rapidly to the advantage of the Vietminh. The strategic advantage gained from locational access to China through Tho territory enabled the Vietminh to receive training in China for 40,000 of their troops by mid-1954, and to get aid from China at the rate of 3,000 to 15,000 tons of war material per month. This included field artillery.[28] The fact that the Tho rallied to the Vietminh in the First Indochina War was indicative of the changes in the balance of power in the highlands. This was eventually to lead to the hemming in of the French colonial forces in the Tonkin plains and to their preoccupation with a defensive posture, harassed as they were by guerrilla actions in the plains. Dien Bien Phu was a dramatic attempt — which failed — to break out of this strategic impasse.

Minorities as a Source of Manpower in Labour-Scarce Zones

Examples abound of ethnic minorities proving useful or vital in the struggle against French sea-succoured power. In the battle of Dien Bien Phu, the factors of availability of transportation over long distances across mountainous country, of sufficiency of food, heavy guns, and ammunition for the army which was to invest, and eventually overrun, the French garrison, was vital to the outcome of the battle.

The French had grossly underestimated the logistical capacity of the Vietminh, and in their strategic planning, expected to meet relatively lightly armed opposition. That the Vietminh were able to supply and re-supply their army in a sustained manner was due to the mobilization of all resources for the purpose of transportation. An important element in this major logistical effort besides human porterage and modified bicycles was the use of pack horses. Vo Nguyen Giap refers in this connection to "convoys of pack horses from the Meo Highlands...."[29] The Meo (Miao), or H'mong as they prefer to be called, were prominent in the preparations for the Vietminh assault on the French fortified plain. Of the porters working on the Vietminh supply routes "the Meo were the most enthusiastic".[30] Also, the heights above Dien Bien Phu overlooking the plain and the airfield were denied to the French partly because of Miao pickets operating on ground familiar to them. At any rate Miao guerrilla units fought actively for the Vietminh in the surrounding areas during the period before the battle.[31]

Another strategic asset that lies with mountain dwelling groups is that they are often the only source of labour in inaccessible areas with diseases which those from other environments could find fatal. The building of the Burma Road, connecting Kunming to Lashio, during the Sino-Japanese War depended entirely on Han-Yunnanese and "hill tribe" labour. Similarly the Ledo road from China to the road network of northeastern India, completed in 1942 after two-and-a-half years' work, depended on more than half a million people of the mountain minorities of China and Burma.[32] During and after the 1962 Sino-Indian border war, Tibetan-speaking inhabitants of the North East Frontier tracts were used by the Indian Army to construct roads. When the Japanese tried to invade northeastern India after their conquest of Burma in 1942, they were hampered by lack of transport and porterage manpower, whereas the British defending Imphal were well supplied by road. Moreover, the British could rely on the considerable Indian "tribal" manpower reserves resident in the foothills of the "tea estates" below Imphal for labour. Nearly 600,000 labourers from the tea plantations were available for the purpose of road construction.[33]

The Malayan Communist Party and the Senoi

The strategic and tactical value of hill tribes can be elaborated upon further, drawing from examples in other countries of Southeast Asia. The Senoi in Peninsular Malaysia were recognized by the British early on in their campaign against the Malayan Communist Party (MCP) insurrection as being the key to success against the MCP in the mountains and deep forests, as opposed to the jungle fringes. Once the MCP armed groups had been driven from the forest fringes where they had been supplied by the mainly Chinese "squatters", their survival in the forested mountains of the interior of the peninsula depended on Senoi co-operation in acting as a "screen" for information gathering, food supply, movement along routes and trails known only to the Senoi, and finally for manpower for porterage, since draught animals are unknown in the high uplands of Peninsular Malaysia.

The MCP on their part also recognized the value of the aborigines. Having failed in 1951 to create bases in the lowlands and jungle fringes near the main population centres, MCP members were forced to retreat into the forested interior. Their policy was to befriend the aborigines and form tactical support groups referred to as "asal clubs" (the term "asal" having an Arabic root denoting "original"). The MCP was the first to dignify the aborigines in their nomenclature, thus rejecting the derogatory and widely-used Malay term "sakai" meaning slaves. In a move imitative of the MCP's, the government subsequently, coined the word "asli" to cover all the tribal groups.

The MCP plan was to have an "asal club" in each valley led by selected young aborigines who would be given training to lead their groups.[34] MCP cadres working with the "asal club" and the aborigines generally were to use tact and persuasion and to abjure violence. The MCP Central Politburo issued directives to this effect:

> All comrades engaged in the work of the Asal must take full responsibility in investigating and studying the habits of living, customs, traditions, rituals and other racial characteristics of the Asal. . . . Information on the foregoing should be compiled for references. This will help us improve our methods of work . . . in order to fully understand the Asal compatriots' way of life . . . we should try to identify with them by adopting their way of living.[35]

By the end of 1953 only about two years after the implementation of this MCP policy of friendship to the Asal, the success of this approach was attested to by the fact that the MCP controlled approximately three-fifths of all aborigines in the country.[36] Considering that a number of aboriginal groups lived in the foothills and lowlands which were largely under government control, the proportion of pro-MCP aborigines in the strategic high valleys and ridgelines must have been considerably more than three-fifths of their number. In following this policy the MCP was only adapting from the experience gained in the Long March in Chinese communist history.

To counter the MCP withdrawal away from the populated areas, the British built a series of mountain-top fortified camps, known as "forts" to block and control movement along the North-South series of ridge-top trails, following the geological grain of the peninsula. These trails, unimpeded by undergrowth, are often the quickest way of travel in the thickly forested terrain. Being on the north-south crestline of watersheds, the trails do not need to traverse streambeds and water courses. They are also generally free of very steep gradients and before the guerrilla uprising were used only by big game and by the Senoi groups; in fact the British often referred to them as game-trails.

In their counter-measures against the jungle-based MCP, the British moved known settlements of Senoi to mountain-top forts in 1954 to give them "protection" from the guerrillas — that is, to deny the MCP of their manpower, their food, and their jungle expertise, important elements in conflict carried out in the jungle. However, these deep forest forts were set up only after an attempt had been made to move the aboriginal groups out of the reach of communist influence by re-resettling them outside the mountains and in the hot, humid lowlands. This policy of strategic re-resettlement (which for the British had worked well with the problem of Chinese farmers and squatter cultivators in the lowlands and which had cut off food and information to the guerrillas) was unsuccessful when applied to the aborigines in the highlands. Many died in the squalid camps while some escaped to join their kinsmen in the forest. Their experience in the British camps persuaded the remaining mountain-dwelling aborigines to move wholeheartedly to the communist side,[37] and to move yet deeper into the remotest mountains where they produced food by swidden agriculture, thus making their settlements food-collecting areas for units of the MCP.

Although the highlands of Peninsular Malaysia are mostly steep-sided and concave-sloped, affording few opportunities for agriculture at the higher levels, there appear to be numerous small elevated valleys at varying levels, the geomorphology of which does not appear to have been examined thoroughly. The better-known of these are at the Cameron Highlands (at 3,500 to 4,500 ft. above sea-level), in the Gunong Tahan massif (at about 5,000 ft. above sea-level), Fraser's Hill (at about 4,000 ft. above sea-level), and in the Genting Sempah area (at about 1,500 to 3,500 ft. above sea-level). There are many others which are not easily accessible.

In the later stages of the campaign when a proportion of them had been won over to the government side, the Senoi were also responsible for the information leading to the successful ambush of guerrilla bands, the identification of food-gathering areas used by the guerrillas, and the location of insurgent camps. The final success of the British campaign against the guerrillas was preceded by an appreciation that it was necessary to move into the guerrillas' own base areas in the deep jungle, to imitate the MCP policy of friendship and materiel support for the aboriginal groups, and to provide them with security, material, and medical aid in their own territory all of which were forthcoming once the mountain forts were built. The greater material resources of the British finally gave them the upper hand over the guerrillas in the competition for the loyalty of the mountain forest dwellers. With the support of these minority groups the British had won over a strategic asset which was instrumental in the defeat and the withdrawal northwards of MCP fighting units.

The importance of psychological warfare and of what the British propagandists have aptly termed "the battle for hearts and minds" is realized by the protagonists. The political and propaganda arms of the MCP work closely with their armed units. The long-range re-infiltration into the mountains due east of the town of Ipoh, evident in 1981, 1982 and 1983, by Betong-based MCP guerrillas involved to a large extent the winning over of the sympathies of several groups of Senoi, or Orang Asli.

The Minorities and War in Vietnam's "Central Highlands"

In the Vietnam Wars, not only the French and the Americans but also their Vietnamese adversaries recognized the strategic value of the Montagnards. U.S. army commanders during the Vietnam War realized the importance of winning over the inhabitants of what were known as the "Central Highlands" of South Vietnam.[38] So did the Vietcong and later on the North Vietnamese. In the U.S. phases of the war, the various Montagnard tribes were split into two groups according to their support for either the U.S. forces or the North Vietnamese and the Vietcong. The fall of the Pleiku and Kontum and the rout of the South Vietnamese army in the highlands in 1975 was to some degree attributed to the support given to the North Vietnamese by Montagnard groups that acted as ancillary troops and who were specialists in jungle fighting and in ambush.

Since the conquest of the South by armies from North Vietnam, the Montagnards have not been entirely compliant to the new Vietnamese policies of moving Vietnamese immigrants from the lowlands of North Vietnam to the Central Highlands. The settlement by Vietnamese which was earlier supported by the Saigon authorities was a contributory factor in the alienation of the southern hillmen from Saigon's cause.

Since the conquest of the South there have been sporadic reports of armed resistance in the Highlands to the Vietnamese. The importance of the many Montagnard groups, both during the Vietnam Wars and the present attempts by Hanoi to consolidate its hold on the South as well as on the "Indochina Federation", lies to a large extent in the strategic location of the territory some of them occupy. In the post-1975 situation it would be in relation to the power balance in the region comprising Vietnam, Thailand, Kampuchea, and southern Laos.

The Sedang and the "Central Highlands" of Vietnam

One Montagnard group known as the Sedang, numbering between 20,000 and 40,000, can be examined in the light of the projection of military power into this particular mountain area. It is said that, "The tactical importance of the Sedang lies in their knowledge of the jungle-mountain area they live in and their ability to move easily about in the jungle."[39] The Sedang it was reported could become excellent guides and scouts for conventional infantry units and in the American assessment, made good material for paramilitary units. The characteristics of the Sedang are common to many mountain minorities of mainland Southeast Asia.

The Sedang are not averse to taking up arms against those they deem to be their oppressors. Their mode of living includes a thorough knowledge of their surrounding flora and fauna and they are expert hunters with their traditional weapon, the crossbow. They thus take readily to modern shoulder-fired infantry weapons. Importantly they, like many other groups in the highlands, occupy territory "characterized by narrow river valleys and steeply rising mountains with sharp ridge lines. The rivers are deep and swift; there are many rapids and waterfalls. This makes the rivers navigable only to shallow draft native dug-outs."[40] Wet season conditions of heavy mist, poor visibility and low cloud cover, torrential rains and muddy slopes, furthermore, make military operations into the region difficult, if not hazardous. Although such seasonal conditions also occur in many other parts of the montane zone, it should be noted that the Central Highlands because of their heights in the path of monsoon winds, both Southwest and Northeast, have exceptionally heavy rainfall.

Apart from the terrain, the location of the Central Highlands is important. Access trails linking southern Laos, Vietnam, and Kampuchea are hidden from aerial observation by the thick three-tiered rainforest vegetation. These trails traverse the general area of the Highlands. Significantly the Sedang tribal lands straddle the area where the borders of Kampuchea, Vietnam, and Laos meet. This area overlaps the base area of the Northern Region of Democratic Kampuchea or Khmer Rouge resistance against the Vietnamese. There has been, in 1980, reported co-operation between the seemingly viable Khmer Rouge resistance in Northeast Kampuchea, the remnants of Montagnard resistance and elements of the Lao right-wing resistance. In any study of the geostrategic function of terrain in Southeast Asia, the Central Highlands of Vietnam abutting on Laos and Cambodia should not be ignored.

Generally, the Central Highlands provide the kind of mountain base area that enables small resistance groups to retire to avoid enemy action, retrain, and resist and avoid incorporation into the lowland political system. Although the Central Highlands of southern Vietnam are merely an outlier of the main highland zone of mainland Southeast Asia, they nevertheless possess most of the characteristics of the main zone, that is, ethnically or culturally-based resistance groups operating in difficult terrain, strategic location, and, especially important, contiguity with more than one state or power centre. However, in terms of dissent after 1975 against Hanoi's policies, the Central Highlands lack the main zone's size and contiguity with the main power centre in the region — the PRC — though this is partially offset by adjacency to Cambodian resistance bases in northeastern Cambodia and thence to Thailand. The Vietnamese appear to be well aware of the value of this belt of highlands which are a miniature of the main highland zone of mainland Southeast Asia. There have been reports of Vietnamese efforts to strengthen their hold on these highlands. It is unlikely that the Vietnamese would readily forego their presence there, even if the lowlands were returned to Kampuchean administration.

The Li of Hainan Island

A little known example of the awareness of the strategic advantages of getting aid, co-operation, or an alliance with hill minorities against lowlanders occurred during World War II in Hainan Island, where conditions resemble in miniature the topography and ethnic compositions of mainland Southeast Asia. The Japanese occupying army was concerned about the security of its bases on the island, and envisaged using the Li minority group of the foothills as a buffer against the Chinese, particularly the Chinese guerrillas, operating from the central core of mountains. An anthropological study was made in 1942 to study the Li in order to find out how they could be used by the Japanese Army in Hainan Island. This may have been a very early, if not the earliest, systematic attempt to study hill groups in the wider strategic context.[41] A conclusion reached by the Japanese was that the Li could be an invaluable source of labour in support of Japanese military efforts.

The Implications of Highland-Ethnic Fragmentation

Much has been written on the differences which are said to exist between highland dwellers and the majority populations of the plains. This antagonism exists from Assam in the west to Vietnam in the east. In the pattern of highland-lowland gap, there are important variations which have to be noted. First of all, it is not always that the inhabitants of a highland region share a common purpose with regard to the lowlanders and their presence in the region. Highlanders can also be divided between upland valley-dwelling irrigated-rice growers like the Shan and Tai and the mountaineers who live mainly by swidden agriculture on the mountain slopes. These two categories of culture would have differing economic interests. While at present it is true that normally there is little open conflict between the various groups of highland peoples, it is also true that the authorities of the lowland state could use, and have used, economic and political power to manipulate intergroup rivalries to their own advantage. This happened, for example, when the Vietminh took advantage of the ridge-dwelling Miaos' (H'mong) apprehension of political domination by the valley-cultivating Tais in the northwest of the northern Vietnamese mountains in 1945-46. At that time Deo Van Long had attempted to assert his authority which was based on the valley-dwelling Tai, with French support, over the Miao.[42] The result was a confrontation between the H'mong and the Tai, with the H'mong aiding the Vietminh while the French received the support of the Tai chieftains. The antipathy between Miao highlander and Tai valley dweller was to have grave consequences in the events which led to the fall of Dien Bien Phu.

In French Indochina, the tensions in ethnic relations not only between Vietnamese and highlander, but also between the different highland groups was exploited by the French as they expanded their influence. A policy recognizing the "politics of race" was advocated by Gallieni, "the pacifier of Tonkin". Basically, it was to make subjugation and control of the colony easier by setting off ethnic groups one against another. This cynically manipulative approach was explained as follows:

> The study of races that occupy a region determines the kind of political organization to give it, and the means to use for its pacification. An officer who has succeeded in preparing a sufficiently exact ethnographic map of the territory under his control is well-nigh close to having obtained its complete pacification.
>
> Every agglomeration of individuals, race, people, tribe or family represents a sum of either common or opposed interests.... There are hatreds, rivalries, that we should know how to disentangle and

utilize to our profit, by opposing one against other and by leaning on one the better to conquer the other.[43]

This strategy of using ethnic rivalry, tension, and conflict as a means of control was recognized by other colonial powers besides the French. The British used it in India, and to a lesser extent in Burma, too. It was also used by the Dutch in Indonesia. In Malaya, British rule in the earlier stages was maintained by using imported Indians as soldiers and policemen. Later, only Malays were recruited into the police and infantry units, in a country where the urban population was almost entirely Chinese.

Some mountaineers can also be hired to harass anti-government groups and foreign intruders in remote areas where the government has little or no presence. The Burmese Government employed Lahu amongst others, as mercenaries to harass the groups of largely Guomindang Chinese who had retreated from China into the Shan highlands of Burma.[44] Mercenary attitudes were made use of by the colonialists who like the British employed Chin and Kachin riflemen to help maintain order among lowland Burmans. The Karens, to a large extent a lowland dwelling minority were also used in similar fashion to control the majority Burmans. The Nung of North Vietnam are well known for their physique and fighting prowess. The French, the South Vietnamese Government, and the Americans in Vietnam used them as troops or as élite guards.

This propensity by some highland groups to mercenary attitudes is related to another feature of mountaineer participation in warfare — that is, that groups can switch sides. This again can be used by central lowland authorities to manipulate them to their own advantage.

Divisions between ethnic groups are not the only kind of characteristic in any hill-based resistance to lowland authorities. Within one ethnic group, there could be sub-divisions which can be exploited by the lowland centre. Thus in northeast India it was found that the Naga resistance suffered from this defect. In Nagaland, there are a number of major "tribes" such as the Angamis, Konyaks, Aos, and Semas. This proved to be an inherent weakness in the Naga agitation and armed resistance against the imposed rule of New Delhi and Naga demands for a separate state. "One of the main reasons for the turning point in Nagaland was that because of the break-up of the underground into various tribal factions, it became possible for Army intelligence to effect a breakthrough — an essential prerequisite for the conduct of counter-insurgency operations."[45] The same source noted that a similar kind of tribally fragmented situation did not exist in Mizoram, where the Mizos have only one major tribe. Mizo resistance groups were less easily penetrated by Indian army agents.

It should be noted, however, that with the possible exception of Vietnam and the Vietnamese military network in Laos, the lowland governments of mainland Southeast Asia are unlikely to have the same political and military intelligence capability that the Indian Army has in northeastern India.

★ ★ ★

Any strategic environment is composed of a combination of diverse factors. Indeed, it may be seen as a result of the blending or overlapping of a number of other environments such as the cultural, the political, and the geographic which includes topography among other things.

In montane Southeast Asia, the strategic environment is to a very considerable extent coloured not only by the terrain but also by the cultural groups which reside in the uplands. The co-operation of these mountaineers has proved important, if not crucial, to armies operating in, and to governments with policies towards, the highlands.

The patchwork of hill peoples have in the past been manipulated by groups based in the lowlands to maintain lowland supremacy over the highlands. The implications of the maintenance of this supremacy will be dealt with in the chapters that follow. Suffice it to say that ensuing highland-lowland cleavages form an integral element in the strategic environment of the region. In this sense, the mountain-based "ethnicities" which are an outstanding feature of the geo-strategic map of the region bears an influence on the strategic environment, out of proportion to the numbers of the highlanders, who are at the macro-level described as demographic and political minorities in the states where they are found. In their own montane habitats, however, the situation at the micro-level may be quite different, giving these habitats a geo-strategic distinctness of their own.

NOTES

1. For want of a better term, "ethnicity" is used here to denote the agglomeration of cultural factors which includes the religious and linguistic and gives rise to feelings of separateness, in varying degrees, by one group from another. The term "ethnic group" is also used.
2. See Geoffrey Powell, *The Kandyan Wars: The British Army in Ceylon 1803–1818*

(London: Leo Cooper and Kandy: K.V.G. de Silva and Sons, 1973), pp. 36–37 (for Dutch experience), pp. 98–101 (for the British).
3. Burton Watson, *Records of the Grand Historian of China translated from the Shih chi of Ssu-ma Ch'ien*, vol. 1 (Introduction to Vol. I), (New York: Columbia University Press, 1961), p. 13.
4. Jules Roy, *The Battle of Dienbienphu*, translated by Robert Baldick, Introduction by Neil Shoehan (London: Faber and Faber, 1965), p. 298.
5. Machiavelli, *The Art of War*, Book 4.
6. C.E. Calwell, *Small Wars: Their Principle and Practice* (London: His Majesty's Stationary Office, 1906), p. 292.
7. Calwell, op. cit., p. 286.
8. G. Johnson, "Terrain: Let's Not Just Add a Multiplier", *Military Review*, January 1982, pp. 38–42.
9. A. Scoffer, "The Wars of Israel in Sinai", *Military Review*, April 1982, pp. 60–72.
10. W.G. East, O.H.K. Spate, and C.A. Fisher, *The Changing Map of Asia* (London: Methuen, 1971), p. 9.
11. Ulrich Schweinfurth, "The Problem of Nagaland" in Charles A. Fisher, *Essays in Political Geography* (London: Methuen, 1968), pp. 166–67.
12. Stuart Schram, *Mao Tse Tung* (Middlesex: Penguin, 1967), p. 187 quoting Liu Po-ch'eng, "Looking Back on the Long March" in *The Long March: Eyewitness Accounts* (Peking: Foreign Languages Press, 1959).
13. *Red Star Over China*, with an introduction by John K. Fairbank (New York: Grove Press, 1961), pp. 213–15.
14. Snow, op. cit., pp. 213–14.
15. Snow, op. cit., p.213.
16. Schram, op. cit., p. 188.
17. Pieter Schier and Manola Schier Oum in collaboration with Waldtraut Jarke, *Prince Sihanouk on Cambodia: Interviews and Talks with Prince Norodom Sihanouk* (Hamburg: Mitteilungen des Instituts für Asienkunde, 1980), p. 30.
18. Ibid.
19. Ibid.
20. B. Fall, "The Pathet Lao; a 'Liberation' Party" in *The Communist Revolution in Asia: Tactics, Goals and Achievements*, ed. Robert A. Scalapino (Englewood Cliffs, N.J.: Prentice-Hall, 1965).
21. *Journal of Ethnology*, no. 2 (1979), (Hanoi): 13–24, translated by Sophie Quinn-Judge in *Southeast Asia Ethnicity and Development Newsletter* 5, no. 2 (May 1981) (Singapore: Institute of Southeast Asian Studies).
22. Gary D. Wekkin, "Tribal Politics in Indochina: The Role of Highland Tribes in the Internationalization of Internal Wars" in *Conflict and Stability in Southeast Asia*, ed. Mark W. Zacher and R. Stephen Milne (N.Y.: Anchor Books, 1974), p. 130 quoting Bernard B. Fall, *Street Without Joy* (Harrisburg, P.A.: Stackpole Co., 1961).
23. John T. McAlister, Jr., "Mountain Minorities and the Vietminh: A Key to the Indochina War", *Southeast Asian Tribes, Minorities and Nations*, ed. Peter Kunstadter (New Jersey: Princeton University Press, 1967), pp. 796, 798.
24. Ibid.
25. Ibid.
26. David G. Marr, *Vietnamese Anticolonialism 1885–1925* (Berkeley: University of California Press, 1971), p. 72.
27. See Huynh Kim Khanh, *Vietnamese Communism 1925–1945* (Ithaca: Cornell University Press, 1982), p. 278.

28. See George K. Tanham, *Communist Revolutionary Warfare: The Vietminh in Indochina* (New York: Praegar, 1961), p. 102.
29. General Vo Nguyen Giap, *Selected Writings of the Military Art of People's War*, ed. Russel Stetler (New York: Monthly Review Press, 1970), p. 159.
30. McAlister, Jr., op. cit., p. 831.
31. Ibid.
32. Howard Liss, *The Mighty Mekong* (New York: Hawthorn, 1967), p. 49.
33. Geoffrey Tyson, *Forgotten Frontier* (Calcutta: W.H. Target & Co., 1945), p. 24.
34. Iskandar Carey, *Orang Asli: The Aboriginal Tribes of Malaysia* (Kuala Lumpur: OUP, 1967), pp. 310–11.
35. Anthony Walker, "In Mountain and Ulu: A Comparative History of the Development Strategies for Ethnic Minority People in Thailand and Malaysia", *Contemporary Southeast Asia* 4, no. 4 (1983): 451–85. This article was first presented at the "Conference on Societies in Transition: Alternatives for the Future" held in India, December 1981.
36. Richard Noone, *Rape of the Dream People* (London: Hutchinson, 1972), p. 152.
37. Walker, op. cit.
38. Wherever possible the term "Central Highlands" will be retained — although it is no longer central in the geography of a united Vietnam — to avoid confusion considering the amount of literature referring to this term.
39. U.S. Army Special Warfare School, *The Montagnard Tribal Groups of the Republic of South Vietnam* (Fort Bragg, North Carolina, 1964), p. 185.
40. Ibid.
41. Kunio Odaka, *Economic Organization of the Li Tribes of Hainan Island* (Ann Arbor: University Microfilms, c. 1950).
42. McAlister Jr., op. cit., p. 824.
43. H. Desschamps and P. Chauvet, *Gallieni pacificateur* (Paris, 1949), quoted in Huynh Kim Khanh, *Vietnamese Communism 1925–1945* (Ithaca: Cornell University Press, 1982), p. 277.
44. In Burma, the Lahu have shown animosity towards Hans. See F.W. Mote, "The Rural Haw of Northern Thailand" in *Southeast Asian Tribes, Minorities and Nations*, ed. P. Kunstadter (Princeton: Princeton University Press, 1967), pp. 487–524.
45. Maj.-Gen. D.K. Palit (Retd.), *Hindustan Times*, 14 July 1975 reprinted in Marcus F. Franda, *Northeastern India in the Wake of Vietnam*, American Universities Fieldstaff Reports, South Asia Series, vol. 19, no. 13 (August 1975).

CHAPTER 2

Interaction between Lowlander and Highlander

There are a number of differences in culture and outlook between plainsmen and hill-dweller. The differences are widespread and pervasive to the extent that they colour the geo-strategic environment of mainland Southeast Asia.

Minorities as Local Majorities

It should be pointed out that while the highlanders are in fact minorities in the respective states which claim their allegiance and are often dismissed as politically and economically unimportant because of the relatively small numbers of each group, these upland people are in fact not minorities *in toto* within the confines of the mountain zone. Here the lowlanders are often in the minority, as are the Burmans living in the Kachin state of northern Burma and who need legal impositions to "protect" them. "[I]n Kachin state, there is a Burman population, which is protected as a minority element."[1] In fact, in Burma as a whole, the "minorities" comprise fully 35 per cent of the total population. Some, notably the Karen and the Mon, however, are to a large extent plain-dwellers, but the high proportion of hill minorities in Burma's population is undisputed.

Vietnamese, or Kinh, are minorities in all the mountain areas of Vietnam although migration programmes initiated from Hanoi may radically alter this pattern. Lowland Lao do not form a clear majority even in the country as a whole, with highland "minorities" adding up to about 48 per cent of Laos' population. Thais are mainly administrators and soldiers in hill regions of northern Thailand and are outnumbered by the highlanders in these areas. In Yunnan's Tai-inhabited Xishuangpanna (Sipsongpanna) area abutting on Burma and Laos, the

Hans are in the minority, as they are in the mountainous frontiers throughout Yunnan and Quangxi and also in Guizhou. In extensive areas throughout the highlands of Quangxi and even in the riverine tracts, the minority Xhuang far outnumber the Han Chinese.

Avoidance of the Highlands by Plainsmen

The existence of a situation wherein highlanders are the majorities in the areas where they live, can be attributed in part to the avoidance by the southern lowlanders of the uplands. In the southern lowland states, that is the states of mainland Southeast Asia, the majority lowlanders have traditionally tended to avoid the highlands. The material culture of the lowlanders does not include the agricultural techniques or skills needed to utilize the unfamiliar highlands. Lowlanders tend to have apprehensions about the forested mountains and their hostile denizens. The diseases common to the mountains are attributed to malignant spirits of the mountain forest. The Vietnamese, for example, disliked the highlands, and the mountainous and forested Ai Lao Dinh was traditionally dreaded by the lowlander Vietnamese. The Court of Annam maintained a prison in the mountains at Lao Bao until 1885. A traditional Vietnamese proverb ran as follows: "For the Annamite to go as far as Ai Lao without risk, he must be preceded by an elephant."[2] The diseases of the mountains are particularly rife in the lower and mid-altitude slopes; the upper elevation is in fact salubrious. Particularly virulent forms of malaria are encountered at these lower and middle elevations. U.S. troops operating in the highlands during the Vietnam War, and the post-1979 Khmer resistance against the Vietnamese experienced these and other insect-borne diseases which are absent or less noticeable in the carefully cultivated lowlands. Victims of malaria and other diseases outnumbered battle casualties among the Khmer resistance against the Vietnamese in the post-1979 period.

 The psychological warfare directed by the United States against the Vietcong recognized this fear which the lowlanders had for the unhealthy forested mountains. It has been noted that the U.S. Army devised techniques "producing horrifying noises at night that reminded the VC of their dreaded forest demons and spirits. . . ."[3] French geographers have also observed the Vietnamese farmer's fear of the highlands and the diseases of the forest. While in Burma, this avoidance was reinforced by the British policies which restricted entry into the Shan States.

Minority Diversities

In any one particular area or even locality the ethnic pattern among the highland dwellers themselves can be so diverse that no single group appears as a clear majority. Over various sub-zones, however, there is often, but not always, a "majority" group. Such regionally localized majorities include the Chins in the Chin Hills, the Kachins in northern Burma, the Shans in much of the Shan plateau and the Xhuang in mountainous and hilly parts of Guangxi province of the PRC. Often it would be useful to see numerical dominance in terms of an altitudinal or vertical plane and not so much as a horizontal "map" spread.[4] This is the case with the high-dwelling Miao or H'mong who are the dominant group in the highest cultivable lands.

The important point remains, however, that the lowlanders of the coastal or the main riverine plains are not strongly represented — except temporarily as members of military campaigns or of garrisons — or may even be absent altogether over large stretches of the mountain belt. Often due to pressure of population growth on the arable land in the plains adjoining the highlands, the main lowland ethnic group finds it has to move into the edges or foothills of the uplands. This is the case in northern Thailand where the lowland Thai have moved into the edges of the highlands in order to follow the practice of swidden agriculture in the foothills.[5] This pattern of lowland population pressure leading to a slow expansion of lowlanders into the outer fringes of the uplands is also the pattern in China and in northern Vietnam, but not as yet Burma or Laos. In southern Vietnam it is part of a government programme to Vietnamize the highlands.

In cultural terms, hill peoples although disunited among themselves, stand clearly apart from the majorities of the plains. It has been pointed out that the Akhar in Assam and the Lamet in Laos living about 500 miles apart have more in common than there is between either group and their nearest valley-bottom dwelling neighbours.[6] Thus in the states of mainland Southeast Asia the territory can be roughly divided into two categories — majority-inhabited and minority-inhabited. This territorial differentiation of ethnicity allied to terrain is basic to the strategic understanding of the problems of mainland Southeast Asia.

Nevertheless, it must be stressed that despite many cultural affinities the dwellers in the hills are not a homogeneous element. Intergroup rivalries, traditional hostility, and the extremely fragmented nature, culturally and politically speaking, of the population owing allegiance usually to local chieftains or village heads lends them to manipulation by a more organized power with a consistency of political aim. The population per square unit of area is also low. This thinly dispersed character of the mountain population inhibits organization for a common political purpose. However, there are certain factors which make for a limited degree of what can be loosely called a common indentification beyond the local area or any one cultural group. These factors may change from time to time, but in periods of oppression or interference from lowlanders, a loose "unity" may sometimes be found amongst various groups, opposed to the "outsiders".

Common Features among Highlanders

In dealings such as in trading exchanges with the lowlanders, especially in the mountain fringes, the languages used are generally some form of the lowland language, but in the highlands there is often one dominant highland language in particular tracts. Jinghpaw is spoken by the largest Kachin group and significantly, its function as a *lingua franca* for northern Burma is spread over an area much more extensive than the political boundaries of Kachin state. Shan is widely spoken by all groups in the Shan plateau of Burma. The Yunnanese dialect of China is spoken over wide areas stretching well into Burma and northern Thailand. In northern Thailand and in montane Burma most male adults among the hill people are bilingual and conversant in two or even three or more languages of the highlands, including Chinese in the Yunnanese spoken form. This facilitates communication between the diverse highland groups and makes for a wider understanding such as that between villages of different cultures and between local inhabitants and travellers from a distant district.

Although there is no single *lingua franca* for the mountain zone as a whole, the existence of a considerable degree of bilingualism or even trilingualism among the hill groups, without having continually to resort to the main lowland language, further strengthens the difference between highland and lowland.

In addition, kinship ties are widespread. Sometimes they cut across cultural divisions and can be of importance in ensuring safety of transit through certain areas. As with many cultures of a lower technological achievement, kinship is an important element in dealings between individuals and groups. As has been noted by Leach, some of these links can be very widely-spaced in geographical terms. They become especially significant when international boundaries are straddled in the process of maintenance of kinship ties. Leach has also observed that while lowlanders and valley peoples in mainland Southeast Asia repudiate marriage with the highlanders who are regarded as barbarians, among the various highland groups themselves there is no objection to such marriages and indeed trade facilitates intermarriage and vice versa. Chinese traders also intermarry with women hill folk. Girls are married on payment of a bride-price involving the transaction of objects which are similar to those that the Chinese traders deal in and which are widely found throughout the mountains. "Thus the ties of official kinship ramify widely, following trade routes and jumping across language frontiers and political boundaries."[7] It should be noted that traditionally most of the main trade routes were in a north-south direction, connecting the village manufactories of Yunnan (producing the simple iron implements and utensils needed by the highlanders) to the sources of precious woods, medical products and gemstones, like jade, which were much sought after by the Chinese. On the question of the widespreading network of kinship, and hence personal, ties Leach records that "[i]n 1942, a Gauri acquaintance of mine from East of Bhamo found himself in a Sinfo village in Assam 250 miles from home, but it took him only a day or so to persuade his hosts that he was one of their relations".[8] During the Vietnam War a H'mong (Miao) fighting against the Vietnamese and Pathet Lao in Laos told his American officers that he had gone a few weeks earlier to marry a H'mong girl living about 200 miles away in China.[9]

Some sacred sites of the minorities like the H'mong are located in China, and whenever possible are visited. Significantly, some of the ethnic groups like the H'mong are historically recent migrants from China. Continued family links can apparently still persist because of the not-too-distant move to the south. A H'mong chief in northern Thailand has been recorded as having known of his grandfather being born in Yunnan. The H'mong are also aware of their historic migration routes,[10] and can trace the southward movements of their families and class. The Lahu and the Yao, too, are notable in this respect.

Of the Lahu, including the Lahu of northern Thailand, it has been noted that folk memory of their migratory route from China to the south is indicated in their funeral rituals. "Today, when the Mawpa or shamans repeat incantations to supposedly make the souls of the dead rest peacefully, they try to escort the souls from Lan-ts'ang to Tien-ch'ih by way of Lin Ts'ang and Seng ch'ing."[11] To many of the highland minorities, especially those who have migrated southwards in more recent times, the state boundaries to do not hold the same kind of meaning as they do to the ruling élite and administrators in the capital cities.

The pattern of relative ease of trans-boundary movement applies throughout the region. In 1962, for example, during the Vietnam War, a

U.S. agent based in northwestern Laos trained Lahu and Yao tribesmen and sent them deep into China's Yunnan province to monitor road traffic and tap telephones.[12] Infiltration across borders is not uncommon, even in the early 1980s.

Grievances and common economic interests among the hillfolk generally set them, or coalitions of them, apart from the lowlanders and from the officials who represent the lowland authority. For example, one case in point is the attempted control by the present authorities of the forest-felling by the swidden agriculturists on the mountain slopes. This attempt at control is based on sound ecological grounds, and on the premise of "national" well-being, but does not take minority cultural and economic interests into full account. The levying of official and unofficial taxes by police or military personnel who are invariably lowlanders and are seen by the hillfolk as the representatives of the lowland government adds to the friction. Highlanders have almost invariably regarded intruding lowland officials as being oppressive.

To the differing economic interests can be added the often undisguised contempt which lowlanders hold for the highland cultural groups. That this animosity, though often only in latent form, exists between highlander and lowland dweller is agreed upon by most observers.

The Vietnamese have referred to the uplanders under the generic term "Moi" which means "savage". This general contempt was shown, for example, during public celebrations and parades in Saigon in the days of Ngo Dinh Diem's rule when participating groups of minority peoples in their traditional costumes were the object of derisive laughter on the part of Vietnamese onlookers. The Laotians of the Mekong Valley call the tribes who live mainly in the foothill zones and who are the group of hill people most frequently in contact with the lowlanders, "Kha" which means "slaves" as indeed they have often been in the past. The Thais of the Central Plains of Thailand also tend to regard the hill people of the kingdom as being non-Thai and of a separate breed. Generally, however, the Thai authorities themselves have tended to take a more benevolent attitude towards the cultural groups that have filtered into Thailand's northern and northeastern mountains so unobtrusively during and before the last century and in the early part of the present century.

Generally, interaction between lowland majorities and highland minorities is minimal. The lower foothills form a physical divide separating sharp differences in culture and in political development.[13] Contrasts in language, religion, mode of economic activity and therefore of economic interest sharpen the political disparities. The introduction of Christianity has in certain areas played a role in this differentiation between uplands and plains. The Nagas in Northeast India and the Karen in Burma are to a large degree Christian. About 60 per cent of the Nagas have been converted from their previous animistic beliefs.[14] Both groups have been prominent in their vigorous resistance against central rule during the post-colonial period.

Lowland Nationalism and the Minorities: The Case of Burma

It is in Burma that the political and security problems deriving from the schism between ethnic groups in most acute. Burma, too, has been relatively well-documented in this respect. To help in the better understanding of the overall regional situation, it would be useful to examine briefly the factors in the development of the situation that existed in Burma from the British withdrawal up to the time of writing.

While it is not intended to explain the causes of the common rift between highlander and lowlander, it should nevertheless be noted that scholars of Burma have attributed an exacerbation of historic, preexisting cleavages to colonial policies. The effects of colonial rule and policies cannot be underestimated.

During the period of British colonial administration, what is now Burma was divided into the lowland "Burma Proper" and the uplands known as the "Frontier Areas". The lowlands were predominantly Burman, with substantial Karen, Mon, and Arakanese minorities. The uplands were the homes of the minorities such as the Shans, Chin, Kachin, Kayah, and other smaller groups. In these upland zones, ethnic Burmans were few and far between. Over large tracts they were absent altogether. The British administrators believed that the cultural differences and the lower level of economic and political development among the upland people required that some form of protection be given them to shelter from the dominance of the more advanced and sophisticated lowlanders.

> The effect of this administrative arrangement was to emphasise the distinctions between the two regions by establishing an official political and cultural divide. On one side of the divide, the British created conditions, for the emergence of a modern, national political movement, a bureaucratic administration, and a monetarised economy. On the other side they presided over the ossification and simultaneous strengthening of traditional political elites, cultural practices, and economies.[15]

When Burma achieved its independence in 1948, the British period had left its stamp in the form of an increased consciousness of difference and division between highland and lowland, between majority and minorities. Nevertheless, British rule had only accentuated the schism between the Burman and the minorities. It did not create the ethnic differences which had existed before the arrival of the British Raj.

The concern of the British rulers for the less sophisticated indigenous minorities had earlier led them to attempt to buffer the Shans from growing Burman restiveness. Of all the minorities the Buddhist Shans, were perhaps the least rudimentary in political organization, having retained a system of ruling princes. A hardening of the divide between Shan and Burman occurred in 1922 when the British established the Federated Shan States. The Shan-inhabited region received a governing instrument covering all the many small Shan principalities. The Federated Shan States' Council consisted of all the ruling Shan princes and the British Governor in Rangoon, and dealt with matters such as health, education, and public works. This separate administrative status meant that the Shan States were largely unaffected by the nationalist movement in Burma proper in the period before the Japanese invasion. The Burman nationalists focused political attention on the overlordship of the British and on the exploitative role of the Indian immigrants, particularly the Chettiars (Tamil money-lenders) who benefited from British rule and who, in lower Burma, had acquired substantial tracts of agricultural land from their Burman cultivators. In the Shan States, however, this was not a political issue for the British had prevented Indian money-lenders, and also Burmans in general, from settling there. The Shans and Shan States were thus largely insulated from the ideals of an independent Burma, as well as from the political and economic progress of the lowlands.

The seeds of internal dissent, ethnic rivalry, and political competition were, in fact, sown in the period well before World War II. The British desire to protect the interests of the minorities, referred to earlier, has been interpreted as being a source of disunity and conflict.

> During this period, developments . . . tended to create tension and violence rather than peace and unity. From the beginning of their rule, the British had sought to protect the minorities from the dominant Burmans. The indigenous minorities, most of whom lived in areas fringing the Burmese heartland — such as the Shans, Kachins and Chins, who collectively occupied approximately 45 per cent of the country's area — were administered under the direct authority of the governor separately from the rest of Burma.[16]

Consistent attempts had been made constitutionally and legislatively by the British to maintain the ethnic divisions in Burma. For example,

Karens who were not entirely a mountain frontier people and most of whom lived intermingled amongst Burmans in the lowlands, were allotted reserved seats in the legislature to protect their group interests. The Indian immigrants were also given special treatment and in 1935 were granted special seats in the elected assembly. This policy of division had been extended along occupational lines including military service.

The Japanese occupation of 1942–45 brought out into the open the differences between Burman and non-Burman. The Japanese had appeared to be solidly behind Burman nationalist aspirations. While Burmans in general, and for the first part of the occupation at least, sympathized with and aided the Japanese, it was the Karens, Kachins, and Chins who remained aloof. Kachin and Chin units, in fact, fought on the Allied side against the Japanese.[17]

The loyalty of the "martial" hill peoples to the British was no mere coincidence. The colonial government followed a policy in which certain minorities were allowed to bear arms for the Crown, while the Burman majority was regarded as a race to be controlled. This was not surprising considering the record of Burman resistance to British rule.

> Using the pretext that Karens, Kachins and Chins made better soldiers than Burmans, the British recruited members of these indigenous groups into the British-Burma army and generally excluded Burmans from its ranks.[18]

It was a cause for resentment among the Burmans to see those they regarded as inferiors, and former subject races, bearing arms.

The initial successes of the post-1946 minority rebellions, especially the Karen attacks into the areas around Rangoon, can be attributed to the earlier training of both officers and men by the British. The identification by Burmans of Karens with British interests has further aggravated the problems of present-day Burma. This mutual hostility has been reinforced by the policies of previous rulers, viz. by the Japanese and the British recruiting from different ethnic groups. While the British used the Karen, Chin, Kachin, Shan, and Arakanese minorities, the Japanese avoided these peoples and preferred Burman recruits.[19]

In addition to the divisiveness brought about by differentiated military recruitment, British policies aimed at aiding Burma towards self-rule within the Commonwealth led, albeit inadvertently, to a further widening of the political gap between Burman and non-Burman. Along with attempts to attain self-rule, a measure of freedom was given, but chiefly only to the Burmans in the lowlands. During the period from 1923 to 1941, the British rulers steadily granted concessions to the

Burmese. Self-government was the eventual aim. The constitution of 1935 set up limited self-government with a lower house and cabinet. The more important ministries — defence and foreign affairs — however, were the responsibility of the governor.[20] This period comprising the approximately twenty years prior to the beginnings of the demise of British rule saw important developments which have implications for the strategic situation of the post-independence period. Advancement to self-rule and eventually independence gave Burmans a consciousness of Burma as a modern nation-state.

Here the consequences of the earlier colonial rule appear again. In a political and administrative decision which was to have far reaching consequences for an independent Burma, the British followed an arrangement which to all effects and purposes instituted an inner Burman Burma and an outer non-Burman Burma. In the 1935 constitution, the governor held direct administration over Frontier Areas, without having to consult parliament or his ministries.[21] Thus was the continued existence of an abiding divide in Burma ensured by the colonial policy of ethnic division. Desiring to lead the Burmans politically to a higher level of parliamentary democracy, and wishing to preserve the political institutions of the frontier peoples, notably the Shans, the British through a series of administrative decrees in effect created the basis for two Burmas.

In post-colonial Burma, moreover, nationalism is identified with ethnic *Burman* nationalism and is moreover narrowed down to be closely associated with Buddhism. It has been pointed out that Buddhism, as a nationalistic symbol and as an integral part of what Burmans see as their political and military power and high civilization before the arrival of British imperialism had played a strong role in the rise of Burman nationalistic opposition to British rule.[22]

The Burman-Buddhist outlook widens the highland-lowland gap since in addition to marked linguistic differences, most of the highland groups with exceptions like the Shan, are non-Buddhists. The Karens who have put up some of the stiffest military opposition to Rangoon since independence are to a large extent Christian, especially their leaders. Over and above economic and political differences the cleavage is thus exacerbated by an ingrained ethnic hostility. It has been observed, perhaps unfairly, that Burma's policy towards minorities "... is a manifestation of ingrained Burman contempt for the different races that populate the peripheries of the country...."[23]

At this stage it would be worthwhile to look yet further back into history. The concept of assimilating the mountain minorities would appear alien to the Burmans. While many observers would tend to the view that British colonial policy was mainly responsible for dissension in Burma, it would be useful, however, to see the problem also in the perspective of cultural relationships in historical or pre-British Burma. While relationships within Burman society itself were not rigid, the relationships between Burman and non-Burman, on the other hand, showed a tendency towards rigidity.[24] Under the Burman monarchical system, no serious attempt was made to Burmanize the mountain minorities, such as the Shan. At the level of royalty, there was intermarriage between conquering Burman and defeated minority groups, but generally there appeared little interaction between lowland Burman and the mountain dweller away from the plains. Discrimination and apartness were features of these social and political relationships.

> Some of the minorities living among the Burmans, particularly the Karens, were treated with hostility and were not accepted as equals. Mons and Arakanese who were captured in war and forced to migrate to Burman population centres found it relatively easy to intermingle and intermarry with their captors. The Burmans did not exert pressure to assimilate or Burmanise the culture of minority groups living in the frontier areas, such as the Shans. As long as the conquered people sent a few sons as hostages and daughters as wives of the Burman monarch and accepted a Burman official at their court, few other demands were made. Thus the Burman political culture treated non-Burmans who did not intermarry or assimilate as separate and different. . . . No serious effort was made to Burmanise the minorities, and the ethnic and cultural diversity developed as part of the Burman tradition has carried over into the modern period.[25]

It would again appear that the separateness in political and cultural identity of the various ethnic groups of Burma existed well before the arrival of both the British and later the Japanese. The British only solidified an existing system for their own political and administrative purposes.

The Minorities in Laos in Relation to the Lowlanders

Burma and Laos are the two countries with the highest percentage of upland minorities in their respective populations. In Laos, as in Burma, there has been antagonism between lowland main ethnic groups and the uplanders. There has been widespread exploitation and subsequent alienation of the hill peoples. Approximately 500,000 Lao Thong of Mon-Khmer and Malayo-Polynesian derivation live in Laos.[26] The lowland Lao used the Lao Thong, whom they referred to as *kha*, as slaves, until the late nineteenth century when the French abolished slavery.

The lowland Lao clearly regard the Lao Thong as second class citizens with minimal rights. As late as the 1960s the Lao Thong of the northern parts of Laos were subject to corvée draft. Traditionally they could be compelled to work for the lowland Lao without payment.[27] As a result of the past injustices inflicted on the Lao Thong "the Lao Thong's attitude towards the lowland Lao is simple hatred".[28] With the exception of a few tribes living in the lowlands, the Lao Thong "resent their slave-like status and the perjorative term *kha* which the Lao use to designate them".[29] The wars in Laos were to a large extent influenced by these attitudes which prevailed widely before the North Vietnamese and Pathet Lao successes in Laos at the close of the Vietnam War.

The Pathet Lao had taken pains to exploit the alienation of the Lao Thong and other groups by promises of autonomy, social and political equality with the lowland Lao, and the right to govern their own affairs.[30] Prominent among the inducements offered to the minorities are the promises embodied in the platforms of the front organizations. The Neo Lao Hak Sat, the Pathet Lao's mass front organization, had guaranteed social and political equality in its platform.[31] But even in the early 1980s, it still remained to be seen whether promises, such as that of autonomy for the mountain monarchs, could be realized.

In Burma, in the colonial and post-colonial periods, events have tended to harden the division between highland and lowland, while in Laos the period of the Vietnam War saw highlanders like the Lao Thong identifying themselves with a national cause led by middle-class lowlanders. Whether this common identity of purpose will last and whether the traditional and ingrained prejudices of the lowland Lao can be eradicated remains to be seen. What is also not yet known is whether the policy of ethnic equality and minority representation in the government will be fully implemented in the Lao People's Democratic Republic. It has been noted that:

> In view of the highly plural nature of its society, the LPDR is unlikely to avoid the ethnic tensions common among its neighbours in Southeast Asia or to escape the demands for power that excluded ethnic groups have been making throughout the Third World.[32]

A communist-ruled Laos has not yet escaped from the geopolitical predicament arising from primordial highland-lowland tensions. Significantly, the derogatory *kha*, signifying the highland peoples, is still commonly used in Vientiane.[33] Due to the high proportion of highlanders in the population of Laos, amounting to approximately 50 per cent of the total, and in view of the political dissatisfaction, and even armed dissent against communist rule among the lowland Lao themselves, the problems of the communist government of Laos will be of such a magnitude that implementation of ethnic equality and the policy of allowing the highlanders to govern their own affairs may not be possible for the foreseeable future.

French Policy in Vietnam

An important feature of the policy of the French colonial government in Vietnam was the exploitation of the divisions between the Vietnamese of the lowlands and the minorities in the uplands. The practical objective was to rigidify the territorially-based cleavage between the various ethnic groups, particularly that which already existed between plainsmen and mountaineers. The French employed ethnic Vietnamese or Kinh as their minions and used them to help administer and control the minorities. At the same time, soldiers were recruited from among the highland minorities and were deployed to suppress Vietnamese uprisings or as prison guards. This policy of the French administration caused resentment between Kinh and the highland minorities.[34]

Some Chinese Attitudes to Minorities

It has been noted that a different situation exists in the mountain regions of South and Southwest China. C.P. Fitzgerald has pointed out that in the Chinese view, "[t]he sense of unity, of belonging to a civilisation, rather than to a state or a nation" has deep historical roots.[35] In relation to China's south, the same author remarks on the Chinese view of their civilization: "It was an ideal which could be transmitted to the southern peoples as they were absorbed by or accepted into"[36] the orbit of Sinic civilization. In this context, historically China has had no fear of threat from its southern border.[37] While the Chinese have "historically regarded the northwestern nomadic barbarians as irreconcilable foes",[38] they have by contrast seen the southern peoples as ". . . merely 'raw' country cousins. Most of the peoples of the southwest did not have physical appearances significantly different from the Chinese. In modern times in southwest China, the expressions 'sheng' and 'shu', 'raw' and 'ripe' (or 'cooked') were still commonly used to distinguish between those non-Chinese peoples who clung to their old customs, and those who had to a great degree accepted Chinese civilisation."[39] Intermarriage between Chinese males and women of the minorities is not uncommon in the hills and is one aspect of the assimilation of the south. In contrast, the Vietnamese, themselves sinicized, very rarely intermarried with hill minorities. There is hardly any intermarriage even with the more sophisticated Tho and Nung who live in close proximity to regions of dense Kinh population.[40]

The sublime faith the Chinese, farmers as well as mandarins and emperors, had in the utter superiority and achievements of their civilization gave them a confidence, and a patronizing yet benign attitude to neighbouring non-Han peoples provided they were not entirely hostile to the Court. This abiding belief of the Chinese in their cultural superiority has been expressed thus: "If distant people are not obedient to China, Chinese rulers should win them over by cultivating their own refinement and virtue."[41] The influence of China over neighbouring states and non-Han ethnic groups was often expressed in moral terms, too. Like the Confucian exemplar who by conduct and example won lesser beings over to good socialized behaviour, the Chinese empire was thought to exude this moral influence and pressure. "The kings of former times cultivated their own refinement and virtue in order to subdue persons at a distance, whereupon the barbarians (of the east and north) came to Court to have audience. This comes down as a long tradition."[42] Furthermore, many Chinese also regard the H'mong or Miao, Yao, Tai, and other minorities as being of the Chinese family of peoples, even though the Miao among others have been subjected at times to punitive campaigns.

Within China itself there have nevertheless been differences in perceptions of a state's role in minority policy and of the generalized relationship between the people of lowland civilization and the mountain cultures. The relationship between the lowland Han and the non-Han in the mountains should not, of course, be exaggerated in terms of amicability. It is alleged that the Guomindang and the warlords, for example, often adopted repressive policies towards the minorities, or had generally neglected them. Friction and tensions have existed and wars have taken place between Han and non-Han. Edgar Snow noted that before the Revolution in the Kunming area ". . . [d]istrust and hostility were mutual" between Han and mountaineer.[43] Generally, however, the overall view held by those of Sinic culture contrast markedly with what has been observed in Burma, or Laos, for example.

Past Han population pressures pushing various ethnic groups southwards have led frequently to competition for, and conflict over, the limited arable land of the highlands. However, this ethnic intermingling together with the existence of a benevolent Chinese attitude towards the highlanders has led to extensive cultural contacts. Historically the technological superiority of Chinese plains culture over that of the hills has led to extensive cultural absorption and assimilation of salient features of Chinese culture by the highland dwellers.

It is significant that several of the hill groups which live in montane Southeast Asia, notably the Yao and even the Nung — the latter living on the Sino-Vietnam borderlands — are regarded as being at least partly, in the case of the Nung heavily, "sinicized". The Nung use Chinese calligraphy and some Nung clans are still referred to by their place of origin in China. To a lesser extent this is also true of the H'mong. The Xhuang of Guangxi, too, are to a very large extent "sinicized". Split loyalties were reported among the Nung and other groups at the time of the Chinese punitive campaign into North Vietnam in 1979. Prior to the communist victory in 1975, some Vietnamese referred to the Nung as being "Chinese".

In some of these groups, the Chinese written script is revered, with Chinese ideographs adorning households. Medicine-men who know the Chinese ideographs are held in high regard. Among many of the hill groups, "sinicization" is noticeable in the adoption of Chinese religious ideas and practice. Among both the Yao and H'mong, for example, the cult of ancestor worship is of great importance.[44]

Chinese Highland Settlement and Some Chinese Affinities to Highlanders

Chinese influence in the highlands was noticeable in cross-border trading activities which were widespread until the "closure" of borders for various reasons in the post-World War II period. It is also seen in the adoption of Chinese styles of living, for example, in the use of Chinese-type household and farming implements, eating utensils, and importantly in the use of forms of the Chinese language. In northern Burma ". . . [f]ree movement across the national boundary with China persisted until 1958. For centuries the only source of agricultural implements like plow-blades and hoes, other goods like swords, and pots and pans has been from China, through seasonal and migratory smiths."[45] The Shans wear, or used to wear, a characteristic broad-rimmed, limp, woven grass hat imported from Yunnan.

This overland trading between Yunnan and northern Southeast Asia goes back many centuries and has been a salient aspect of Chinese dealings with the southern peoples. In the case of northern Thailand and northern Laos, the local population are familiar with Chinese settlers and traders mainly from Yunnan, many of them Muslim and in the local Tai term "Haw". It has been noted earlier that the Yunnan dialect of the Chinese language is widely used among the mountain peoples. In 1876, the Qing suppressed a Muslim rebellion in Yunnan based on a quasi-independent Muslim "kingdom" centred on the Dali

(Ta-li) basin. Many of the defeated Chinese Muslims settled in what is now Burma and northern Thailand to escape reprisals. In the 1950s the numbers were increased following a further influx of refugees when the People's Republic of China (PRC) was set up.[46]

Currently, about half of the estimated 30,000 Haw Chinese in northern Thailand are Muslim. The hill-dwelling Chinese are to be found mainly in the mountainous Fang district of Chiang Mai province, and in Chiang Saen district of the province of Chiang Rai. The swidden farming of hill rice and trading are their main occupations.[47] By the early 1980s they had taken to farming of cash crops, including fruit and high-grade market gardening. The Chinese movement into mountainous upper Burma and northern Thailand is typical of most of the other southward ethnic movements in montane Southeast Asia, in that it was caused mainly by turmoil and strife in southern China. The Chinese of these uplands are not typical of the mainstream of Chinese settlement in Southeast Asia which has been, and still is, mainly urban in character and which was water-borne in origin.

In the gradual process of movement south by refugees when the PRC was established, many permanent Chinese communities of agriculturists have been established in the highlands especially in northern Thailand. In addition many highland villages have resident Chinese in their midst, usually as shopkeepers. Chinese settlements tend to be separate ethnic entities but there has also been considerable intermarriage between Chinese traders and shopkeepers to local upland women.[48] The Chinese presence is felt in many villages, culturally as well as in economic activities. Many Yunnanese men who have settled as traders in upland villages have taken Chinese wives, and together with their families form effectively Chinese households in "tribal" villages. The Chinese residents in the mountains generally maintain amicable relationships with the other highland dwellers. It has been noted that:

> [with] . . . hillmen whose own connexion with China is by no means forgotten, especially Yao and H'mong but to a lesser extent Lahu and Lisu as well, these Chinese families in their midst are more than simply tolerated, they are represented as representatives of a high culture, well worth emulating.[49]

Chinese, in the form of its southwestern dialects, is widely understood and spoken in the highlands of mainland Southeast Asia. In the case of Burma — where Burmese is also widely known in the highlands — and northern Thailand, the Chinese dialect is Yunnanese, a northern "mandarin"-type form. In areas adjacent to Guangxi, the western

Guangxi dialects are widely known. In addition, as noted earlier, most hillmen are at least bilingual if not trilingual or even quadrilingual, often with a knowledge of Chinese included. In addition to feelings of cultural affinity, exemplified in one aspect by knowledge of the Chinese language, the Chinese settlers enjoy mutually satisfactory economic relations with the other groups.

In the case of northern Thailand, it has been observed that:

> Many highlanders, especially the Lisu, the Akha, the H'mong and the Yao, also prefer to deal with Chinese shopkeepers rather than with Yuan[50] market sellers. One of the reasons is that these highlanders often know Chinese, as spoken by the Yunnanese, while they often do not know Yuan, the language of the demographically and politically dominant groups in northern Thailand.[51]

Other reasons for this preference are the hospitality given by the Chinese shopkeepers, a bed to sleep in, advice on where to obtain other services, and how to deal with the official authorities from the lowlands. Lowland Tai Yuan market vendors deal only in the mornings in selected places whereas the Chinese shopkeeper has what amounts to a permanent base in the hills, often open for business at all times. Besides, the Tai Yuan traders are often women whereas the hillmen prefer to trade with members of their own sex. As traders, the Chinese generally operate *in situ* or else travel from, and return to, fixed bases, usually a shop in a village.

The settled nature of the Chinese in the hills is most clearly seen in their agriculture. They tend to have a greater diversity of crops than do their neighbours and are willing to grow cash crops whenever these can be sold. These settlers also have an advantage in that they have been able to adapt fairly intensive methods of cultivation to a mountainous environment. It has been noted that their influence has been positive for highland agriculture, as is the case for northern Thailand. Although their agricultural techniques are "fifty years behind the most advanced agriculture in Japan or Taiwan, . . . [they are] to a similar degree in advance of the agriculture at present practised by all about them".[52] Technologically, the Chinese of montane Southeast Asia are perhaps the most advanced of all the upland groups. Of all the peoples of essentially lowland cultures bordering on the montane zone, only the Chinese have been able, without official encouragement, to adapt to the highland environment and to settle there permanently. Those who have settled in these northern mountains are almost entirely anti-communist, having fled from China after the communist revolution.

The Chinese — not necessarily communist[53] — presence in the mountains and the use of Chinese as a language of trade and communication between different ethnic groups is a pointer to the relatively weak presence in terms of language and culture of the southern lowland states. This pattern appears to be the case in northern and northeastern Burma and the Shan plateau, northern Thailand, and northern and northwestern Laos. The distribution of individual Chinese and their connections with the hill groups is significant in terms of the unanswered question: where do the real boundaries lie? This question has been raised earlier in another context by E.R. Leach when he discussed it in the nature of the frontiers of the region. Perhaps more important is that within the size and diversity of China, there have developed Han groups who are equally at home, socially and agriculturally, in mountain as in plain. The Yunnanese and the men from Guangxi — as well as the Hakkas who are not strongly represented in northern Southeast Asia except in isolated pockets in the uplands adjoining the border — in a way put the men of the southern lowlands at a disadvantage in any political or economic competition in the highlands.

Coastal Plains Authority, Minority Areas, and the Highlands

The governments of the lowland states are essentially governments of lowlanders with access to the coast. The plains have usually been more advanced than the highlands in technological terms. The attainment of this superiority is partly related to trade and access to the sea. The sheer physical size of the main cultivable plains and their higher productivity meant also that the lowland cultures were superior in the size of the economies. The plains authorities with greater resources of richer land could therefore muster larger food reserves, more people, and labour and thus larger armies. Food reserves, and men not needed for agricultural production were vital for the power of the state. Thus the annual post-harvest season, when grain and men were available, was the time for the various monarchs and princes to launch military campaigns against rivals. The historic Burmese campaigns into Thailand are good examples.

In modern times, as well as with most historical epochs, the balance of power measured in numerical counts of men and wealth, has tilted, and tilts heavily, towards the plains. Historical exceptions have been when the plains were disunited and weakened by internal strife or crumbling kingships thus enabling a strong mountain leader or coalitions of mountain minorities to overrun the plains or parts of the plains. This happened with the spread of Shan military power in Burma and into northeast India in the period following the crumbling of the Pagan Dynasty of Burma towards the close of the twelfth century.

In this respect, the Burmans and Thai themselves can be said to represent the remnants of waves of southward migration of warlike, essentially highland people overcoming previous plains civilizations, notably the Mon-Khmer. In China, Tibetans and Luoluos have in the past swept into the neighbouring Han-inhabited valleys and lowlands in short-lived expansions.

Intermontane Flatlands

In the interaction between highland and lowland, it is important to differentiate the different kinds of lowland or valley authority which the highlanders have had to deal with in the past. This will give a clearer picture of interaction between highland-based military power and that of the lowlands.

Plains-type authority and military power are of two kinds — those which are essentially based on the coastal or riverine plains opening onto the coast, mentioned earlier, and those of the smaller inland valleys or basins. Examples of power centres in the coastal plains or plains within easy reach of the coast by river are those of the Arakan coast of western Burma, the Irrawaddy and Salween drainage systems of Burma, the Central Plains of Thailand drained by the Menam Chao Phraya flowing into the Gulf of Thailand, the Tonkin plains or Red River delta of northern Vietnam, the Mekong delta, the small coastal plains on the central Vietnamese coast, and the large plains of the Cambodian basin centring on the wet lands around the Tonle Sap.

Military power based on plains within easy access of the sea has the advantage over inland power bases, unless the latter have access to aid from external sources. The role of the sea in the accumulation of wealth and military power is seen in the Thai economic resurgence which after the fall of Ayudhya was based on sea-borne trade with China.[54] This same process was continued in the early Bangkok period, with much of the trade being controlled by the royal household. This trade included the import of strategic materials, like metals and saltpetre, from China.[55]

There are two sub-types of intermontane lowlands. The weaker and most widely scattered type is that found in the numerous narrow ribbon-like valleys, on the alluvial bottoms of which irrigated rice can be grown. Such valleys are found throughout the highlands. Throughout the region these are invariably inhabited by Shans or Tais. The second more important category of inland plains comprise the numerous, scattered, old lake basins like those of the Shan plateau in Burma,

Mogaung in the northern part of Burma, Menglai and Dali in Yunnan, the Chiang Mai and Chieng Rai basins in northern Thailand, and the Dien Bien Phu valley in the mountains of northern Vietnam.

With the exception on Han-populated upland basins in Yunnan, the ethnic groups most often identified with valley bottoms and lake basins are the Tai-speaking ones — Tais, Shans, and also the Xhuang of Guangxi. The Tais and the related Shan have generally been politically predominant in the highland region from northern Vietnam into the Shan States of Burma. The Tais and Shans are invariably alluvial valley bottom dwellers, with an economy based on wet or irrigated rice cultivation using buffalo-drawn ploughs. The soil and the technology gives the Shan greater surpluses of grain compared to the shifting or swidden agriculture of the mountain slope dwellers. A sign of Shan power derived from the agricultural surpluses are the size of valley settlements and towns, which are centres of small principalities. Leach has pointed out that in the Shan and Kachin states of Burma the Shans are the only inhabitants in the valleys. Where there are no Shans, the valleys are deserted.[56] Although the Tai or Shan are valley dwellers, they are included here as "highland" peoples as opposed to the plains' dwellers of the main riverine lowlands.

Mainly because of colonial acquisitions as in the case of the Shan valleys and Dien Bien Phu, these intermontane basins have been incorporated into the main coastal lowland states. On occasion in the past they played a role balancing the power of the rising lowland states. This was especially so when they had access to material technology from China by overland trade routes. The Chiang Mai power, once at odds with that based in the central plains of Thailand is now part of the Thai kingdom. Dien Bien Phu, once controlling much of the northern highlands of Vietnam, is now part of Vietnam, and the sources of Shan power, once a rival to the Burmese, are now part of the territories of the Union of Burma.

Coastal and Inland Authority and the Montane Belt

It has to be emphasized that in terms of resources that can be mobilized, the inland power bases are small and weak compared to the potential of the coastal plains. Historically, however, in the period before the coastal lowlands (with their heavy swamp forest cover and the floods which were difficult to control) were fully developed, the inland basins were political and military rivals of states established in the plains closer to the coast. Because of their size and the annual flooding, the coastal plains presented difficult problems of water control to technologically weak or underpopulated states.

In modern times, intermontane sources of economic power and manpower, small though they may be, represent highly strategic outliers of the central power base, and convenient military and political bases, from which central lowland authorities can control the surrounding uplands. This applies to both the southern states as well as to the northern part of the montane zone. They provide, for example, not only easily available rice for the provisioning of troops, but as the Chinese in Yunnan and the French in Dien Bien Phu have found they are the only suitable locations for modern air bases.

From its possession of extensive tracts of the massif, China is to its immediate neighbours to the south, a state which has to be reacted to, or dealt with, in a montane environment. From the perspective of both the lowland coastal powers of Southeast Asia, with the exception of Vietnam, and of the inhabitants of the montane zone, the Chinese plains-based power to the north is to all effects and purposes an "inland" or continental power and is from the southern lowland perspective, a largely montane power. Vietnam, but not Laos, would see China as both a montane, continental power and a power with strong maritime interests, as witnessed in the disputes over the Paracels, the Spratleys, and areas of the South China Sea's northern shelf.

Thus we have a picture of a broad montane zone, separating a single large plain-based power to the north from a series of smaller coastal plains powers to the south. Within the mountain zone, partitioned politically between the various plains states, there are no centres of power comparable to that to the north and to those in the south. But there are in the confines of the mountainous belt numerous small basins and ribbon-like valleys and flatlands which form convenient bases for forward military power.

From another perspective, it is important to note that although access to the sea gives the plains-based authorities decided advantages over the land-locked sources of military power in the minority-inhabited frontier areas, the latter in fact can and have in the past relied on overland trade and cultural contact with the Chinese civilization, in order to draw on its technology, including military technology. The political and military decline of these intermontane basins, accompanied by the gravitation to the sea coast of the seats of authority has put distance and rough terrain between the capitals of the southern states and the Chinese border, and has further reinforced the belief that China and Southeast Asia are both separate and distinct.

The widely-held view has been to assume that, like the Himalayas, this east-west mountain belt of mainland Southeast Asia acts as some kind of dividing or at least buffering zone separating to some extent China from "Southeast Asia". In fact this is one of the criteria used by geographers in the delimitation of "Southeast Asia". The minority-inhabited montane zone of mainland Southeast Asia will be examined later on in this study in the perspective of its "separating" function in state-to-state relations in the region.

Antagonisms in the Geo-Strategic Context

While it is true that a lowland state's authorities can manipulate mutual suspicions or hostility between mountain people living in the territory, it can be equally true that a larger, stronger, or more influential state bordering on the highland belt would be well placed to attempt, should it suit its overall interests, to co-ordinate highland groups, using ideology and common highland grievances as linking factors to counter the influence and power of the lowland state. The welding influence of dissenting and revolutionary ideology, particularly communism, in states whose governments are non-communist, yet authoritarian, should not be underestimated.

A situation in which the authorities of a lowland state depend on manipulation of inter-highlander feuds and rivalries to maintain the paramountcy of its administration is, however, not conducive to the stability of the state itself. In contrast, it can perhaps administer the mountain population as part of the national polity through political integration with the lowlands on terms acceptable to the highlanders; or through an integration achieved by conquest — that is, drawing on an example beyond the region under study — by a thorough military subjugation, as in East Timor. A relatively weak lowland government does not have the luxury of indulging in political experiments and ethnic manipulation *in vacuo* within sealed borders. While inter-group rivalries allow for government manipulation as a means of asserting the lowland state's authority over the mountains it is, however, equally likely to invite external involvement. In such a situation the mountainous possessions of a lowland state could slip out of the control of the centre.

Ethnic Relations and the Strategic Situation

In the southern states, the general pattern of ill-feeling between highlander and lowlander is reinforced by mutual ignorance. Except in the cases of individuals and isolated settlements, there is minimal interaction between highland and lowland; rather, there is ethnic stereotyping by lowlanders of the hill peoples, and exploitation of the materially less advanced and poorer highlanders by individuals from the lowlands, trader as well as official and soldier. This hostility and suspicion is widespread and reciprocal.

The existence of insurgencies and resistance against central rule, constitutional disputes, and charges of "law-breaking" (mainly in terms of alleged smuggling and misuse of the environment), made by the authorities against the highlanders are symptoms of a cleavage between highlands and the lowland centre. It is also a sign of a lack of understanding of the problems that beset both hillmen as well as the government that rules them.

In any assessment of the geopolitical and strategic elements present in the highland-lowland dichotomy of mainland Southeast Asia, due emphasis should be given to the marked difference in economic levels and cultural and technological achievement existing between plains and uplands. Exploitation of the usually penurious and less well-organized inhabitants of the highlands is well-known and needs no recapitulation here. The exploitation is basic to these differences, expressed in tensions and conflict which it exacerbates. This cleavage between highland and lowland within states and in the region as a whole is further complicated by an inadequate system of boundaries between states in the region.

The Question of Independent Land-Locked Mountain States

It would not be inappropriate to end this chapter with a discussion of the question of independent montane states. The situation in the mountains does not approach the stage where any mountain power or state is likely to arise, as was the case with the historical Shan power. Through a French colonial decision, Laos remains as the last example of an inland and mainly mountainous Southeast Asian state. Historical cases of such non-coastal states were often to be found in what are now the mountainous parts of China, Burma, Thailand, and Laos beginning with the case of the legendary "Nanchao".

In passing, it would be useful to turn briefly to the question of the possible development of "internal" or "indigenous" sources of power. "Internal" is meant here to denote sources of power developed solely within the montane zone and which are distinct from the main sources of power in the lowlands.

Although there may be sufficient ground for the creation of mountain states, the existing state of international affairs does not allow for any idealized mountain state or confederation of mountain states, even though this concept has been mooted by the leaders of several mountain dwelling ethnic groups.

Referring to Burma, it has been stated that the Shan of the former British Shan States display some of the characteristics necessary for the creation of a separate mountain state.

> Of all the non-Burman peoples, the Shan have the soundest claim to be treated as a nation. Had the British drawn the borders of Burma differently, had they followed the practice of the French in demarcating Laos, they would have created a separate British Shan states colony. But such a Shan state would have been no more capable of defending or financing itself than Laos has been. If the Shan State were juridically as sovereign as Laos, the Shan people would have to consider the necessity for cooperation not only with the central government of Burma but also with Thailand and China. It is difficult to believe that the Shan state region would be more secure, independent or peaceful than it is now if it were formally independent like Laos, as some Shan leaders would like it to be.[57]

Moreover, it should be noted that for any hypothetically independent mountain state to exist in mainland Southeast Asia, it would be necessary for its leaders to accept the paramountcy of the interests of neighbouring lowland states over its own. A form of quasi-independence which recognizes the leadership of a stronger neighbouring state as in the Laos-Vietnam relationship gives rise to possibilities, provided that other neighbouring states, particularly the PRC, accept the situation.

An interest in a confederation of mountain nation-states stretching from Assam to Thailand was reported to have been expressed by Nagas, Ahoms, Shans, and other groups.[58] A.Z. Phizo, leader of the past Naga resistance against Indian rule, had in the past called for military cooperation between the insurgents of Nagaland, Manipur, Tripura, and those of the Mizo Hills, as well as with the Shans and other hill groups. Phizo also held views on what he considered the appropriate political reorganization of the hill peoples.[59] The strategic and political environment is inimical to any such form of political unity. For the foreseeable future, then, analysis should focus only on existing "lowland" states and how power relationships in the region interact and are influenced by the existence of the highland-lowland dichotomy.

★ ★ ★

It can be said, without undue exaggeration, that in mainland Southeast Asia the highlands and the lowlands are two separate worlds. Traditionally lowlanders have avoided what they saw as the hostile environment of the uplands. Mountain peoples are minorities in the post-war states where they find themselves, but in the mountainous frontier tracts, the lowlanders are few or absent altogether. Beyond the topographical basis of differentiation, the issues of mutual, and age-old, hostility divide lowlander from highland dweller. Sharp differences in the mode of agricultural production and of economic interest deepens this cleavage. There has been a tendency by the centres to regard highland minorities as being uncivilized, lawless, and beyond the pale. Neglect, economic exploitation, and political repression by lowlanders have given rise to deep antagonism. The gap between lowland majority and upland minorities was in some instances widened by the colonial powers which manipulated rivalry and hostility to suit their own interests. While lowlanders as a rule have not been able to adjust to the highlands, the Chinese from mountainous southwest China have been able to adapt to both the physical as well as the social environment of the mountains. To the southern lowland states, the rugged face of Southwest China would appear to give China the features of an essentially montane power. The historical importance attached to the intermontane basins as sources of power has declined, and has been supplanted by the growth of coastal plains power made possible in part by the improvement in the technology of artificial drainage and by the development of overseas trade. This has led to a shift southwards of the seats of authority, lending credence to the widely held perception that Southeast Asia is indeed sheltered from China by its northern mountains, which ironically are the homelands of often estranged ethnic groups harbouring a variety of resentments towards the lowland majority governments.

NOTES

1. Maran La Raw, "Toward a Basis for Understanding the Minorities in Burma: The Kachin Example", in *Southeast Asia: The Politics of National Integration*, ed. John T. McAlister Jr. (New York: Random House, 1973), p. 345.
2. Arthur J. Dommen, *Conflict in Laos: The Politics of Neutralization* (New York: Praeger, 1971), footnote p. 342.
3. Edgar O'Ballance, *The Wars in Vietnam 1954–1973* (New York: Hippocrene Books, 1975), p. 97.
4. For a description of the many ethnic groups, see Frank M. LeBar, Gerald C. Hickey, and John K. Musgrave, eds., *Ethnic Groups of Mainland Southeast Asia* (New

Haven: Human Relations Area Files Press, 1964).
5. Cornelis Lodewijk Johannes van der Meer, *Rural Development in Northern Thailand: An Interpretation and Analysis* (Groningen: Rijsuniversiteit te Groningen, 1981), p. 85.
6. E.R. Leach, "The Frontiers of 'Burma' ", in *Southeast Asia: The Politics of National Integration*, ed. John T. McAlister Jr., (New York: Random House, 1973), p. 330. This article was originally published in *Comparative Studies in Society and History* (Cambridge: Cambridge University Press, 1960).
7. Leach, op. cit., pp. 330–31.
8. Leach, ibid., p. 331.
9. George Osborn III, private communication.
10. Hugo Adolf Bernatzik, *Akha and Miao: Problems of Applied Ethnography in Farther India*, translated from German by Alois Nagler (New Haven: Human Relations Area Files 1970), pp. 30–31.
11. *Kuang-ming Jih Pao* (Beijing), 18 January 1957, quoted by Anthony R. Walker, "The Lahu of the Yunnan-Indochina Borderlands: Ethnic Groups and Village Community" (D. Phil. thesis, Oxford University, 1972), p. 56.
12. Alfred W. McCoy, Cathleen B. Read, and Leonard P. Adams II, *The Politics of Heroin in Southeast Asia* (New York: Harper and Row, 1972), p. 265.
13. Leach, op. cit.
14. Ulrich Schweinfurth, "The Problem of Nagaland", in *Essays in Political Geography*, ed. Charles A. Fisher (London: Methuen, 1968), p. 167.
15. Robert H. Taylor, "Burma's National Unity Problem and the 1974 Constitution", *Contemporary Southeast Asia* 1, no. 3 (December 1979): 236.
16. Josef Silverstein, *Burma: Military Rule and the Politics of Stagnation* (Ithaca: Cornell University Press, 1977), pp. 16–17.
17. For the Japanese impact on militarization of the lowland peoples, particularly among Burmans, see Joyce C. Lebra, *Japanese Trained Armies in Southeast Asia* (Hong Kong: Heinemann, 1979).
18. Silverstein, op. cit., pp. 16–17.
19. James F. Guyot, "Ethnic Segmentation in Military Organisations: Burma and Malaysia", in *Political-Military Systems, Comparative Perspectives*, ed. Catherine McArdle Kelleher (Beverley Hills: Sage, 1974), pp. 27–37. A more recent study states that Chin troops saved Rangoon during the Karen attack on Insein in 1949 and that the military itself called in Chin troops on several occasions to put down unrest in the capital. The leadership remains firmly in Burman hands. There is also no shortage of Burman recruits at all levels since a military career is held to be rewarding and honorable. David I. Steinberg, "Constitutional and Political Bases of Minority Insurrections in Burma", in *Armed Separatism in Southeast Asia*, eds. Lim Joo-Jock and Vani S. (Singapore: Institute of Southeast Asian Studies, 1984).
20. Silverstein, op. cit., p. 14.
21. Silverstein, op. cit., p. 15.
22. See for example, Fred R. von der Mehden, "The Growth and Development of the Religio-Nationalist Movement", in *Southeast Asia: The Politics of National Integration*, ed. John T. McAlister, Jr. (New York: Random House, 1973), pp. 128–29.
23. Michael Armacost in "Comments on Robert W. Schwabb III, 'America's Golden Triangle'", *Journal of Contemporary Asia* 8, no. 4 (1978): 584–94.
24. Silverstein, op. cit., p. 11.
25. Ibid.
26. Frank M. LeBar and Adrienne Suddard, eds., *Laos: Its People, Its Society, Its Culture*

(Conn.: New Haven, Human Relations Area Files 1960), p. 42.
27. LeBar and Suddard, op. cit., pp. 73–74.
28. Gary D. Wekkin, "Tribal Politics in Indochina: The Role of Highland Tribes in the Internationalization of Internal Wars", in *Conflict and Stability in Southeast Asia*, ed. Mark W. Zacher and R. Stephen Milne (New York: Anchor Press, 1974), p. 132.
29. Wekkin, ibid.
30. Wekkin, op. cit., p. 138.
31. Ibid.
32. Joseph J. Zasloff and MacAlister Brown, "Laos: Coping with Confinement", *Southeast Asian Affairs 1982* (Singapore: Institute of Southeast Asian Studies, 1982), p. 212.
33. Zasloff and Brown, op. cit., pp. 211–12.
34. Viet Chung, "National Minorities and National Policy in the DRV", in *Vietnamese Studies*, no. 15 (Hanoi, 1968), p. 4.
35. C.P. Fitzgerald, *The Chinese View of their Place in the World* (London: Oxford University Press, 1969), p. 6.
36. Ibid.
37. Wang Gungwu in *Vietnam-Kampuchea-China Conflicts: Motivations, Background, Significance*, ed. Malcolm Salmon. ANU Working Paper no. 1. Canberra, March 1979.
38. Fitzgerald, op. cit., p. 6.
39. Ibid.
40. "The Family and Family Relationships of the Tay and Nung People", *Journal of Ethnology*, no. 2, (Hanoi, 1979) pp. 13–14, translated by Sophie Quinn-Judge in "Southeast Asia Ethnicity and Development Newsletter" 5, no. 2 (Singapore, 1981).
41. *Analects* in J.F. Fairbank, "China's Foreign Policy in Historical Perspective", *Foreign Affairs*, April 1969, p. 457.
42. Ta-Ming chi-li (collected ceremonies of the Ming Dynasty) quoted in *The Foreign Policy of China*, ed. King C. Chen (Seton Hall University Press, 1972), p. 18.
43. Edgar Snow, *The Other Side of the River* (London: Victor Gollancz, 1966), p. 604.
44. Nusit Chindarsi, *The Religion of the H'mong Njua* (Bangkok: The Siam Society, 1976), pp. 32–34; Anthony R. Walker, "Highlanders and Government in Northern Thailand", *Folk* 21–22 (Copenhagen, 1979/80): 426. This attractiveness of a valley civilization for a hill people is not often found in the southern states. There is one notable exception occurring in Burma. There the "Chins are regarded as the community which has most easily adjusted to inclusion within the structures of the central Burma state. . . . The reasons for this are complex and related to the cultural attractions of valley civilization for the Chins." Robert H. Taylor, "Perceptions of Ethnicity in the Politics of Burma", *Southeast Asian Journal of Social Science* (Singapore) 10 January 1982. Also F.K. Lehman, *The Structure of Chin Society* (Urbana: University of Illinois Press, 1963).
45. La Raw, op. cit., p. 345.
46. F.W. Mote, "The Rural Haw of Northern Thailand", in *Southeast Asian Tribes, Minorities and Nations*, ed. P. Kunstadter (Princeton, 1967), pp. 487–524. Also M. Yegar, "The Panthay (Chinese Muslims) of Burma and Yunnan", *Journal of South-East Asian History* 7, no. 1 (March 1966): 73–85.
47. Gordon Young, "The Haw" in *The Hill Tribes of Northern Thailand* (Bangkok: The Siam Society, 1966).
48. Walker, op. cit., p. 425.

49. Walker, op. cit., p. 424.
50. Tai Yuan or the Northern Tai, the lowland people of that region.
51. W.Y. and A.Y. Dessaint, "Economic Systems and Ethnic Relations in Northern Thailand", *Contributions to Southeast Asian Ethnography*, no. 1 (Singapore, September 1982), p. 79.
52. Mote, op. cit., p. 506.
53. In fact, a major influx of Yunnanese and other Chinese into the region after the defeat of the Guomindang brought in a large number of individuals, both soldiers and civilians, who were anti-communist or else fleeing the aftermath of the revolution.
54. Sarasin Viraphol, *Tribute and Profit: Sino-Siamese Trade 1652–1853* (Harvard: Council of East Asian Studies, 1977), pp. 140–59.
55. Hong Lysa, "The Evolution of the Thai Economy in the Early Bangkok Period and its Historiography" (Ph.D. dissertation, University of Sydney, 1981), pp. 77–123.
56. E.R. Leach, *Political Systems of Highland Burma* (Boston: Beacon Press, 1968), pp. 36–37.
57. Taylor (1979), p. 237.
58. Robert D. Crane, *The Role of Ethnic Nationalism in the Modernization and Stabilization of the Third World*, Hudson Institute, Discussion paper, 13 December 1967.
59. Gordon P. Means, "Cease Fire Politics in Nagaland", *Asian Survey* 19 (October-November 1971): 1025 and footnote.

CHAPTER 3

Interstate Boundaries and the Frontiers

Boundaries are designed to divide land or sea space between states. In this chapter, the question of this dividing role is examined, and the topography of the border zones is reviewed in relation to the role of the boundaries.

The Significance of Boundaries

Mainland Southeast Asia is divided by boundaries into a number of sovereign states. The concept of boundaries — that is, demarcations between the territories of neighbouring states — needs to be discussed in some detail, as it is fundamental to the very special role that the montane zone of mainland Southeast Asia plays in the pattern of power distribution and in state-to-state affairs of the region.

A boundary, precisely surveyed and appearing as a line on a map, attains its full meaning only if it separates two states which are able to project their sovereignties, exemplified in the sustained enforcement of the authority of their governments, to the very limit of their respective boundary lines, or claimed boundaries. If conditions on both sides of the boundary bear no relation to this state of affairs which we would normally expect from territories properly administered by established governments, then a distinct geo-strategic environment would emerge.

Boundary Policies and Functions

The governments which rule contiguous territories are normally supposed to have a set of priorities in boundary policy. If boundary policies are not in harmony, or if both sides, or one side, of the boundary line are in disorder or turmoil, then the boundary often can be no longer meaningful in the political, and often in Southeast Asia in an ethnographic, context.

If one side chooses in such a situation to exploit the blurred nature of the line arising in times of turmoil or lack of control, then the boundary loses even more of its originally intended function. If conditions on one side of the line are chaotic while on the other the neighbouring state's sovereignty is exercised to the full, backed by all the necessary accoutrements of power, then needless to say, if any overt competition arises, the strategic advantage lies with the more organized state.

Depending on the more organized state's policies, the status of such an international boundary line is no longer the dividing line it was set up to be, but instead takes on a new significance in state-to-state relations in which the supposedly legal dividing line can be, and often is, ignored if necessary. The boundary *per se* then losses its original function.

Types of Boundaries and Frontiers

In the pre-colonial era the present boundary lines which were imposed on the maps by the intruding European powers did not exist. States and rulers recognized the extent of their authority in relatively imprecise terms. Mountainous areas, often thickly forested, served as "frontier regions" between states. Such frontiers were broad belts of difficult territory with a separating — as distinct from the dividing — function between states. These frontiers, recognized as such by both sides, served geographically as political buffers. In these zones there was often no clear demarcation between each state's zone of influence, although such influences spread with varying degrees of effectiveness into the frontier belt from the lowlands on either side. Often, too, there was interaction in cultural terms between the cultures that the frontiers were supposed to separate.

Frontier zones need not necessarily be confined to mountainous belts. Marshy land has also served this same function. Riverine tracts did not usually act efficiently in this role, since both banks of a river are usually part of one system, politically, economically, and even socially. Separating zones in riverine tracts tend to be unstable like the situation which existed between the expanding Vietnamese territory and the Khmer lands in the lower Mekong region. Culturally, rivers have served as links rather than dividers.

The use of rivers to divide land between two states was an imposition on the cultural and political map dictated by the needs of the colonial powers to define each other's zones of control so as to facilitate their setting up of internal administrations and to avoid possible conflict. The use of the Mekong by the British and French is the classic example of this in Southeast Asia. In other words, the pre-colonial, broad, separating zone was deemed insufficient to show the limits of each state's authority.

In insular Southeast Asia a potentiate based on a river mouth and controlling the trade which passed through, would define the extent of his realm in the direction of the mountains ringing his river valley as being so many days' journey away from his capital at the confluence between sea and river. If a boundary line had been imposed between two states with this kind of behaviour towards sparsely populated inland territory, it would then, at that stage of development in state-to-state relations, have had very little meaning, and indeed would have been unnecessary.

Some Existing Boundary Situations

Various boundary situations exist in the mountainous parts of mainland Southeast Asia. The boundary separating the People's Republic of China (PRC) and Vietnam is an example of a mutually recognized line — with certain exceptions like the ridge called Fakashan in China's Guangxi province, but which is claimed by Vietnam — separating two relatively firmly administered territories belonging to relatively stable states. Of all such lines in Southeast Asia, the Sino-Vietnam boundary is the one which most closely resembles the boundary lines in Europe where the concept of the linear demarcation between two sovereignties evolved to its fullest extent. Yet even the Sino-Vietnamese line especially in its more westerly or mountainous portion has until very recently served in an ambiguous role, with the preventive or dividing aspect of its function being blurred and not very different from that of the other boundaries in montane Southeast Asia.

While the Sino-Vietnamese boundary had grave import for the French forces which respected it — for fear of wider consequences — in their pursuit and bombardment of Vietminh troops during the First Vietnam War, it had a different meaning for the Vietminh who used it as a protective shield allowing access into a then friendly China. The PRC thus applied the European concept of a boundary in its attitude towards the French forces in Vietnam, while at the same time adopting the pre-colonial stance with respect to troops of a friendly power. With the consolidation of Vietnamese power based on a highly organized plains-dwelling population the Sino-Vietnam border condition has, with some exceptions, reverted more to the European pattern.

It is clear from this that the Sino-Vietnamese line is in this respect different from most of the other boundary lines in montane Southeast Asia, that a "Western" style interpretation was given it by both the Chinese and French. After 1975 with the rise of Hanoi's power the Western style function and interpretation of the boundary were given even firmer emphasis though in fact severe porosities still remain.

The boundaries between Burma and China and also that between China and Laos are examples of lines set up in an attempt to separate states of vastly different power status. They are also colonially imposed linear demarcations between what is now the territory of a relatively firmly controlled power — but during the earlier period weak and yielding to Western pressure — contiguous to a former colonial territory or territories previously firmly administered, but now characterized by political and administrative weaknesses or even disorder. This is a partial reversal of the positions obtaining during the colonial era when the colonial possessions were relatively firmly administered. The drawing of the boundaries were in fact at the expense of the earlier zones of influence of imperial China.[1] The British and French set up these boundaries to separate their own colonial gains from the loosely administered and relatively lawless territory of China. Reliance by the Laotian Government on Vietnamese assistance after 1979 partially rectifies for Laos the weakness of its colonially inherited boundary.

The boundary dividing Thailand and Burma shows characteristics of abnormal conditions on both sides of the line, particularly on the Burmese side. While it is largely free of border demarcation disputes, the central government on the Burmese side has been powerless for sustained periods to extend its sovereignty to the limits of its territory, while Thai policies have tended until very recently to ignore the poor, mountainous frontier zone to the north, north-northeast, and west of the country. Functionally the Thai-Burma boundary zone resembles in many respects the pre-colonial dividing zones.

The Indo-Burmese boundary runs through high, rugged terrain. In British times both the Indian and Burmese sides were neglected and thinly administered or else unadministered. The boundary itself was imprecise. In the Naga Hills area "a nominal administrative delimitation was believed to run right through the hills, and with independence of both India and Burma this line has become an international boundary...."[2] Approximately 500,000 Nagas live on the Indian side and about 100,000 are in Burmese territory.[3] The Indo-Burmese boundary, like the Thai-Burma boundary, bears some resemblance to the historical dividing frontier zones, although the Indian and Burmese governments have agreed on a definition of the boundary. The British were less attentive to the Indo-Burma boundary because of the wild nature of the country and because the imperative of defining a foreign power's territory *vis-à-vis* their own was absent.

Boundaries and the Wider Strategic Situation

Boundary lines, however meticulously they may be surveyed and then represented in maps, have to be studied in the context of prevailing political and security conditions in the regions through which they traverse. This may apply even if the international boundary lines have been the subject and result of previous negotiation, "legal" processes, and treaty. It would apply with added force if the boundaries traverse sparsely populated, uninhabited, or ethnically fragmented territory.

In montane Southeast Asia at least, the flux arising from changing political and military conditions have at times meant that international boundary lines serve different purposes in differing strategic situations. The role of boundaries can change with changes in regional power balances, and perceptions of their primary role as dividers — whether linear or zonal — can change with the changing strategic impellants of different historical periods.

The China-Vietnam Boundary: A Historical Background

The demarcation of part of the boundary between China and present-day Vietnam was agreed upon in a Sino-French accord of 1887 on the Tonkin boundary. This agreement followed the June 1885 Treaty of Tianjin, in which China acknowledged French rule in Tonkin. French annexations of territory in Laos led to a western extension of the line dividing French and Chinese territory. The boundary between China and the French possession of Tonkin which, except for a narrow coastal plain bordering on the Gulf of Tonkin, traversed hilly country from the sea to the Black River, was extended westwards to the Mekong River.

The French movement inland and westwards was prompted in part at least, like the British expansion in India and Burma, by a desire for secure frontiers. Weakening of Qing authority in the 1860s and 1870s in the southwest led to armed Chinese bands in Laos and the Tonkin highlands, exerting what the French considered to be an undesirable influence on the Laotians and their rulers. To prevent deterioration of the situation in the western Tonkin highlands, the French annexed the Sip Song Chu Thai in 1888. The Sip Song Chu Thai is a group of Tai principalities and includes the basin of Dien Bien Phu. The French were, like the British in Burma, also attracted by the prospect of control of the Mekong which was thought then to be a potential major trade route leading into the interior of China with its supposedly rich resources and large market for industrial goods.

The largely French-determined line was extended to hive off Laos from China and eventually joined effectively the British held territory in Burma. To illustrate the attention to detail of the way European colonial powers divided up territory between themselves — a reflection of the heritage of the concept of boundary lines brought from Europe — the *thalweg*, or the deepest part of the water channel, of the Mekong was recognized by both British and French as the line of demarcation between British Burma and French Indochina.[4]

It has been asserted that in the negotiation leading to the Treaty of Tianjin the Chinese position was in fact one of some strength, since the French had been handed a military defeat in Langson by the Chinese in 1885.[5] There was thus a degree of mutuality in the drawing up of the line that divides China from Vietnam.

The Terrain of the Sino-Vietnam Boundary and Military Operations

Although not very high, the mountains of the borderlands are nevertheless of a considerably rugged nature in many places, with many steep, almost vertical limestone outcrops overshadowing narrow winding canyon-like valleys many of which are veritable culs-de-sac. It was in this type of country around Langson that a French expeditionary force was routed by Chinese irregulars in 1885.

The Vietminh were later to repeat this performance in their war against the French in the same general area, making skilful use of terrain. Langson, the scene also of the final battle in the Chinese punitive campaign into northern Vietnam in 1979, lies in this terrain and the southernmost significant ridge of the highlands dividing China from Vietnam in fact lies south of Langson. The easily defensible nature of these mountains on both sides of the proposed line was probably a factor which influenced Chinese acceptance of the Treaty of Tianjin. Distracted by internal problems, by turmoil in its other borderlands and by European encroachments on its sea-coast and ports, the court in Beijing would have needed a boundary agreement of the western type in order at least to ensure that further French encroachments by land would be halted or at least checked temporarily. In this instance the western concept of a regularizing boundary line was acceptable not only to the western power in question but also to China.

Permanency of the Sino-Vietnam Boundary?

It has been pointed out that the boundary created between 1887 and 1895 has "stood the test of time, and the present Chinese regime would seem to challenge neither its alignment nor its treaty basis".[6] In the friction and conflict between the PRC and Vietnam after the fall of Saigon in 1975, the alleged Vietnamese "ingratitude" for help given during the Vietnam Wars, its subsequent ill-treatment of ethnic Chinese in Vietnam, and its attack on Kampuchea were, from Chinese pronouncements, the main causes of conflict. Although there was rhetoric by China over the "unequal" boundary, it was not in fact a cause of conflict. Or more precisely, slight differences in interpretation of the actual alignment of the boundary markers did not impinge on vital interests of both parties to a degree that would initiate conflict. Military disputes over isolated hills continued after the Chinese incursion but these have been of tactical not strategic significance. It should be noted, however, that such situations could get out of hand or else be exploited and made the *casus belli* for a more widespread conflagration involving wider interests.

The situation is, nevertheless, different in the case of the marine boundaries between the PRC and Vietnam. The disputed boundary in the Gulf of Tonkin involves proven deposits of offshore petroleum and gas resources, while longer-term conflict is latent over the Chinese held Paracels and the conflicting claims over the more southerly Spratley Islands.

Boundaries, Unequal Treaties, and Conflict

The other mountain frontier area in which China has fought an open, conventional war is the Himalayan line between India and China. The 1962 war in the Himalayas, described as a war over the exact demarcation of a boundary line, has to be seen not only in terms of Nehru's insisting on the inheritance of the farthest limits of imperial British claims,[7] but also against the sum total of a neighbouring state's behaviour in terms of antagonism or accommodation to what the PRC would describe as its vital strategic interests. The Chinese road in the Indian-claimed Ladakh plateau — the western sector of the boundary in dispute — joining western Tibet to Xinjiang is a vital strategic link between two Chinese territories which have been prone to dissidence and restlessness and which were otherwise practically inaccessible to one another.

Indian adherence to maximum British colonial claims, which China rejected in terms of principles of equity, were thus seen, especially in the westerly Himalayas, as threatening the PRC's security position. Colonial boundaries incorporating land yielded by neighbouring countries into what are now the post-colonial states remain a source of potential friction.

Boundaries as Indicators of Mutual Policies by Neighbouring States

Boundaries and the ways in which boundary problems are solved particularly those traversing thinly populated "negative" areas, can be a signpost indicative of the state of mind of the policy-makers of two neighbouring states facing one another. For example, the conciliatory and even accommodating attitude of the Chinese in the negotiations which led to the boundary agreements of the early 1960s with Burma and Nepal contrast strongly with the Chinese posture adopted towards India's claims to the McMahon Line. Conciliation was shown to those who posed no threat. The condition — that is, neglected, unguarded, or unnoticed — that the boundaries themselves are in, can be seen as an index of the perception of the strategic environment by the centres of two neighbouring states. It also indicates the limitations the centres face, in the management of their frontier regions. The limitations are connected with sheer physical separation of the frontiers from the centre which may also be faced by more pressing economic and political problems in areas far removed from the frontier zones and boundary lines.

The Historical Context of the Sino-Burmese Boundary

The present Sino-Burmese boundary line, drawn up by protocol in October 1961,[8] follows closely the line established between the British and the Chinese administration of the Qings and follows in the main the lines which reputedly demarcated the areas of actual Chinese occupation from the line of British advance into the interior from the coast. There are two significant exceptions in the Namwan Tract in the north and the Panlao area east of the Salween in the northeast, where post-colonial adjustments have taken place.

Like the Sino-Vietnam boundary which was drawn up by treaty between the Chinese and the French, the Sino-Burmese boundary is one which can be said to be mutually accepted, as a political dividing line between China and independent Burma. It would appear that "plainly the Chinese view [is] that the current boundary does not take its course because of certain treaties concluded with an imperial power in the past, but because this is an acceptable boundary to two independent Asian countries".[9] The rejection of boundary lines imposed by the colonial powers is implicit in all Chinese actions towards her southern neighbour. If existing boundary lines are accepted, it is because it suits the interests of China, as a power in its own right, dealing with another independent state.

On a government-to-government basis there has been, between Burma and the PRC, a mutual recognition of previous lines which the Chinese, however, had not entirely accepted in their dealings with the British authorities ruling Burma. Much of the *de facto* acceptance prior to the 1961 protocol was due to distance of the boundaries from the centres of authority in the neighbouring states and because there was no immediate urgency by either side to force a decision on the matter. This again is a reflection of the frontier character of the trans-border region.

The Terrain of the Sino-Burmese Boundary

A description in some detail of the topography traversed by the China-Burma boundary is instructive, as it shows that the extended massif of mainland Southeast Asia, however difficult it may seem to be in terms of transportation, does not in fact constitute a complete barrier between states. The Sino-Burmese boundary begins at the junction between the three states of India, Burma, and China.[10] It follows in the northernmost section high ridge lines, rising steeply to heights of 3,500 – 4,000 metres above sea-level. These ridges can in fact be classified as being southeasterly extensions of the Himalayan system.

As the boundary approaches the edges of the Yunnan plateau it traverses ridges which are considerably lower and less rugged. Eastwards up to the banks of the Mekong, the boundary traverses the relatively low (compared to the Himalayan section) Yunnan plateau, dividing it into Chinese and Burmese sectors. Heights in this part of the border area are seldom more than 2,000 metres above sea-level.

The term Yunnan plateau is a misnomer. Far from being a flat-topped tableland, the Yunnan plateau is, in fact, through the action of fluvial or riverine erosion, a complicated maze of isolated groups of mountains and low ridges. These are separated by valleys, some of which have flat bottom lands and which are relatively wide. Chief among these flatlands are the valleys of the Mekong, Salween and the Schweli, and those of their tributaries.

The floors of the valleys of the Yunnan plateau are only about 500 metres above sea-level and have a pronounced warm, wet tropical climate. Importantly, they form the basis of an intensive, wet-rice based agriculture with the resultant relatively dense valley populations, they also provide routes for movement between the north and the south, that is, between the areas under Chinese and those under Burmese administration. These rivers, in most general terms, flow from areas of Chinese control into Burma. On the Chinese side and in the immediate trans-border zone the population is denser than in the other Burmese border areas. In addition there is also an ethnic diversity stretching on both sides of the boundary, with Shans inhabiting the valley bottoms on both sides of the border, but especially on the Burmese side.

Mountains, Boundaries, and Warfare

Contrary to widely held opinions that the northern frontiers of Burma comprise a "negative" zone of difficult, disease-ridden, country, which provides a barrier to movement between north and south, these frontiers are in fact fairly wide gaps of relatively open country as far as movement is concerned. They have not prevented, though they may have hampered, the traversing of the area by invading armies from the north.

Historically, large northern armies, unaccustomed to tropical conditions, moving in columns through disease-ridden, malarious valleys, have been the victims of disease, debility, and ambush. However, in the modern situation, especially after the refinement of irregular warfare in the period since Japan's "China Incident" application of power by one state to another across such a mountainous frontier zone and the technique chosen need not be that of a massive movement of columns comprising a conventional army.

In the words of Arthur Huck, the Maoist concept of revolutionary warfare "promises no Napoleonic crusades".[11] The cult of Maoism is clearly no longer in favour in China, and this was clearly discernible by 1979–80. It is not suggested that the PRC has a policy of infiltration into Burma. However, any strategic analysis of the ethnic insurgencies and the activity of communist parties such as the Burma Communist Party (which borrows from the Maoist concept of revolutionary warfare) should be seen against the background of the combination of factors which in total comprise the environment, physical as well as political, in which the warfare takes place. In this case, the natural ecology of warfare embraces the factors of terrain, alignment of natural routes, geographical spread of populated areas, sources of food supply, ethnic composition of the zone under study, and the attitude of the local populace to representatives of the central authority. Easily infiltrated border areas and boundaries are just one factor in the mix.

The Yunnan plateau portion of the Sino-Burmese boundary, then, provides one of the sectors where the terrain is conducive to movement, clandestine or otherwise, between the territories of the neighbouring two states, China and Burma. This is important, and would be crucial should the PRC decide in the future to fully support insurgencies in Burma. However, a later section in this study will also show that in a situation in which China does not wish to antagonize the Rangoon Government by openly giving supplies to the Burma Communist Party (BCP), an important direction for outflows of easily saleable country produce or contraband or inflows of supplies is not on a north-south alignment, but would lie rather on a west-east axis across the grain of the country in the search for the easiest outlets to the sea.[12] In this kind of strategic ecology, appropriate technology in the form of trains of draught animals is important as well as the securing by force, negotiation and compromise, bribery or the paying of toll charges, of fords and ferrying points across the many strong-flowing rivers. The grain of the country facilitates north-south movement but does not entirely prevent east-west communication.

The Other Boundaries in the Region

The other boundaries of the region follow the same general pattern already described. They transverse thinly populated highlands separating the main plains. The Indo-Burmese border is particularly difficult, crossing high, rugged, and thickly forested country. On the Burmese side the undeveloped area lies in a broad belt adjacent to the boundary, and approach to the boundary is rendered even more difficult. On the Indian side, the development of tea estates in the foothills of Assam in the last century has brought in a network of roads and the approach to the boundary is in this way facilitated.

The Sino-Laotian boundary traverses high land and is particularly porous especially to mountain ethnic groups dwelling in the vicinity. Cross-border movement and smuggling have been prevalent in the past. The Chinese-built strategic highway in northwestern Laos crosses the boundary and reaches into the Mekong lowlands. The Chinese have always had an interest and influence in northwestern Laos. This part of Laos had been recognized by the Anglo-Chinese Convention of 1894 as belonging to China. China ceded it to France in 1895. The PRC could raise claims to this region.[13]

The Laotian-Burmese boundary is also traversable even by large groups. The Mekong in the main divides Laos from Burma and is fordable in several places during the dry season.

The Thai-Burmese boundary follows high ridge lines and the border zone has been largely neglected by both governments. The ridges are steep but can be crossed by two main routes — the Three Pagodas Pass in the southern section and the route leading from the Burmese Shan State to Chiang Mai in northern Thailand. Both routes have been used by Burmese armies invading Thailand in the past. The Thai-Laotian boundary lies along the *thalweg* or the axis of the deepest channel of the Mekong River.

Between Vietnam and Laos is a belt of forested highlands. The crest of this runs in a general north to south direction and serves, with exceptions, as the common boundary. Of all the boundary lines, that dividing Laos from Vietnam, despite the difficult terrain, has been the one most frequently traversed by armies and their supply trains in the post-1945 period. A regular network of trails comprising the Ho Chi Minh Trail, some motorable in dry weather, facilitated movement from north to south during the Vietnam War. The network of routes straddled the boundary, helping movement not only from north to south, but also from east to west. Several Vietnamese-built all-weather highways leading from Vietnamese ports across the mountains into the lowlands of central and northern Laos have meant that the highlands dividing Laos from Vietnam are no longer a significant barrier to large-scale movement.

Although the Vietnam-Laos boundary appears to have stabilized, there are several sectors where this has been disputed. At a time when Vietnam was still divided, Pham Van Dong told Prince Souvanna Phouma in 1957 that, "[t]he border between Vietnam and Laos concerns all of Vietnam. In southern Vietnam there are numerous regions in dispute as in the north. . . ."[14] The Plain of Jars is one area where friction arose during the 1950s. The Plain is well suited for growing cold climate vegetables and potatoes, and both French and North Vietnamese governments had encouraged Vietnamese immigration into the region. Vo Nguyen Giap is reported to have regarded the Plain as of high strategic value to Vietnam.[15] In an inaccessible part of Xieng Khouang adjacent to Vietnam, the Vietnamese in 1954 had occupied a Lao-inhabited valley north of Nong Het, bringing in civil servants and farmers as settlers. In subsequent negotiations, "the Vietnamese were unable to answer Lao demands that they produce Vietnamese names for the peaks, streams and various villages. . . ."[16] The Lao delegation produced the standard French map of Indochina which showed the area to be on the Laotian side of the boundary, but the North Vietnamese dismissed it as an "imperialist legacy".[17] The boundary between Vietnam and Laos, although quiescent by the early 1980s, still remains a source of potential friction between Vietnam and Laos, especially if Laos in the future finds powerful allies in the region.

The boundary lines drawn by the colonial powers are often mere markers of convenience when they traverse inaccessible mountain regions. With the development of power imbalances between neighbouring states, the argument of "imperialist legacies" may be heard more often.

Movement across Boundaries

In the past there has been considerable movement by peoples across the boundaries of the region. These boundaries traverse sparsely populated areas and for long distances have been and still are largely unguarded, with the exception of the Sino-Vietnamese line. Migrationary movements of entire groups have taken place frequently, such as that of the H'mong from China into Thailand in the last century. As a result of this southward movement most of the mountain ethnic groups have representatives in more than one country. Tai-speakers are spread over the entire mountain region encompassing territories of five states — China, Vietnam, Laos, Thailand, and Burma. The H'mong are found in China, Vietnam, Laos, and Thailand, with by far the largest number living in China. Lahu are to be found in China, Burma, and Thailand, while the Karen, found mostly in Burma, also form the main mountain minority group in Thailand. Mountain groups have tended to ignore boundary lines whenever possible. The porosity of these boundaries is shown by the frequent movement of hill people across these unmarked lines even during times of vigilance on the frontiers.

In 1917 when the British power in Burma was secure, the boundaries they had drawn up were nevertheless trespassed with impunity by large groups, including Chinese traders and smugglers. It has been recorded that in March 1917 a Chinese caravan of 300 men and 200 horses left a village in Yunnan for Rangoon, the capital of Burma. The round trip took 172 days, the object was to trade in opium, and the caravan was armed with 170 rifles and pistols. Such cross-border trade and smuggling was a primary means of accumulating wealth in the densely-populated Han-inhabited intermontane basins of Yunnan.[18]

During the First Indochina War, the Vietminh could find sanctuary in China and, unknown to the Thai Government, in the mountains of Loei province in the north-northeast of Thailand. Troops of the Communist Party of Thailand (CPT) could find refuge across the border in Laos when the Indochina War was still in progress. There is evidence that guerrillas of the BCP do not remain solely on Burmese territory while during the Naga insurgency dissidents have been able to move across Burmese territory into China and return to Nagaland (though not without serious loss). Karen insurgents when hard pressed by the Burmese Army retreat across boundaries into parts of Thailand which are practically inaccessible from the Thai lowlands.

Attitudes to Highlands as Barriers

In these mountainous frontier zones, the existence of even high ridge lines should not be assumed as having a "natural" separating function, politically, economically, or even in military terms. In fact, dwellers in the highlands may not find mountains a hindrance to movement. Observers from cultures evolved in an essentially lowland or urban environment, on the other hand, may come to the conclusion that uplands pose a constraint; yet it has been pointed out that "[t]o mountain peoples mountains do not necessarily constitute barriers. This is a concept of lowlanders."[19] This perception is important to the strategic issues of the region.

On the question of accessibility and armies operating in mountains, the Prince of Ligne has been attributed as saying that "[i]t is known that an army can pass wherever a goat has passed: it is possible to hoist cannon with ropes into the highest mountains . . . to lay waste an enemy camp which did not expect to see a hail of cannon balls fall from the clouds".[20] In Dien Bien Phu the Vietminh demonstrated the truth of Ligne's assertion.

★ ★ ★

Where there is movement in mountain areas, the trend or direction of the main ridge lines encourages, or sometimes even determines, the direction of movement including the migrations of large mammals, traders, smugglers, cultures, guerrillas, and entire ethnic groups. Thus in the uplands of mainland Southeast Asia much of the historic migratory movement has followed the north-south trend of the landscape. Where movement is against the "grain" of the country — as in the case of the BCP attempts in 1982 to move west to the lowlands and the Government of Burma's attempts to move east to rebel strongholds — the impediments are much greater but not insurmountable.

Mountain regions do not necessarily constitute barriers to uplanders nor to those determined to cross them. If boundaries were drawn through mountainous terrain on the assumption that the topography would strengthen the barrier function of boundaries, then it can equally be said that remoteness and terrain render surveillance difficult thereby weakening the very role of such boundaries. This paradox is abundantly manifested in mainland Southeast Asia, where river valleys and crest lines which are natural routes cut across invisible boundary lines in hundreds, if not in thousands, of places.

The boundaries in the extended massif are based on the lines previously drawn by the colonial powers. These Southeast Asian boundaries are supposed to divide the region and to rigidly separate the territories of neighbouring sovereign states. The nature of the terrain, the lie of natural lines of communication, the boundary-straddling cultural groups, and problems of control of faraway boundaries combine to give rise to imperfections in the boundary system as applied to the deep hinterlands of mainland Southeast Asia.

A boundary line is fully meaningful and operatively functional only when all the parties on both sides of the dividing line unreservedly accept all aspects of its inalienable nature. As such, a boundary line is as much a condition of the mind as it is a line drawn on the ground.

NOTES

1. It is important to note that the British and French territories were administered more thoroughly than were the Chinese only in *relative* terms. Much British and French held territory was in fact thinly administered.
2. Ulrich Schweinfurth, "The Problem of Nagaland", in *Essays in Political Geography*, ed. Charles A. Fisher (London: Methuen, 1968), p. 171.
3. Ibid.
4. See Lee Yong Leng, *The Razor's Edge: Boundaries and Boundary Disputes in Southeast Asia* (Singapore: Institute of Southeast Asian Studies, 1980).
5. Alastair Lamb, *Asian Frontiers* (New York: Praeger, 1968), pp. 174–75.
6. Ibid., p. 175.
7. See Neville Maxwell, *India's China War* (London: Cape, 1971).
8. For the text of this protocol, see "Sino-Burmese Boundary Protocol, October 13, 1961", *New China News Agency*, 13 October 1961; also *Survey of China Mainland Press*, October-November 1961, no. 2602, pp. 23–24.
   For the text of the treaty of agreement on the boundary and general alignment, see "Boundary Treaty Between the People's Republic of China and the Union of Burma, October 1, 1960", *China Today 1960* 5, nos. 45 and 46, pp. 12–17; also *Burma Weekly Bulletin* 9, no. 24 (13 October 1960): 187–89.
9. J.R.V. Prescott, *Map of Mainland Asia by Treaty* (Clayton: Melbourne University Press, 1975), p. 347.
10. The material presented here on the terrain of the Sino-Burmese boundary relies considerably on Prescott, ibid.

11. Arthur Huck, *The Security of China: Chinese Approaches to War and Strategy* (London: International Institute of Strategic Studies, 1971), p. 53.
12. See *Far Eastern Economic Review*, 18–24 June 1982, pp. 26 and 29.
13. See Lamb, op. cit., p. 175.
14. Arthur J. Dommen, *Conflict in Laos: The Politics of Neutralization* (New York: Praeger, 1971), p. 336.
15. Dommen, op. cit., p. 259.
16. Dommen, op. cit., p. 337.
17. Ibid.
18. Hsiao-Tung Fei and Chih-I Chang, *Earthbound China: A Study of Rural Economy in Yunnan* (London: Routledge & Kegan Paul, 1948), pp. 282–83.
19. William Kirk, "The Inner Asian Frontiers of India", *Transactions* XXXI (Institute of British Geographers December 1962): 156.
20. As quoted by Jules Roy, *Dienbienphu*, translated by Robert Baldick (London: Faber & Faber, 1965), p. 98.

CHAPTER 4

Boundaries as Symbols in International Relations

It would be useful at this stage to examine boundaries and the concept of boundary lines in the montane zone. The question to be examined is the ritualistic aspect of a boundary's function. Viewed in this way boundaries can be seen as convenient markers of a nation's existence spatially and in relation to its neighbours, rather than as actual lines of division between one territorial sovereignty and another.

Colonial Boundary Practice and the Region's Political and Cultural Ecology

The fact that illicit trade and unauthorized movement of people[1] take place frequently and freely across the boundaries in the region is well known and needs not be recapitulated in detail. Why does such movement take place? The problem is perhaps best understood if the region is seen once more in the light of previous colonial policy and practice, and what can be termed the pre-colonial pattern of behaviour towards frontiers, especially in what are essentially distant marchlands.

It has been pointed out that the colonial powers took great pains to demarcate the boundaries between various territories. In this they were merely following what has been called the European concept of boundaries, reflecting their concern for the limits of territorial sovereignty, absolute in nature and undiminished in space.

However, it was difficult then for the colonial administrations and is even more so now for the southern lowland states to maintain firm administrative control up to the furthest limits of the colonially gained territory as defined by the boundary lines.[2] Confronted by the problem of holding onto a greatly expanded piece of real estate, "[t]he colonialists concentrated on hardening the perimeter, neglecting as both their pre-

67

decessors and successors have done, to build out to the fringe on a sound administrative basis".[3] With the withdrawal of the colonial powers, the perimeters have not remained hardened nor are they under firm administration. Moreover, effective administration, more often than not, has not been built out to the fringes.

Boundaries and Protective Distance

As in India, the British in Burma and the French in French Indochina, pushed the boundaries of their colonial possessions as far away from their political seats of power as was possible. Distance and the intervening terrain provided security and a measure of protection in depth. However, it was left to the inheritors of colonial rule to make optimum use of the extended territorial possessions, which included large tracts of culturally alien lands and which were ecologically unfamiliar and to that extent unusable by farmers of the main ethnic group. It would appear that the advantage of protective distance carries with it disabilities in terms of state expenditure and efforts needed to bring about political control. This condition is most apparent in Burma and Laos, but is also evident in milder form in Vietnam. Thailand, despite its lost outer territories still retains a large enough proportion of marginal highlands to show the same kind of condition.

An analysis which refers to Chinese historical expansion into the northwestern steppes states that further advances into Mongolia were halted "because a line of diminishing returns had been reached. A further advance would have thinned out and dissipated the strength of the expanding state; increased revenue would have been far less than the costs."[4] The strategy of obtaining security through maximizing distance between frontier or boundary and capital city carries with it its own inherent disadvantages and distinct liabilities.

A Consequence of Expanded Colonial Boundaries

The failure to build outwards from the centre, and the consequent leap frogging to the furthest attainable frontiers which the neighbouring state was willing or forced to concede, meant that behind the legally demarcated line lay considerable tracts of strategically "soft" territory. These were inhabited by peoples who were not, and in a few cases never had been, under the complete administrative control of the centre. Perhaps the colonial powers did not have sufficient time to accomplish this. In contrast, the relatively slow culturally-based southward movement of China over a much longer period and culminating in the administrative and political reorganization of its southern highlands after the PRC was proclaimed meant that the cultural fringes of Han China, were in relative terms close to its actual frontiers.

In the region as a whole there is at present evidence of a lack of political and military capacity at the outer edges of the southern lowland states, with the exception of Vietnam. This state of affairs persists not only along the actual boundary lines, which have theoretically at least to be guarded, but also in some of the areas between boundary and centre. This thinness of political control is an indication that boundaries as delineators of national sovereignty are often not in tune with the existing realities. In the thinly populated region the paucity of control is often associated with an avoidance of all forms of lowland authority. This has been vividly described with regard to northern Thailand. "Without a word, all my informants and spectators . . . seized their belongings and . . . disappeared into the forest. I did not understand what was going on until, almost three hours later, several Thailand gendarmes appeared, who, after a short rest, again left the village. They had scarcely disappeared, when my Lahu, with friendly smiles, appeared again."[5] The weak presence of central authority in the border areas is made even more ineffective by cultural considerations (referred to in an earlier chapter).

The Traditional "Asian" Concept of Boundaries

In contrast to the Western-derived boundary concepts there is what observers have called a traditional "Asian" boundary concept which regarded landspace, especially space in the outer fringes, as being less valuable than that nearer the capital city. The degree of "sovereignty" was thus accepted as being diluted in some parts of a state, and territory or landspace was seen as a negotiable element in the preservation of sovereignty in the face of external threat. This has been referred to as "territorial diplomacy",[6] wherein land is considered an essential part of a bargaining process, the ultimate objective being preservation of the kingdom as exemplified in the capital city and the areas immediately around it. Implicit in this concept is the idea that boundaries are never rigid nor once and for all time.

The historical behaviour of the pre-colonial Southeast Asian countries indicated a pattern of political thinking in which adherence to absolutes such as boundary lines in the Western sense was considered alien. Instead, preference in this context was given to broad and sometimes imprecise dividing frontier tracts (which have already been referred to). Officials were content with approximations, until the arrival of the colonial powers. A vivid illustration of this traditional view of the separation of one state from another is drawn from the Shan highlands between Burma and China. "For instance, it would be perfectly satisfactory to say: 'Kengtung is bounded in the north by Monglem and Kenghung, in the east by Kengcheng, in the south by Chiengrai. . .'."[7] Where the intervening land was sparsely populated or uninhabited, a state's or kingdom's territory was measured by the number of days march upstream from the nearest administered population centre.

It has also been stated with reference to states in the montane zone, that historic "Nanchao should not be thought of as a state with borders but as a capital city with a wide and variable sphere of influence".[8] This description of Nanchao and its territory gives a clear indication of the strategic relationship between capital or seat of power and lands subject to it in the traditional setting. Before the colonial era, there were only loosely "interpenetrating political systems" and fluid "zones of mutual interest"[9] instead of firmly set tracts of "national sovereignty."

However, a possible exception to this general pattern occurred as early as 1364 between the Lao King of Lon Xang and the King of Annam. The 1364 agreement stands as one of the oldest border treaties in existence, and fixed the boundary in the vicinity of the Ai Lao Pass.[10] In Souligna Vongsa's reign, a famous treaty fixed the boundary line according to the geographical distribution of housing-types and was based on whether the homes of the inhabitants were built on stilts or on the ground.[11] These treaties are exceptions and arose partly because of the proximity of Vietnamese inhabited lowlands to the territory of Laos. Moreover despite the seeming precision of the demarcation the boundary at the Ai Lao Pass was only at a point or a short sector on a traversable route and was not a long line precisely dividing all the territories of one state from the other. The division on the basis of house design was not a precise definition because large tracts of mountainous forestland divided Lao valley settlements built on stilts, and the Chinese-style Vietnamese houses built on the ground in valleys on the other rise of the ranges. It was an ethnic divide, but it still left the highlands to the mountain tribes. It was more a demarcation of each kingdom's area of control, on the criteria of ethnicity, in order to prevent encroachment of each other's ethnically settled territory.

Traditional "Asian" Boundary Concepts in the Modern Context

In the broad context of political situations influenced by ideas of the negotiability of land space, there have been precedents of using space as a negotiating counter in dealings with neighbouring states in times of conflict or stress. In this practice, landspace and rights over territory were traded for assurances that the central ethnic heartland and the royal seat would remain undisturbed.

In modern times, territorial diplomacy has allowed for the use, but not the permanent occupation, of "national" space by foreigners. Sihanouk has pointed out during the Vietnam War that he knew the North Vietnamese used northeast Cambodia, particularly the province of Ratanakiri, for transit of men and supplies to the south. He was also aware of Vietcong sanctuaries in eastern Cambodia bordering on South Vietnam. However, Sihanouk made it clear that he had been compelled to allow it chiefly because Cambodia was too weak to prevent these Vietnamese intrusions and not because his country had agreed to it. The point was that these incursions occurred in geographically outlying and inaccessible lands which were, in the circumstances, not vital to the survival of the Cambodian state. However, it should be noted that this attitude, when applied to the Khmer-inhabited lowlands of the Mekong delta, was a reflection of acceptance of the inevitable. It has been stated that in 1966, Sihanouk admitted that the National Liberation Army (NLA) or Vietcong troops were using Cambodia for "rest and refreshment".[12] Nevertheless it still falls into the category best described as territorial diplomacy, for Sihanouk was willing to exchange rights in an outlying territory for amicable relations with a well-armed force. Besides, it was hoped that this loss would only be temporary.

Thus another aspect of territorial diplomacy is the willingness to accept temporary incursions into a state's territory. The GMD armies which retreated into Burma after the communist victory were similarly regarded as a tolerable nuisance at first. The Burmese dislodged these GMD troops only with the help of People's Liberation Army (PLA) forces which took part in a pincer movement against the Chinese Nationalist divisions. This toleration of incursion and even of what was hoped would be only temporary occupation by organized armies has been evident since the withdrawal of the colonial powers from the region. The pattern of behaviour in the region also has been to tolerate or ignore peaceful tribal migrations across boundaries even when these involved armed men and when they have been brought to light.

The borderlands, too, have been used for refuge by beleaguered political groups. Ho Chi Minh took shelter from French attempts to capture him in the mountains of north-northeastern Thailand. This was an area made remote from Bangkok by distance and absence of communication lines. The unguarded, and therefore open, boundaries make this kind of clandestine movement possible and difficult to detect. In this connection, it is interesting to note that the Democratic Kampuchea (Pol Pot) Government had reason to believe that Vietnamese troops were still present in Mondolkiri and Ratanakiri provinces prior to the conflict with Vietnam in the late 1970s.[13]

The Western-inherited concept of national sovereignty with regard to territory, defined ideally by geodetic survey and wherever possible by boundary markers on the ground, has led to other repercussions in the modern setting of new "nation states" in the region. For example, demands can be made internally by domestic political groups that the professedly unwilling "host" government formally condemns the incursions. This was the case in Burma when the Guomindang troops took refuge in the Shan highlands after their defeat by the Red Army in 1949. On the other hand, state authorities can also pretend in their public statements that they have no knowledge of unauthorized entry or remain silent on the subject. In such instances they could work diplomatically, openly, or in secret, for either withdrawal or assurances that occupation would only be temporary.

Tolerance of uninvited armed groups seeking sanctuary has to be accommodated to protestations of sovereignty. Where feasible, such groups are utilised for the overall security interests of the "host" state. Thailand's policy allowing the independent Guomindang armed groups which have based themselves in northern Thailand to remain, is linked paradoxically to concern for border security. The anticommunist Guomindang groups were said to be serving as a useful buffer and as forward listening posts against communist infiltration from the Burmese highlands.

Reactions from willing or unwilling "host" states are in many respects necessarily ritualistic in view chiefly of their lack of the capacity of power projection in their frontier areas. Western concepts and principles of boundaries and attachment to the formalities of sovereignty incline states to one course of action, even though these may be merely verbal, while the traditional concepts of frontiers impel them on the other hand to behave in accordance with the existing geo-strategic realities of power. More often than not, the policy adopted would be one of compromise between the two courses of action open to a "host" state. It has been noted that "because so much importance has been attached to the formal aspects of sovereignty, these incursions take place on a *de facto* basis".[14] Territorial diplomacy in the modern setting is essentially a policy of geo-strategic impotence.

However, whenever possible the Western concepts appear to be adhered to in the "open" relationships between states. The boundary negotiations between Burma and China have been alluded to earlier. Attention is given to detail in the manner of Western boundaries. In 1982 and 1983 negotiations on the exact alignment of the Burma-Thai boundary was the subject of negotiations between Bangkok and Rangoon because a stream recognized as forming the boundary had changed course. However, this kind of attention to detail in the mutual recognition of one another's territorial sovereignty is necessarily tempered by the realities of porous and unguarded, or unguardable, boundaries. The "open" relationship exists alongside strategic realities which are largely hidden, at least from the public and international eye.

In the strategic context of the montane region of mainland Southeast Asia, boundary lines, so painstakingly staked out and jealously guarded by the colonial powers to enclose their maximum territorial gains, now acquire at times a more symbolic significance. This state of affairs is, in fact, a partial reversion to the pre-colonial practice of regarding economically "negative" zones such as mountains and swamps as conveniently broad buffer belts separating one country's vital economic regions from those of its neighbours.

The Impact of European Ideals on Current Boundary Attitudes

It should be noted that when faced with boundary disputes, India in contrast has attempted to uphold the imperialist ideal in its frontier and boundary policies by maintaining firm claims, backed by military force, on the boundary lines drawn up by the British, as for example, the outermost interpretation of the McMahon Line in the North-East Frontier Region and also in Ladakh.

It has to be recognized that boundaries as symbols of national integrity can also be used as emotional rallying points to defend the nation's so-called "sacred soil", as happened in India during the 1962 Himalayan War.[15] It is significant, however, that the state in Southeast Asia most liable so far to such incursions, Burma, and which also has perhaps the most nationalistic feeling among its citizens, or at least the ethnic Burman segment of its citizenry, has not used border incursions for arousing its people to a concerted or total national defence effort.

Any increase in the capacity by the lowland authorities in mainland Southeast Asia to administer frontier regions will lead gradually to the extension of the state's administrative capacity to its territorial limits, thus hardening its spatial perimeter. This spatial extension of central power in turn can lead to new kinds of disputes.

Increased Boundary Control and Regional Stability

Boundary and national sovereignty are linked in such a way that it has been observed:

> Increasing ability to administer boundaries is necessary if what purports to be the symbol of sovereignty is to become actual sovereignty.[16]

In mainland Southeast Asia, the greater the coincidence between states' control of their respective land spaces with their degree of attachment to the idealized nation-state concept of the Europeans, the greater the chances for escalation of direct conflict involving one state against another. This has taken place between the PRC and Vietnam in 1979 and along the Sino-Indian border in 1962. Both wars involved substantial conventional armies.

Increased internal power together with greater administrative and military control would mean greater internal stability in individual states but could also lead to greater regional instability because of the increased risks of state against state wars. The brief but full-scale Sino-Vietnamese war of the spring of 1979 is of considerable significance because it indicates that the increased ability to bring outlying mountain areas under central control leads to greater internal stability of states but is not necessarily concomitant with increased regional stability. Thus it could be hypothesized that mild and persistent instability in the montane belt of mainland Southeast Asia would in fact, contrary to most views, be a pointer to greater regional security — that is, a situation precluding large-scale war between states. This would be so only if the instability in the mountains is contained and managed so as to limit it and to prevent it from spreading to the lowlands. Significantly, this containment was already successfully achieved by Burma and Thailand in the 1970s and early 1980s.

Ethnic Dispersion and Border Friction

The pattern of ethnic distribution renders boundary management extremely difficult. Generally, the upholding of Western-style boundaries tends to be weakened by the well-known straddling of these boundaries by the geographical dispersion of the mountain and high-valley dwelling groups. This has been exacerbated by movements caused by upheavals such as war. The refugees often carry their old animosities along with them. It has been noted that the settling of H'mong who have fled from Vietnamese and Laotian punitive action, in north-northeastern Thailand poses what is regarded as a serious threat to Thailand's security,[17] because of possible intervention by neighbouring states, either to make use of the H'mong for their own ends (such as the PRC recruiting them to re-infiltrate into Laos) or to eradicate the H'mong problem, which is a Vietnamese objective.

Options in Boundary Policy for a Weak State

When a state, weaker than its neighbour, is faced with a problem of boundary management it has two courses of action open to it. One is to rely on the Western derived and colonially superimposed system of fixed borders and on the largely Western developed body of international law, in which is embodied the concept of negotiation between equals as a means of regulating state-to-state relations. This has been one facet of the relations between Beijing and Rangoon and has been manifested at times in the mutual concern about the Sino-Burmese border. The other course of action, at another level, has been observed in relation to inter-state affairs, and is stated as follows: "Asian traditions were based on hierarchical relations formalised... from one level of power to another."[18] This second condition existed in mainland Southeast Asia before the colonial era. The two courses of action are not mutually contradictory and may in fact be used in tandem. Thus border agreements can be carried out as if they were between equals, but in fact the total relationship of the weaker to the stronger, of which the boundary relationship and the border policies are but one facet, could contain aspects of the second hierarchical type of accommodation.

To the extent that differences in military strength and internal political cohesion exist in sharp contrast and in such close proximity, the evolution of a uniquely Southeast Asian system involving some form of agreement based partly on the traditional hierarchical approach cannot be discounted altogether. Indeed, it has been asserted in the context of border disputes, that in view of the difficulty in reconciling legal and political claims to territory, "the traditional means utilised by most Asian states are the most practical for resolving the border disputes that exist".[19]

The Western style of boundary management enhances the legalistic aspects of boundaries, whereas the "Asian" or "Southeast Asian" approach to the problem strengthens their symbolism without any explicit rejection of the previously, that is, colonially, superimposed order. In fact, this modern, modified "Asian" approach by its symbolic recognition of the delineations of the Western-derived model strengthens its own position by the inclusion and recognition of the "legal" and "moral" issues which are the roots of the legitimacy of action demanded by Western influenced élites and their followers. In the region both the traditional and the Western or legal means have been apparent in the montane region and particularly in Sino-Burmese and Vietnam-Laotian relations.

With Vietnam, however, Hanoi's rejection of the traditional methods employed to smoothen interstate relations with China has led to conflict, to the 1979 war and to continued political combativeness accompanied by low-key military actions between the two. On the other hand, Vietnam at the same time appears to be adopting the traditional, hierarchical method in its dealings with its two weaker neighbours, Cambodia and Laos, through the concept of an Indochinese grouping of states.

Both analysts and political practitioners in the region tend to see the "state" with linear demarcated limits in the Western sense. However, the strategic circumstances of the region have compelled some states and their leaders to adopt features of the traditional approach to boundary and territorial issues. A complete reversion to the historical approach would, however, appear to be unlikely in the context of the modern situation which incorporates the elements of superpower mobility, their capacity to intervene to buttress allies in the region, and the existence of the various fora for the airing of international opinion and grievances. Moreover, it has been argued that "the longer the political boundaries remain intact, the more they will be accepted as the proper political boundaries".[20] A major reshuffling of boundaries is most unlikely. Present boundary functions, however, would not be totally on the Western model.

Boundaries, Centres, and Concentric Peripherality

It would be useful at this point to bring out one aspect of the traditional method of boundary management which has deep implications for any analysis using the geopolitical approach with its emphasis on the relationship between space, location, and power. The traditional approach has also been seen as conforming to "the concentric cosmological world concept of Hindu mythology, with the throne in the centre of the kingdom, and with the capital, the outlying provinces, vassalages and neighbouring realms represented as a series of concentric rings".[21] The statesman would then be provided with a "ready-made schedule of priorities".[22] This schedule of priorities is the basis of the use of territory as a means of the preservation of power in the centre. While the centre retains its sovereignty, this is achieved at the cost, considered acceptable, of yielding territory to a stronger power, although it is hoped only temporarily.

The concept of territorial diplomacy in relation to the centre in a state or kingdom is said to have been derived from the thinking of Kautilya of the Mauryan era in Indic history who enunciated a set of rules or principles for statesmanship in the period *c.* 321–206 B.C. Kautilya was among the first to advocate the trading of land space for the continued security of the centre.[23]

This kind of perception in terms of international order has also been observed in the traditional behaviour of Imperial China. "Stability in the Chinese view depended ... on the recognition of a natural order which corresponded roughly to the actual situation of Imperial China in her heyday. The heartland, the traditional Eighteen Provinces, was the seat of Chinese civilisation. Beyond this in roughly concentric zones, lay regions of different importance and interest to China. The contiguous non-Han regions ... were clearly of the greatest importance."[24] In this model of concentric rings of diminishing strategic value the difference between Imperial Chinese perceptions and practice on the one hand and Kautilya's pronouncements in an environment of small warring states on the other was only one of scale.

The categorization of national priorities by concentric geographical belts has its advantages in the assignment of security priorities. When the leadership of a lowland country, for example, is faced by external enemies and is hard-pressed by internal problems and strife, it is tempted to follow this traditional approach. The outlying stretches, often in the mountains, are then usually given the lowest priority that is, regarded as being most dispensable.

Thailand as the only independent state during the colonial period showed astute use of territorial diplomacy, with all that is implied in the concentric ring concept of state priorities. Thailand witnessed the loss of its territories in the Mekong valley, in western Cambodia, and in northern Peninsular Malaya but saw the retention and the preservation of the Thai ethnic and economic heartland.

China also followed this course of action, having been forced into it by military defeats or pressure at the hands of the sea-borne Western and land-borne Russian imperial powers. During the period of British encroachment the royal court of Burma can be seen as having progressively traded space which was "outer" in relation to the Burman cultural heartland in the dry but productive irrigable central zone of the Irrawaddy basin in Burma, for the political survival of Mandalay.

Centres, Peripheries, and Ethnicity

In the analytical framework of the centre-cum-concentric periphery, the location of the centre in mainland Southeast Asia is more often than not associated with ethnicity. The location of the numerically and politically dominant group in the typical state is related to topography, namely that of alluvial lowlands, while the extensive uplands or the watershed of the core valley makes up the peripheries of the state. The relationship between ethnicity, centres, and concentric peripheries will be elaborated upon later in this study. At this stage, however, it is necessary to indicate the kinds of problems which are created by a coincidence of ethnicity and concentric peripherality. The ethnic separation on a territorial basis within a new state poses problems when the ideal of national integration becomes the objective of the rulers of the new states. National boundaries, in this context, can be said to encapsulate groups with highly diverse sentiments.[25] These sentiments roughly correspond with territorial differentiations giving a spatial aspect to the problem of nation-building.

Boundaries, Frontier Zones, and National Integration

Imbued to varying degrees with Western or Western-derived ideals, the leaders of the post-colonial territories have striven for the creation of countries modelled after the nation-state based on an identifiable nationalism which in turn would have taken root and form in the anti-colonial struggles or would have been nurtured in the period of negotiations with the colonial powers for the attainment of independence. The manner in which the boundaries of colonial territories were drawn has meant that the new rulers, the inheritors of colonial power — particularly in Rangoon and Vientiane — became *de facto* managers of problem-ridden *territory*, rather than of cohesive states, inherited from the departed colonials.

The concept of a nation-state is universally accepted by these leaders, and embraces sovereignty, uncompromised, over the entire territory which had been and still is defined by firmly drawn and firmly claimed, but often weakly administered, boundary lines. It has been noted that "contemporary international and national requirements preclude the continuation of historically indeterminate borders and seem to call into question . . . amorphous ethnic and group alliances that were elements of traditional . . . control over peripheral areas".[26] Thus the new managers of these heterogeneous territorial units are faced by a dilemma. While there has been some inclination to territorial diplomacy, viz. overlooking sovereign rights over distant lands, there is little or no inclination to allow people inhabiting the state territory to have alien allegiances.

The solution would most apparently lie in policies which could successfully bring together, in a satisfactory manner, two sets of factors which are often in contradiction to one another or even in conflict. Firstly, such policies would have to consider, indeed be formulated by, the ideals of the mainstream "nationalism" that had been both the force and the instrument which had translated serfdom into freedom. Significantly, however, this mainstream "nationalism" would have been more appropriately described as "ethnic nationalism". Secondly, the formulators of pan-territorial policies of integration would have had to enforce, or implement, the objectives and values of this "nationalism" onto territories and their inhabitants, many, if not most, of whom would not wholly share, or have not participated in, this new state "nationalism". The heart of the problem with those post-colonial states which show this dualism is seen in the lack of coincidence between the territorial extent of the mainstream nationalism which resides chiefly in the main ethnic group heartland and the extent of the territorial sovereignty claimed by the new state.

It is precisely this lack of fit between claimed boundaries and ethnic dispersion together with the formalistic territorial and loyalty dictates of the new states, modelled after the nation-state, that compound the strategic problems faced by the administrators of these new states. Contemporary political mobilization rejects what was historically an amalgam of seemingly inconsistent "but nonetheless effective, symbiotic and hierarchical relationships among peoples".[27] With reference to Burma, it has been stated: "The Burmans had a reasonably correct tacit understanding of the nature of their relations with bordering people, tribal and non-tribal. That Burma seems to have lost this understanding today is almost certainly directly attributable to the importation of very explicit European ideas about a nation's societies, and cultures, and the kinds of phenomena that they are taken to be."[28] Space and boundaries play a basic role in this post-colonial search for a viable form of the new state for the inconsistencies, and even outright contradictions, arising out of the clash between loose historical political arrangements and management philosophies springing from unequivocal European ideals are clearly based on the same piece of land.

The nature of this problem has been pointed out or implied, though not in territorial terms, by various scholars. Referring to the creation of new nation-states, Deutsch has stated that in addition to facilities for enhanced communication so that a national infrastructure is laid to help create links and so to bring people together in shared values, shared experiences as well as a shared sense of common identity are also needed.[29]

Clifford Geertz has warned that a limit to national integration is created by the contrast between civil politics and what are termed as "primordial" sentiments. In civil politics, reward is obtained more from merit and performance, while "primordial" attachments include those of region, tribe, religion, and ethnic group.[30]

It has also been stated by Rupert Emerson that the elements of territory, language, common historical tradition, and what Emerson refers to as the intricate inter-connection between the state and the nation need to be studied. Though important in aggregate, however, all these cannot outweigh the crucial human feeling among a group of people who hold to the belief that they constitute a nation.[31] A variation of this has been expressed in the concept of a "state-idea", which is described as a statement of common purposes which citizens of a state can subscribe to and identify themselves with.[32]

The prerequisites put forward by Deutsch for the growth of a nation, namely shared experience and a shared sense of common identity are scarcely to be found throughout the post-colonial states. More often than not differences in political, economic, and social experiences, sometimes over prolonged historical periods, coincide with differences in ethnicity and with territorial separation or differentiation. Few such common links of experience or shared identity, on any extensive scale, are to be found between lowland people and the bulk of the masses living in the highlands in the frontier regions adjoining the boundaries of the state.

As for the contradiction between civil politics and the existing "primordial" sentiments, as expressed by Geertz, it can be said that the approach of civil politics when adopted by state leaders who are invariably of lowland ethnic origin, would be confronted with "primordial" feelings both in the highlands as well as among members of the lowland ethnic groups who might oppose any concessions to the highlanders. In any case, what are essentially "primordial" sentiments set the frontier regions apart from the central lowlands. The highland-lowland dichotomy is to a marked extent a symptom of the occurrence of Geertz's "primordial" attitudes within the spatial confines of the new state. "Primordial" sentiments when given expression in territorial terms take on a new dimension in the geo-strategy of the region.

Apart from the inclusion of various groups in a single territorial unit, none of the elements of language, common historical tradition, or identification are to be found permeating both the lowlands and the border regions to the same degree. Indeed, from the viewpoint of historical tradition and language the population of the lowlands and those of the zones adjoining the state's boundaries are more often than not quite separate and distinct, although in the exceptional case of Vietnam, attempts are being made to erase these distinctions. The state and the nation in such internally differentiated political entities are again two distinct elements which do not necessarily coincide with one another territorially. The people living close to the state boundaries would with good reason assert that they do not constitute a nation together with the people of the lowlands. The Shans of post-independence Burma could with good reason feel that Shans and Burmans do not constitute a nation.

The ethnically-based highland estrangement from the values of lowland ethno-centric nationalism and the objectives of the lowland-centred governments is central to the problem of stability in mainland Southeast Asia. It is precisely in those states where wide belts of mountains fringe the state boundaries that national integration is least advanced. The internal situation in such states is further complicated by the fact that their mountain belts which the lowland-based governments are unable to subjugate or to control effectively are wedged into the strategic central massif which has periodically been an arena for turmoil from which there is little possibility of effective insulation.

* * *

A thorough return to traditional methods of frontier management or control in relation to behaviour towards a neighbouring state is unlikely to take place in the foreseeable future. The force of Western-style, legalistic approaches would be too strong to be ignored especially when the world community, as a whole, adopts these Western practices in settling disputes. Besides, the "sacred soil" — and it should be noted also increasingly the "sacred seas" — of the fatherland or motherland is a factor that cannot be shrugged off by state leaderships in the region, and which has in fact, been employed to whip up national emotions or to mobilize popular support for state policies.

What is more likely to occur is a symbolic attachment to international boundaries, accompanied by unpublicized deference to the concept of hierarchical relationships. This would apply especially when a strong state is contiguous to a markedly weaker one, without the capacity, organization, will, or external alliances to help maintain the ideal standards of Western behaviour in connection with its boundaries. Needless to say, such traditional approaches to frontier problems are more likely to be successfully applied if the two contiguous states have the benefit of the buffering effect of intervening broad frontier zones.

Where the geographical limits of effective rule — backed by a readiness and an ability to deploy and use military force — of two contiguous states come physically into contact, such as in the case of China and Vietnam, then the traditional solutions of separation through the buffering or filtering effects of frontier zones are less likely to succeed. The Vietnamese-Cambodian boundary in the Mekong lowland sector was also not buffered by intervening "neutral" or peripheral tracts. The Khmer ethnic heartland reached to the borders with Vietnam in the lower Mekong plain. After centuries of Vietnamese and Thai encroachment, Cambodia had no more outer rings of territory which could be disposed of without hurting its sovereignty over its own Khmer people and the land they worked, as opposed to sovereignty over the sparsely minority-inhabited peripheries.

The imperfections in the European-type boundary model as applied to the hinterlands of mainland Southeast Asia and the southern borderlands of China give rise, perforce, to an attendant symbolism to these boundaries and their stated functions. There is an accompanying widening of policy options in a state's border policy. This in turn has grave implications for the progress of nation-building efforts of states whose boundaries function imperfectly in the European sense and which adopt through force of circumstances, some features of the "Asian" boundary model. This poses major problems for post-colonial states which aim at the ideal model of the European-type nation-state, wherein homogeneity, in a political context and on a spatial basis is generally the rule. Symbolic or partially symbolic boundaries, on the other hand, encourage the further development of existent internal disparities which work against the interests of the modern state leaderships both internally as well as in relation to other states. Symbolism of boundaries is the antithesis of the concept of a modern nation-state. Yet this same symbolism may indicate the existence of a larger regional stability overshadowing lesser instabilities, however persistent these may be.

NOTES

1. Such movements of people and goods would be illicit if one or both sides legally recognized the boundary as separating two sovereignties.
2. Thailand not having been ruled by a colonial power is an exception in this case. In fact, Thailand was a loser, a victim, in the scramble for landspace during the colonial expansion.

3. Robert L. Solomon, "Boundary Concepts and Practices in Southeast Asia", *World Politics* 23, no. 1 (October 1970): 1–16.
4. Owen Lattimore, "The Periphery as a Locus of Innovation", in *Centre and Periphery: Spatial Variation in Politics*, ed. Jean Gottmann (Beverly Hills, London: Sage 1980), pp. 206–207.
5. Hugo Adolph Bernatzik, *Akha and Miao; Problems of Applied Ethnography in Further India*, translated from German by Alois Nagler, Human Relations Area Files (New Haven, 1970) p. 702.
6. Solomon, op. cit., p. 12.
7. Sao Saimong Mangrai, *The Shan States and the British Annexation*, Data Paper No 7, Southeast Asia Program (Ithaca, New York: Cornell University Press, 1965), p. 275, quoting G.E. Harvey, *Wa Precis*, 1932, p. 140.
8. E.R. Leach, "The Frontiers of 'Burma'", in *Southeast Asia: The Politics of National Integration*, ed. John T. McAlister Jr., (New York: Random House, 1973), p. 322.
9. Ibid.
10. Arthur J. Dommen, *Conflict in Laos: The Politics of Neutralization* (New York: Praeger, 1971), p. 333.
11. Ibid.
12. Edgar O'Ballance, *The Wars in Vietnam: 1954–1973* (New York: Hippocrene Books, 1975), p. 95. Also pp. 156–57.
13. John Holdridge, *Straits Times* (Singapore), 15 June 1981.
14. Solomon, op. cit.
15. This kind of language was used both by Indian political leaders and the Indian press in the period before and during the 1962 border war with China. As the fighting was concluded and when China began returning Indian troops captured in the brief war, the official Indian information bureau released pictures of returned "jawans" kneeling and kissing the earth of the motherland. It could be debated if this kissing is alien to traditional Indian attitudes.
16. Matthew M. Gardner, Jr., "The Heritage of South Asian Borders", *SAIS Review* 13, no. 2 (Winter 1969): 30.
17. See M.R. Sukhumbhand Paribatra, "The H'mongs of Ban Vinai; A Future Factor in Thailand's Security Equation?" *ISIS Bulletin* 1, no. 1 (Faculty of Political Science, Chulalongkorn University, Bangkok, July 1982): 3–9.
18. Gardner, Jr., op. cit., pp. 28–29.
19. Ibid., p. 30.
20. Robert O. Tilman, ed., *Man, State and Society in Contemporary Southeast Asia* Introduction (London: Pall Mall Press, 1969), p. 7.
21. Solomon, op. cit., p. 14.
22. Ibid.
23. Kautilya, *Arthashastra*, translated by R. Shamasastry, 8th Edition, (Mysore: Sri Raghuveer Printing Press, 1951), pp. 268, 335, quoted by Solomon, op. cit.
24. Arthur Huck, *The Security of China: Chinese Approaches to Problems of War and Strategy*, (London: Chatto and Windus for the Institute of Strategic Studies, 1971), p. 25.
25. Tilman, op. cit., p. 7.
26. David I. Steinberg, "Constitutional and Political Bases of the Minority Insurrections: Burma", in *Armed Separatism in Southeast Asia*, ed. Lim Joo-Jock and Vani S. (Singapore: Institute of Southeast Asian Studies, 1984).
27. Ibid.
28. F.K. Lehman, "Ethnic Categories in Burma and the Theory of Social Systems", in

Southeast Asian Tribes, Minorities and Nations vol. 1, ed. Peter Kunstadter (Princeton: Princeton University Press, 1967), p. 103.
29. Karl W. Deutsch, "The Growth of Nations: Some Recurrent Patterns of Political and Social Integration", in *Southeast Asia: The Politics of National Integration*, ed. John T. McAlister, Jr., (New York: Random House, 1973), pp. 18–41.
30. Clifford Geertz, "Primordial Sentiments and Civil Politics in New States: The Integrative Revolution", in McAlister, Jr., ed., op. cit., pp. 42–54.
31. Rupert Emerson, "The Nature of the Nation", in McAlister, Jr., ed., op. cit., pp. 55–69.
32. Preston E. James, "Some Fundamental Elements in the Analysis of the Viability of States", in *Essays in Political Geography*, ed. Charles A. Fisher (London: Methuen, 1968), p. 33.

CHAPTER 5

Power and its Territorial Basis

In order to examine some concepts of power, it is necessary to set them in a spatial or territorial context. The issues arising from the condition of frontiers, loose boundaries, and the internal cohesion of states are directly related to the generating of the aggregate power available to state leaderships.

Frontiers, Boundaries, and the Organization of Land Space

We have seen that the montane zone in the region acts merely as a filter between the various centres of power and is not a barrier between states. The role of this montane zone mirrors that which Gottman saw for frontiers in general, namely:

> The frontier is a partition, that is, a screening instrument in the organization of accessible space. It screens and to some extent controls the movement in and out of the territory.[1]

The boundaries, as distinct from frontiers, of the region need to be understood in the perspective of this screening and organizing role of the montane zone as a whole. In the case of boundaries, both Gottman and the German political geographer. Friedrich Ratzel, perceived boundaries as merely the result of wider, deeper movements. Ratzel saw a form of organicity in the expansion and contraction of the spatial limits of states, depending on their levels of "culture" *vis-à-vis* their neighbours. Ratzel was much influenced by Darwinism, the principles of evolution, and the new findings of natural science of the late twentieth century. Boundaries were not fixed for all time, states with higher levels of culture, in his view, expanded at the expense of those with lower culture which were thus by definition the weaker states. He placed special emphasis on frontiers and boundaries which he regarded as outer organs of a state, which were evidence of a state's strength or weakness, growth or decline.[2] Gottman states that ". . . examination of the modern role and evolution of international boundaries confirms the feeling of fluidity, of constant changes, of search for a new international order. The decisive element cannot be found in the boundaries, which are the symptoms, effects determined by deeper causes. The 'causes' are to be found . . . largely in the internal organization of the territory."[3] In mainland Southeast Asia the boundaries whose functions are modified by the montane environment are a symptom of the geopolitical and geo-ethnic condition which crystallized in the post-colonial era. It should not be forgotten that this era of post-colonialism is but a phase in the history of the region.

Where there is the phenomenon of a marked differentiation, arising out of geo-ethnic variations, in the degree of central control within the spatial holdings of a "nation-state", as is the case with the southern states of mainland Southeast Asia, the condition can be related to what Gottman saw as the "causes" of the condition of boundaries in the internal organization of a state. Thus, it is in the internal organization of a state that one perceives a relationship with the functioning or malfunctioning of its boundaries. If there were malfunction, why this condition came about or was allowed to come about would explain in part the relative strengths and weaknesses of the various states concerned. The boundary lines in the region are to a large extent symptomatic in Gottman's terms, of wider situations, both internal to a state as well as the external.

The wider situation embraces geo-ethnicity, the highland-lowland dichotomy, estrangement from mainstream, lowland nationalism, and most basic of all the existence and location of the central strategic massif abutting on six states. How this montane belt impinges upon the "organization of accessible space" will be dealt with later in this chapter.

The Power Domain of Karl Deutsch

At this point, it would be useful to examine an appropriate concept of power and to attempt to link it to the question of the territorial bases of power.

Karl Deutsch has pointed to the fact that power is linked to domains. The relevance and value of this approach goes beyond the often adopted technique that consists essentially of a summation of the perceived elements of power of which territory is only one. In this kind of element-aggregative approach, size of territory is considered very important. Deutsch, on the other hand, states that a power domain consists of the people, together with the resources they own, control, or have access to.[4] Deutsch defines a power domain in the following manner: "A . . . possible meaning of the domain of power might include not only the persons subject or obedient to it, but also those amounts of land, capital goods and general resources controlled by them . . . . This . . . view of the domain of power comes close to our . . . notion of power defined in terms of a collection of resources."[5] It is framed in terms of people, and in this sense is not geopolitically propounded. Nor is it defined in the framework of aggregates of economic resources *per se*. This kind of approach would be appropriate when analyses are made of power in geo-strategic terms.

Within the scope of this definition given by Deutsch, a clandestine movement can also conceivably possess a power domain, even though its individuals which *in toto* comprise its source of power are scattered and do not occupy any discernible block of land or territory inside any one state. This kind of domain, too, can be physically scattered throughout the world, as in the case of international revolutionary movements. This is because the emphasis placed on Deutsch was on people, on individuals, and on collections of individuals. The Palestinian Liberation Organization (PLO), apart from its foothold in West Beirut and parts of Lebanon before it was evicted through Israeli military action in 1982, had a definable power domain which drew on people and resources scattered widely over West Asia and North Africa. Thus also it can be argued that, in Deutsch's terms, the H'mong insurgent groups, mobile and difficult to define or locate geographically, possess domains of power. Similarly during the Vietnam War, the Vietcong domain of power was spatially intermingled with that of the Saigon Government. On a wider scale, Israel would also have a domain of power stretching well beyond its borders, with a substantial contribution coming from its supporters in the United States. Domains of power, in this sense, can override international boundaries and need not be solely vested in visible phenomena. Domains can also overlap one another.

Deutsch's Power Domain and Mainland Southeast Asia

Deutsch's concept is rich in strategic implications. If used more broadly in a geo-strategic frame it allows for considerably deeper and more sophisticated analysis of strategic issues occurring in various parts of the world. Applying it to mainland Southeast Asia, we can see that domains of power, that is, zones where groups of people controlling resources submit to a common authority, are discernible in each state. The domains of power of the administrations residing in the capital cities of Rangoon, Bangkok, the urban centres of the Laotian and the Cambodian lowlands, and in Hanoi are, in this definition, essentially plains-based. This is especially marked in the case of Rangoon.

Concentration of potential power in the plains springs from a combination of factors. The density of population, that is the number of persons living in any one unit area of land is highest in the plains. So too is the absolute number of people. This is a direct consequent of topography, soil conditions, water supply, and a ready means of transportation of goods. The mix of the relative fertility of the plains, a more reliable and manageable water supply for rice cultivation, and the availability of labour — which arose in the first place from the food growing potential of the plains — leads to higher production *in toto* and a higher productivity per unit of labour input. The capacity to produce surplus grain, which is not easily perishable and which is the base of wealth accumulation, and an economic surplus was the basis of earlier writings on the "key economic areas" in Chinese history. Physical concentration of people and resources itself facilitates organization and control, and the subsequent creation of a power domain. When the population of the plains is effectively controlled by the centre, then a domain of power, spatially defined, comes into being.

The grouping together so closely in a spatial sense of the factors of production means that the sources of power are to that extent more easily controlled and manipulated by the managers of state authority. If power springs from population and the resources available to this population, then the densest concentration of power is to be found in the plains. This is quite apart from the attitudes and allegiances of the people concerned. Where these attitudes are positive with respect to the government, it adds further impetus to the formation of a power domain.

The Highlands and the Concept of Power Domains

Conversely, in the hills ringing the plains the inhabitants are thinly spread out, are fewer in number, and cultivate land that is relatively unproductive. Returns in relation to resource input per unit area in the highlands as a whole are generally low compared to the plains. This marked thinness in the highlands of the essential ingredients for an economic surplus lead to a paucity of potential power in the highlands. This would coincide with widely held views of the potential in terms of wealth and power of deprived regions.

Some distinctions need to be pointed out. It is true that the wide dispersal of men and their resources lessens the power potential of the hills. However, it is this very dispersal which also adds an element of difficulty of control in the hills. Difficulty of control and management mean that any political or insurgent movement internal to the hill region will find that this wide dispersal — not to speak of the diversities existing — is an obstacle to the mustering of power to challenge intrusions of external power such as that of the plains state. Beyond this, however, the same difficulties of organization presented by wide dispersion also mean that any attempt by the lowland authorities to impose their own administration or system of management for men and resources would also meet with the same kind of difficulties and would need heavy expenditure in order to overcome the hindrances innate in the highlands. The hill regions can at the same time sap the power of the lowlands if continuous attempts are made to control the hills without the popular consent of the inhabitants.

"Ethnic Reliability", Territory, and Power

In mainland Southeast Asia, "ethnicity" — which for lack of a better term can be described here as a "racial" expression of culture — as well as topography and territory are crucial to the location, extent, and the spread of the central power domains. The consideration of ethnocultural factors is important to any understanding of the territorial basis of power in mainland Southeast Asia. The ethnic cleavages between plainsmen and hill folk are central to the question of state power.

A fresh dimension can be added to this problem by the introduction of the concept of the "ethnic map" in the political and institutional sense. The "ethnic map" was not, however, conceptualized in strategic or geopolitical terms. The main concern centred on how "ethnicity" was manipulated by state élites in order to achieve their overall objectives. Loyalties, of fighting men for example, in the service of the managers of centralized power are discerned in terms of distance from what can be called a "reliability" core. Thus in the perception of the state élite, the least reliable ethnic groups are placed farthest from the core in an ideal "security map"[6] which, however, is not a map in the geographical sense, but is actually a chart diagram or what has been called a "mental map". Perhaps the term "security chart" should have been used because, as mentioned earlier, this notion did not seem to have been meant to be applied geographically but only in terms of political control of states by élites.

If, however, this idea is applied in expanded form and adapted to strategic and geopolitical thinking, it can in conjunction with the analysis of Deutsch's domains be of value in studies of mainland Southeast Asia. For in actual fact as far as the lowland-located centres or capital cities are concerned, the least reliable, in general terms, of their citizens or people they claim to be their citizens or national subjects, are more often than not those residing in spatially distant areas, which are by definition, unreliable, fringing areas farthest from the lowland power domain. This geopolitical-ethnographical map of ethnic reliability would be a territorial-based expression of Enloe's ethnic chart or mental map.

A new element, namely that of "ethnic reliability", is therefore added to the picture of domains of power, in order to better comprehend the nature and extent of power domains as they occur in mainland Southeast Asia. "Ethnic reliability" reinforces the pattern of delineation of power domains and underlines the differentiation between various types of power domains. This is a topic which will be dealt with in the next chapter.

Administration and the Frontiers in British Burma

There are considerable difficulties in enforcing effective administration in the uplands. Even the British at the height of their imperial powers did not push their authority in Burma, that is, the mainly Irrawaddy valley based power, to the maximum claimed geographical limits. Despite the control of routes and attempts to police the frontiers by setting up isolated forts and outposts, parts of Burma were up until the Pacific War incompletely or ineffectively administered by the British.

While the frontier fringes of Burma were British-administered and were influenced to some extent by the Indic culture from the plains, it was the Chinese, because of relative proximity and the traversibility of sections of the highland frontiers, who had the most direct physical contacts with Burma's outer limits. The contacts were largely economic and cultural. The trade in jade and precious animal and vegetable products was only part of this general contact between the deep hinterlands of the southern power and the Han-inhabited lands of the north.

E.R. Leach has observed in this context that he had firsthand experience of a number of areas in northern Burma which were what he called "unadministered territory", throughout the period of British rule.[7] In the late 1960s it was observed that the "so-called Sagaing District of northern Burma is unadministered, and no influence is felt there from far away Rangoon".[8] In view of the across-the-border trade and the economic activities of groups of Chinese merchants with their armed escorts, it can be argued that this was also in fact an outer zone of influence of the Chinese power. At the very least it was a zone of overlap of the power domains of two adjacent states.

In the case of northern Burma with its majority group, the Kachins, the British were unable to impose their view of law and order until 1935. It was only then that the Kachins gave up resisting the British.[9] This gives a clearer picture of the difficulty of control of men and resources even under a relatively strong and efficient administration, such as that of the British Raj.[10]

In the broadest terms the British ruled Burma in the sense that their control over much of Burma, in terms of imposing the law, especially in the lowlands, was thorough. This was especially so in cases of suppression of rebellion, enforcement of the rule of law, and revenue collection. This, however, does not dispel the fact that in the accounting for the men and resources that constitute a power domain, in Deutsch's terms, even the British Raj was satisfied with much less than perfection.

Historical Factors and Frontier Administration

The status of boundaries, whether effective or ineffective, can be examined in the historical context. For example, it could be argued that the imperial power would, by using distance as a defensive factor, push the boundaries of their possessions as far as was possible away from the rich lowlands and from the capital city or administrative centre by the coast. In this way, territories beyond the plains and with inhabitants hostile or potentially hostile to control by plainsmen would be included in the colonial possession.

The inheritors of colonial power in a post-colonial "state" thus formed, would also inherit along with the transference of power the problem of closing this gap. Insistence on Western boundary concepts creates problems of internal control and eventually of "civil" war, because of traditional ethnic animosities and colonial policies which actually manipulated these cleavages.

As noted earlier, colonial policies tended to reinforce the cleavage between lowland majority and highland minorities. The practical aim of French ethnic policy in Vietnam had, indeed, been to create a rigidity in the territorial divisions between various ethnic groups, and particularly that between plains and mountains. Resentment had been caused by the French use of Vietnamese underlings to administer and control the minorities, while troops recruited from among the highland minorities were deployed to suppress Vietnamese uprisings or as prison guards.[11] The British policy of preventing Burman settlement in the Shan States and their policy of isolation of Shans from the mainstream of Burmese political movements, which were largely Burman-based, has also been alluded to earlier.

On the other hand, even in Thailand which in the colonial period had never been ruled by an external or imperial power, the ethno-territorial and topographical factors have been strong enough to assert themselves in the pattern of uncontrolled or weakly controlled minority-inhabited frontier zones though this has been much less marked than in the case of Burma or Laos.

The imperial Chinese approach to the problem of the lawless frontiers was through a combination of military action, Han agricultural settlement, and a form of indirect rule at local level through manipulation of the princelings and traditional chieftains using various means, including bribery, and the appointment and the conferring of official status on petty potentates and officials who were given recognition as tax-collecting agents for the Court. All these appointed functionaries worked in a role subordinate to Han officials. These techniques were backed up by the inherent belief on both sides of the superiority of Han culture.[12] Population pressure on land resources in China aided the process of absorption through Han settlement, whereas in the southern states, population pressure on agricultural land has not been a feature of their development. The single exception is to be found in Vietnam and then only in the north, which in many respects is closer to the Chinese model than to patterns prevalent in mainland Southeast Asia.

Although much has been written about colonial concern for the hinterland boundaries, this was in fact subordinate to the overriding concern of the colonial governments which was to develop and exploit the economic potential of the coastal lowlands. Economic and cultural orientation towards the overseas metropolitan power, among other things fostered among lowland élites an outward-looking consciousness which devalued distant and unruly highland possessions.

Geo-Strategic Orientation, and Seats of Power

It is proposed that the concept offered here of the geo-strategic orientation of states cannot be discounted in any analysis of the territorial basis of power and the strategic issues of mainland Southeast Asia. The landward segments of these states have been neglected both politically and economically. In mainland Southeast Asia, the seaward orientation of the states is a factor in the neglect of their landward or northern zones. These zones have come to be of a low priority in the states' main interests and outlooks. These states, with the main controllable domains of population, resources, and production close to the coast or along rivers, giving access to the coast, tend to look seawards.

In mainland Southeast Asia the orientation and also the seats of power of each state tend to be southwards away from the mountains. Historical maritime contacts with the Hinduistic and Buddhistic civilizations of the Indic subcontinent, and the sea-borne trade with China, would have to be considered as being of prime consideration in this outlook towards the seas. In line with this historical pattern, the modern trend — accentuated by colonial rule and its accompanying links to the imperial metropolitan centre — to overseas trade and towards emphasis on international contacts via the sea, enhances the seaward outlook with the states invariably turning their backs on the northern highlands, unless compelled to do otherwise.

The case of Thailand is both typical and instructive. The Siamese Government established its rule over what is now northern Thailand through a process which began in 1874 and was completed in the early 1900s. Before that the Prince of Chiang Mai or the Prince of Lamphun was content to hold a nominal lordship over the local hill peoples, consisting mainly of Lua and Karen. This loose relationship was symbolized in acts of respect such as gifts of rice, roofing materials, beeswax, and other hill and forest produce. In return the princes of the intermontane basins recognized the right of the hill peoples to occupy the highlands, which at any rate, were of little or no interest to the lowland ruler. The princes also settled disputes among the various highland tribes. The hill peoples had military experience gathered in their movement southwards and did not always submit themselves to the lowland authority. They were prepared to give all necessary allegiance to the basin princes. However, there was an element of reciprocity in that the highlanders in return expected to be left alone and that there should be respect by the prince and his followers for their own social, cultural, and political autonomy. They resorted to arms whenever this autonomy was threatened, and if further pressed they would migrate to another area where there was less interference or oppression. The leaders of the Tai valley dwellers "were usually content with no more than symbolic authority over the hill country" and "had neither the people nor the will to colonize for themselves what they regarded as inhospitable country".[13] The avoidance of the highlands by the lowland rulers and their lowland subjects, the negative attitude to the highlands and the absence of any need to colonize the highlands was and is, typical not only of Thailand, but also for all the southern states.

The establishment of a distant bureaucratic and centralized government in Bangkok, political heir of the Tai Yuan basin princes in the highlands, led not only to a continuation of the *laissez-faire* attitude towards the northern hills but, in fact, widened the gulf between lowland authority and hill men, who felt ignored. "Hill leaders ... had no call to confer with lowland authority and lowland bureaucrats exhibited the centuries-old Thai distaste for the hills. For the next fifty years the Thai authorities paid little, if any, attention to the hill people."[14] The bureaucracy of Bangkok had not been able to play even the minimal role of the earlier basin princes whom they had supplanted.

In the meantime migration continued southwards into Thai country of thousands of H'mong, Yao, Lahu, Lisu, and Akha. Despite the size and extent of these movements, the Bangkok authorities remained unaware of this in-migration into their country.[15] It was only after the end of the Pacific War and in the early 1950s with the establishment of the PRC and the instability in neighbouring states (resulting from warfare between the Burmese Army and mainly Shan dissidents and the factional turmoil in Laos) that the Thai Government recognized at last that it could no longer ignore the northern hills which were then seen as being both strategic and vulnerable. Even then, apart from the teak they produced, the hills were not seen as economically valuable territory.

This general perception which de-emphasized the value of the northern hills was strengthened by the Thai experience in the period after the fall of Ayuthia when the power of the kingdom was revived through the benefits of overseas trade which was officially sponsored and encouraged.

This kind of orientation, in a different context, has been noted in traditional Indonesian attitudes where it has been observed that Indonesians tend to look away from the Indian Ocean and inwards towards their archipelagic waters over which they show great concern. The modernization of the port of Cilicap on the Indian Ocean coast of Java and the sharing of a common border with Papua New Guinea have partly offset, but not radically altered, the general posture and outlook away from the open ocean. This orientation is clearest in the case of Java which can be regarded as the seat of Indonesian power. Rough seas, lack of good harbours and coastlines hemmed in by mountains reinforce this outlook. "By and large, the Indonesians have turned their backs toward the Indian ocean throughout their recorded history, as it is still true today."[16] An ancient animistic practice in Javanese culture, observed even by modern leaders, is to propitiate the pagan deity Njiai Loro Kidul, described as the Queen of the Ocean, who if not appeased, exacts her toll of victims.[17]

Japan, too, can be said to have a southward orientation. The warmer regions facing the southern seas are referred to as *omote-Nippon* or "front Japan" while the parts looking northwards, or facing the Sea of Japan, exposed to cold Siberian winds are termed *ura-Nippon* or "back Japan". The Japanese culture, its artefacts, and its technology did not appear to encourage settlement in cold regions. When they conquered Northeast China, or *Manchukuo* as they termed it, the Japanese themselves were reluctant to settle there in the harsher, colder environment especially in the agricultural pursuits. In contrast, for long periods in its history, and due mainly to reasons of defence, Imperial China as a whole turned its back to the sea and faced the troublesome tribes of central Asia, although the southeastern maritime provinces, particularly Fujian, were oriented whenever imperial surveillance relaxed, to a seaward outlook to the southerly rims of the South China Sea.[18]

The important point to bring out is that the countries of mainland Southeast Asia, with the possible exception of Vietnam in its north, have for some length of time neglected their seemingly inhospitable landward, or northerly, territories and have tended to have a coastal or lowland-centred outlook as is reflected in their policies of political structuring and economic development. Even then it must be said, however, that the Vietnamese until recently were not interested in the hills *per se*. Vietnamese ambitions in the past were both southward and westward. In their moves into Laos and the middle valley of the Mekong, the hill tracts were areas which had to be negotiated and thus in themselves were not of primary interest. Where attention has been paid more recently to the hills, as in Thailand, the results of centuries of neglect still remain. The premium placed on the more agriculturally productive, southern lowlands in its turn further strengthens the dichotomy between lowland power and the less controlled northern, highland frontier zones. If the general hypothesis of the existence of geo-strategic orientations in the cultural and policy-making perceptions of a state is acceptable, then in the context of mainland Southeast Asia, it could go some way in explaining the inability of state governments to recognize the value of their share of the strategically overarching massif to their north.

"Territoriality" and Control

While the ethno-centric lowland states were oriented seawards and southwards, the mountainous northern belts were left largely uncontrolled. In this condition, the mountain zone adjacent to each lowland state did not constitute the ideal function of barriers but nevertheless served the frontier function of a "screening instrument in the organization of accessible space".[19] The accessible and controllable space until the arrival of the European colonial powers would have been comprised essentially of the productive belt around the capital or the royal seat. This inner, lowland belt was also the heartland of the ethnic group which supported the throne, especially in economic terms, and was ruled by it.

Previously it was common for people to be used for or be involved in the extension of national territory and to control the new acquisitions. For example, the expansion of the Chinese empire from its cradle in the northern plains westwards and especially southwards, was essentially through a process of the outward, and mainly southward, movement of Han people as conquerors and fighters, agricultural colonizers, or as bearers of a higher technology and representatives of a superior civilization. Through movement into and contact with the fringes, the Hans made accessible hitherto inaccessible space. The Vietnamese expansion southwards into the Cham territories was also a Kinh-oriented and Kinh-based control of extended acquired territory. The Imperial Tsarist movement eastwards to the Pacific was a similar kind of process though it involved fewer numbers of ethnic Russians, and then more as explorers, trappers, administrators, and soldiers rather than as settled agriculturalists. Thus people were the instrument to control territory.

In the colonial and post-colonial eras, however, an opposite process can be discerned. The territorial gains made through the pushing outwards of boundaries has meant the inclusion of previously inaccessible space containing unwilling, unco-operative, or even rebellious ethnic groups in the new post-colonial "national" land spaces. This was led to a situation where two related western-derived concepts of (i) the inalienable sovereignty over, or ownership of, the land space gained through the inclusion of these spaces by the process of (ii) legalized boundary lines, have come together to create a hitherto unique approach in which territory is used as a major *raison d'être* and instrument of control. This is embodied in the concept of "territoriality".

As mentioned earlier, control can involve contact, especially of people, in spatial terms. However, control can also be attempted by using territory, or ownership of territory, to control people. In this approach, "territoriality" has been defined in the following terms:

> We will use the term to mean the attempt to affect, influence, or control actions and interactions (of people, things and relationships, etc.) by asserting and attempting to enforce control over a special geographical area.[20]

The framework of the concept of "territoriality", though originally couched in the frame of political geography is highly relevant to the understanding of the strategic issues of Southeast Asia.

Summarizing the connection between territoriality and power, the expansion of Chinese power southwards into the montane region as mentioned earlier was essentially one derived from the sinicization of indigenous peoples, through the contact of such peoples, as individuals or groups, with Hans as representatives of the Sinic civilization. In contrast, the expansion of post-colonial states of mainland Southeast Asia has been based not on people-centred contact but on an outward burgeoning of territory beyond the main ethnic heartland and deep into relatively inaccessible space. This led to the control or attempts to control, partly on the basis of the legality of ownership of land *and* of the people contained by the expanded territory. This distinction is important for it helps explain some of the internal weaknesses and the retardation of "national" unity in the southern lowland states where unintegrated minorities form a substantial part of the population. The distinction between control of territory through contact between people, and the kind of legalistic control of people through the ownership of territory is often blurred and appears to have eluded observers in the past.

In a different framework, it has been claimed that the new post-colonial countries may have a transethnic identity of legitimacy of their own, but that the very presence of a new state lends added purpose to the various ethnic components since they feel compelled to scramble for the political, economic, and social rewards that the new state has to offer. Thus ethnic consciousness and parochial tendencies are sharpened.[21] This scramble was true of post-colonial Burma, but only in the period immediately following British withdrawal. Should minority ethnic groups fail to obtain what they consider to be their fair share of state resources, the resulting disenchantment can lead to dissidence and rebellion, thus rendering the implementation of central policies incorporating territoriality even more difficult.

The concept of territoriality has given the lowland states the necessary legitimacy in carrying out measures for controlling people and their resources by asserting legal ownership over geographically peripheral areas. The linkage between land space and minority problems, that is, territorially-based minority dissidence and thus "national" disunity, is recognized as a major problem for the states which have succeeded the colonial powers.[22] The ensuing resistance by those thus incorporated leads to sustained conflict and perennial instability.[23] This process is still evolving and creates outer rings within a state which are distinguishable from the former ethnic heartland.

Territoriality can undoubtedly be used as an instrument of control of men and hence as on implement for the accumulation of national power. However, space, in the areal or geographical sense and as implied in the concept of territoriality itself, possesses a function beyond that of a mere territorial arena containing politics. It has been put forward that another process can take place thus:

> The political process organises the space within which it develops. . . .[24]

Thus while territoriality may be used as a means of furthering a strategic policy, it is also possible that its implementation may bring about a process which involves a tacit reorganization of both the space and the people it contains. One visible aspect of this process would be the appearance of conflictual patterns expressed in areal terms. Territoriality and the organizing or reorganizing role of territorial space are not contradictory. In mainland Southeast Asia, they have together produced the phenomena of concentric belts in areas of differing political character, which carry with them significant modifications to the concept of power domains. This question will be enlarged upon in the next two chapters.

★ ★ ★

An understanding of the nature of national power can be facilitated by using the idea of power domains as an analytical tool. A power domain, as defined here, gives a conceptual linkage between people, their resources, and their allegiances on the one hand and territory on the other. These are both the foundations of state power as well as being the indispensable materials for nation-building.

The adoption by states of colonially fostered territoriality is of major strategic significance. It helps explain the predicament of new postcolonial states in attempting to reconcile territorial sovereignty with sovereignty of the state over all its people. This when seen together with traditional geo-strategic orientation (which channels state preoccupations to certain points of the compass while ignoring others), the general weakness of boundaries, the nature of the terrain, primordialism and the cultural predispositions within states, and mental maps of ethnic reliability indicate that the concept of a power domain can be further developed. There is a need to refine it in order to distinguish more clearly between the varying power disparities within states and also to examine the relevance of these to further strategic analysis of regional affairs.

NOTES

1. Jean Gottmann, *The Significance of Territory* (Charlottesville: University Press of Virginia, 1973), p. 138.
2. For convenient summaries in English of his arguments see Norman J.G. Pounds, *Political Geography* (New York: McGraw-Hill, 1963), pp. 28–29; Saul B. Cohen, *Geography and Politics in a Divided World* (London: Methuen, 1964), p. 36. The writers quote Friedrich Ratzel, *Politische Geographie* (Munich: R. Oldenbourg, 1897), and "Die Geztze des raumlichen Wachstums der Staaten", *Petermanns Mitteilungen* (1896): pp. 97–107.
3. Gottman, op. cit., p. 143.
4. Karl W. Deutsch, *The Analysis of International Relations* (New Jersey, Englewood Cliffs: Prentice-Hall, 1968), p. 29.
5. Ibid., pp. 28–29.
6. Cynthia Enloe, *Ethnic Soldiers: State Security in a Divided Society* (Middlesex, England: Penguin, 1980). A more recent study gives another perspective to the problem of cultural identity and the formation of nation-states. Thus in a new nation-state there is a perception of a cultural divide between majority ethnic group, which gives its own definitions to the nation-state's nationalism, and the minorities. There exists "a well-defined ethnic sense which becomes the basis for a nation-state's self-image and around which a national cultural boundary is created with minority groups tending to fall outside". Ruth McVey "Separatism and the Paradox of the Nation-State in Perspective", in *Armed Separatism in Southeast Asia*, ed. Lim Joo-Jock and Vani S. (Singapore: Institute of Southeast Asian Studies, 1984).
7. E.R. Leach, "The Frontiers of 'Burma'", in *Southeast Asia: The Politics of National Integration*, ed. John T. McAlister Jr., (New York: Random House, 1973), p. 330. Originally published in *Comparative Studies of Society and History* 3 (1961).
8. Ulrich Schweinfurth, "The Problem of Nagaland", in *Essays in Political Geography*, ed. Charles A. Fisher (London: Methuen, 1968), p. 171.
9. Maran La Raw, "Toward a Basis for Understanding the Minorities in Burma: The Kachin Example", in MacAlister Jr., ed., op. cit., p. 340.
10. For an account of the conditions under which the British operated, see *Military Operations in Burma, 1890–1892: Letters from Lieutenant J.K. Watson, K.R.R.C.*, ed. B.R. Pearn, Data Paper no. 64, Southeast Asia Program (Ithaca, New York: Cornell University, 1967).
11. See Viet Chung, "National Minorities and National Policy in the DRV", *Vietnamese Studies*, no. 15 (Hanoi, 1968), p. 4.
12. For a detailed description of the methods used by the various Imperial Dynasties, see Herold J. Wiens, *China's March Toward the Tropics* (Hamden, Conn.: Shoe String Press, 1954).
13. Anthony R. Walker, "Highlanders and Government in North Thailand", *Folk* 21–22 (Copenhagen, 1979–80): 428.
14. Walker, op. cit., p. 428.
15. Ibid.
16. Guy J. Pauker, "Indonesian Perspectives on the Indian Ocean", in *The Indian Ocean: Its Political, Economic and Military Importance*, ed. Alvin J. Cottrell and R.M. Burrell (New York: Praeger, 1972), p. 221.
17. Pauker, op. cit., p. 223.
18. For an elaboration of the theme of the linkage between China, the South China Sea,

and Southeast Asia, see Lim Joo-Jock, *Geo-Strategy and the South China Sea Basin: Regional Balance, Maritime Issues, Future Patterns* (Singapore: Singapore University Press, 1979).
19. Gottmann, op. cit., p. 143.
20. Robert D. Sack, "Territorial Bases of Power", in *Political Studies from Spatial Perspectives: Anglo American Essays on Political Geography*, ed. Alain D. Burnett and Peter J. Taylor (Chichester: John Wiley and Sons, 1981), p. 55. While Karl Deutsch, among others, emphasized the role of "nation-ness" in the evolution of modern nation-states, the concept of territoriality would necessarily put much more weight on another aspect of state function, namely, the ability of its central apparatus to coerce, if necessary through the deployment of force. For a study emphasizing the importance of the state as a source of order, see Samuel P. Huntingdon, *Political Order in Changing Societies* (New Haven: Yale University Press, 1968).
21. Ali Mazrui, "Ethnic Stratification and the Military Agrarian Complex: The Uganda Case", in *Ethnicity: Theory and Experience*, ed. Nathan Glazer and Daniel P. Moynihan (Cambridge: Harvard University Press, 1975), pp. 420–549. Cf. Elliot P. Skinner, "Competition within Ethnic Systems in Africa", in *Ethnicity and Resource Competition in Plural Societies*, ed. Leo Despres (The Hague: Mouton Publishers, 1975), pp. 131–57.
22. See Michael Leifer, *Conflict and Regional Order in Southeast Asia*, Adelphi Paper No. 162 (London: International Institute for Strategic Studies, 1980), pp. 6–7.
23. In this context, interethnic conflict has also been seen in a different light. It has been stated that ethnic militancy is basically a movement, or process, from colonial-racial conflict to national-ethnic ("tribal") conflict. Cynthia H. Enloe, *Ethnic Conflict and Political Development* (Boston: Little Brown, 1973).
24. Jean Gottmann, "Organising and Reorganising Space", in *Centre and Periphery: Spatial Variation in Politics*, ed. Jean Gottmann (Beverly Hills, London: Sage, 1980), p. 217.

CHAPTER 6

Territorial Power, Power Isobars, and Core and Peripheral Domains

Having pointed out the spatial basis of power as manifested in the occurrence of power domains, it would be useful to try to examine any variations of power that may exist within these domains.

Power and Administration

Proceeding from the basis of K. Deutsch's definition that management of people and the economic resources that they own or control is the foundation of a power domain, one more element could be added to give the concept a more fully spatial context or frame of reference. In other words the aim here is to modify, adapt, and expand upon the concept of a power domain. To achieve this one must first of all distinguish between geographical areas which show differing levels of degrees of effectiveness of central control.

Needless to say the first requisite in the management of the people and their resources which comprise a power domain would be a firm and effective administrative system. As an initial step in this direction the drawing up of inventories by the authorities or holders of power is essential. A system incorporating these features was introduced into the lowlands of Burma, and previously in India, by the British colonial administration in which civil servants in charge of each administrative district were required to submit detailed reports of population numbers, occupational groups, soil and water conditions, cropping systems, valuations of rice, oil seeds, tree crops and livestock, and an annual assessment of harvest and yields per acre. Wherever possible, the British Indian Civil Service produced the needed data in the form of the *Land Settlement Reports* and *The Revenue Reports*. This was the basis for an efficient land taxing system.

Administration for power to be consistently effective has then to be based in the first place, on a total, or close to total, inventory of the human and other resources involved. Human resources are, indeed, primary to the whole issue under discussion. Following the power domain concept, power and all other resources would flow from the control of human resources. In other words, control and the power accruing therefrom is based on and goes hand in hand with effective marshalling of human resources and springing from that, the land the people live on and cultivate. This can be seen as an accounting or enumerative approach to the issue of power.

Degree of Control and Power Domains

In some areas of the state this accounting, management, and control of resources through political, legal, and even military means would be thorough and thus create an effective administrative basis for a power domain. Yet in other areas, the instrument of management viz. the administrative network and the control exerted through it would be incompletely carried out by the central administration. This could be because of distance and remoteness, lack of communication lines, an ineffective bureaucracy, a weak political centre with insufficient military capacity or with an inability or unwillingness to incorporate the population of these areas into the national body politic. The lack of a universally felt sense of unity militates against effective control, as does the absence of a common and shared historical experience. The parallels with the problems of national integration as seen by Deutsch, Geertz, and Rupert Emerson need to be recognized.

Control by the central authority could also be evaded, or accepted on a nominal basis or as a mere token by the inhabitants of some remote areas. In such cases, if the central authority is not imposed or reimposed as the case may be, doubt could be then effectively raised as to whether the power domain of the central authorities translated into geographical or territorial terms extends effectively into such areas. This doubt would exist even though these areas may lie well within the legally demarcated boundary lines enclosing the land space which the central state authorities concerned would regard as their territory wherein the "national" sovereignty, in terms of international relations which they represent is asserted. For continuity of control to be established, it would be essential not only to secure physical control but also to ensure the legitimacy of the central government in such areas. Difficult as the first requisite may be, the second is very often the more problematic.

Furthermore, there may yet be other tracts of inhabited land within the confines of the state's boundaries where the central administration is completely unable to impose their chosen system of management of human and other resources. At the most, in such cases, the authorities would be capable of imposing their will on the local population only as a result of a concerted and prolonged application of military force.

Moreover, such efforts are often only temporary or merely intermittent or seasonal as when the dry weather after the mid-year monsoons facilitates military movement. In the absence of the projection of force, or when force cannot be used because of climatic or other reasons, control may be absent altogether. The question could then again be raised as to whether the people of these areas are in fact even a part of the territorial power base of the state which claims them as citizens or subjects. Seasonally, as well as territorially, large segments of a state's claimed population could not then be included in its power domain.

Power Isobars and a State's Internal "Power-ness"

In geopolitical terms, it is possible therefore to draw lines through the map of a state with such an affliction, as an aid to a better understanding of the strategic situation within the country and the influence of this condition on its international relations. The "demarcation" is done in order to distinguish between areas of effective control, partial control, areas where control is intermittent, and finally territory where such control from the centre is entirely absent. Such lines would show the varying levels of government authority and power on a spatial basis. Such lines as postulated here would, in fact, adapt an unusual definition of international boundaries as being "political isobars".[1] Ancel applied the political isobar approach to the study of boundaries dividing states. Strictly, however, this is not entirely consistent with the definition of an isobar. A line dividing states in fact divides two different sets of elements or sovereignties. An isobar on the other hand is a line which demarcates two areas showing differing levels of the same element. In this study the common element would be the power, or exercised sovereignty of the state's centre. In other words, both sides of what is in fact a *power isobar* are dissimilar in degree but not in nature. The difference may not be necessarily measurable. In keeping with the meaning of the term isobar, the line is thus a visual attempt to show which side has more of one element than the other.

Here, in the context of power domains, the inequality in the degree of the effectiveness of government administration is the basis for the location of the lines, or power isobars. The line would divide geographical areas with differential levels of effectiveness of central state control of a population and of the resources available to it. The identification of these areas through use of the power isobar would indicate the location and extent of the power base of the centre. The power isobar can be used to show the extent of power domains in spatial terms. Needless to say, the concept of an isobar is more suitable in its application to the delimitation of power domains than to international boundaries.

Finally it should be noted that there are varying shades of power, merging one into the other. The use of the term "power isobar" implies that within the areas divided by the crucial isobar there are different shades of control, reflecting gradations or contours of the state's internal "powerness". In an insurgent-ridden country, for example, the areas completely under the control of the centre, both day and night, would be enclosed by one isobar. Then the next isobar would show the extent of areas where diurnal control is complete by day but only spasmodic by night. The next line might include regions where control is only seasonal, and so on, until areas are reached which are completely out of the government's control at all times. Needless to say, such lines are not fixed, but are liable to move to and fro.

The Ladai Garh of Northeastern India

Perhaps the clearest physical manifestation of the distinct geopolitical separateness of two kinds or shades of power can be found in the westernmost part of the montane zone of mainland Southeast Asia.

The Ladai Garh in northeastern India is a traditional line dividing the Naga from the Assamese plains dwellers. Since India obtained its independence, the Naga state government has been in dispute with the central government over the problem of a common boundary. The Nagas, invariably hill and mountain dwellers, have protested against what they consider to be encroachments by Assamese settlers from the plains into their traditional hill territory and the opening up of the foothills forest zone for Assamese agricultural settlement.

In 1866 when the Naga Hills District was first established by the British, it included the forested Rengma Hills, a foothills zone, and extended far beyond its present boundary. During the period from 1898 to 1925, the British transferred substantial tracts of foothills land from the Naga Hills District to the plains district of Assam in order to increase administrative control in areas desired for the Assam Railway, and for tea growing or mining.

> The British also created a belt of reserved forests along the foothills to reduce conflicts by keeping Nagas and Assamese apart. These forests

were placed nominally within the plains districts to facilitate administration. Today these lands are controlled by the Assamese government which, over the past five years, has prohibited their use by Nagas and opened the forests for settlement by Assamese cultivation.[2]

The British had promised the Nagas that the land in question would remain in perpetuity for the use of Nagas. While the Assamese insist on holding on to the foothills which were transferred to them by the British for ease of administration, the Nagas in turn claim that the western boundary between Nagaland and Assam should be the traditional boundary that was drawn by the Shan-derived Ahom kings who ruled the plains and which divided Ahom-controlled plains from the Naga Hills. This boundary, the Ladai Garh, was mutually recognized and defined by the Ahom kings until the arrival of the British in the nineteenth century.

The Ladai Garh was an example *par excellence* of the line that divided the core from the periphery. The Nagas frequently raided into the plains, denoting lack of control of the hill lands by the Ahoms. The Ahom kings built the line which they referred to as the Ladai Garh as a security road to check raiding parties. It was recognized as a *de facto* boundary that ran roughly between the plains and the foothills along the lower edge of the reserved forests. Thus the existence of a power zone beyond that of the plains core of the Ahom kingdom was implicitly recognized by the building of the Ladai Garh as a defensive boundary.

Another aspect of such a recognition of a power isobar is seen in the Great Wall of China. While the Ladai Garh was essentially a marker dividing plains culture and power from that of the hills and is thus illustrative of the pattern in mainland Southeast Asia as a whole, the Great Wall was built and valued because it gave precision to the differentiation between what was Han-controlled and what was not, in a steppe and desert region which encouraged fluidity and rapidity of movement. The desire for a stable and precise line fencing off the nomadic turmoil of the north, over which China exerted at times only spasmodic influence and little actual control, contrasted with Chinese attitudes to the generally more peaceful and acquiescent southern frontier regions where the local inhabitants went through a continuous process of sinicization. In the north "what could not be included must be excluded",[3] which was also one function of the Ladai Garh. Both the Ladai Garh and the Great Wall of China were physical expressions of a politically and militarily motivated desire to mark out a power isobar defining the limits of effective state control, and fencing off outer tracts where the state's influence was felt but where administration was difficult or impossible. For some post-colonial states, however, such power isobars exist *within* the confines of the state and hence add considerably to the complexity of the state's problems.

The traditional boundary of the Ladai Garh is still visible and can be found in many locations where traces of the road and its bund remain discernible. It is also clearly marked in the 1926 Survey of India topographical map.[4] The Ladai Garh can be regarded as the westernmost extension of the particular combination of geopolitical and cultural factors which make for the kind of strategic environment to be found in montane Southeast Asia.

Not only is the Ladai Garh a clear example of the division between a plains-based core state and the peripheries which it is unable to control, it also clearly expresses the essence of the cultural and physical separateness existing between lowland and highland as seen in mainland Southeast Asia. The Ladai Garh is thus the epitome of the most significant and most widely occurring power isobar in mainland Southeast Asia.

Core and Peripheral Domains Defined

The term "core area" has been widely adopted by political geographers and sociologists alike. It is most often used to define the part of state which is economically dominant, and has also been found in analyses of the development of the nation states of Europe. In this latter context it is the area "in which or about which a state originates".[5] Karl Deutsch has also pointed to this natalistic aspect of a state's core area in his investigation into the manner in which nation-states emerge. In the pattern of integration he described, appearance of core areas was characterized by "unusual fertility of soil, permitting a dense agricultural population and providing a food surplus to maintain additional numbers in non-agricultural pursuits; geographic features facilitating military defence of the area; and a nodal position at an intersection of major transportation routes".[6] This definition approximates that contained in the idea of the "Key Economic Areas" around which Chinese political and military history have apparently revolved.[7]

It has also been said "that once an area has been organised into a coherent unity, it has marked strength, whether of influence or direct power, over adjacent regions less effectively integrated; it has the capacity to grow, to expand geographically not merely as a political realm, but as an area of coherent political integration".[8] This definition by Hartshorne concentrates on the capacity of a unified central area to expand its influence or power.

The term *core power domain* or *core domain* used here, however, denotes the core area over which the centre has effective control of people and resources. It is that part of the state's territory from which accrues the power available to the centre. Although the definition proposed by Hartshorne and that given here for core power domain are not mutually exclusive, the presence of such a core domain does not necessarily imply the beginning of a politically and territorially integrative process, though this may well be so. Rather it denotes a particular type of condition or internal state of *malaise*, which if recognized as such could serve as a useful framework within which to analyse the strategic problems of the post-colonial era in mainland Southeast Asia.

In the case of the southern states of mainland Southeast Asia it would be possible, in this manner, to show the general extent or the spread within a state of the categories or levels of a state's real power. Around the richest agricultural lowlands within easy access of the capital city, there would usually be a belt which can be defined as the core power domain. In a broad fringe around this core domain, usually stretching from the furthest, innermost edge of the lowlands through the foothills and into the more accessible parts of the rim of highlands overlooking the central coastal lowlands can be found a zone which could best be described here as a *peripheral* or *partial power domain*. In such peripheral domains control of people and their resources by the centre is limited.

This differentation between core and periphery has been described, in a different context, in the following terms:

> The typical 'Burma' state consisted of a small fully administered territorial nucleus having the capital as the centre. Round about, stretching indefinitely in all directions, was a region over which the King claimed sovereignty and from the inhabitants of which he extracted tribute by threat of military force. These marginal zones all had the status of conquered provinces, and their populations were normally hostile to the central government. Insurrections were endemic and the political alignments of local leaders possessed the maximum uncertainty.[9]

A feature of the differentiation between core and peripheral domain in the modern context is often the occurrence of conflict between the two.

A peripheral power domain would usually stretch from the fringe of the core domain to the boundary limits of the state. The characteristic level of incomplete control by the centre is very approximately inversely proportionate to distance from the centre. Factors which alter this generalized pattern would be the existence of modern communication lines that would tend to bring linear tongues of otherwise peripheral territory into the core domain; terrain; effectiveness of local resistance to central rule; and foreign intervention at the border belt.

In the remotest parts of the highland country there would be tracts of territory where the central authorities can hardly control the people or utilize the local resources that are undisputedly beyond the control of the centre. Historically, such outer areas would have been a common feature of the political map and accepted as such. In post-1945 Southeast Asia, there has been a tendency for this pattern of an *unaccounted domain* to reappear albeit without the paraphernalia of "silver trees" and related tribute.

In this respect, it should be noted that the normal thoroughness of administration in Britain's Indian Empire and its pragmatism and ability to concede when conditions were difficult, gave rise to a tacit recognition of the existence of outer, unaccounted domains in northeastern India. Thus in the Naga Hills, the tribes nearest the plains were firmly controlled in order to stop their raiding habits, and the frontier was pushed forward to protect them from their wilder neighbours beyond in the deeper mountains. There then evolved three kinds of administrative zones. These were

> [F]irst, the one nearest the plains which was regarded as being fully administered, and was subsequently called the "Naga Hills District"; secondly, a belt of partly administered country ("control area") into which British officers made sporadic visits rather in the nature of expeditions; and thirdly, the remoter hills which remained unadministered . . . the principle of British administration, once it was assured that there would be no more raids into the plains, was to leave the Nagas to themselves.[10]

The concentric pattern of decreasing administrative presence was a direct reflection of the existence of core, peripheral, and unaccounted power domains. With the British in northeastern India, this pattern was to a large extent self-imposed.

The Tax Criterion in Differentiation

Effective management of people and the resources they control is the key factor underlying the formation of a power domain. On the other hand, ineffective management or lack of management altogether is the basis for the formation of a peripheral domain. The following sets of conditions, then, could be used to distinguish a peripheral domain from a core domain: when the central government is not in a position to collect taxes, when taxes are unpaid or remain uncollected, when taxes are collected only intermittently, when taxes are paid to both government and anti-government forces, or when force has to be used whenever taxes need to be collected by the central government. When taxes are paid only to a non-governmental authority then the situation is clearly one in which the area concerned is no longer any part of the government's domain, whether core or peripheral. It would be an outer, unaccounted domain. In this instance, the case of the communist "Northeast Military Region" in Burma, east of the Salween, is revealing. In this region which in 1978 comprised an area of about 28,148 square kilometres with a population of 436, 875, there were difficulties in feeding the insurgent troops because of poor agricultural conditions and because taxes had been lowered after "liberation".[11] It was stated by the Burma Communist Party (BCP) chairman in 1978, "I wish to make a point about taxes. We collect a tax on crops which is ten per cent at the most. If we can extensively boost the masses production program we can obtain more taxes without burdening the people."[12] The taxes paid or dues rendered to Caesar is close to the essence of the matter of a power domain in this contemporary setting.

Peripheral Domains as Strategic Elements

Such parts or regions most remote from the main core power domain would comprise land nominally recognized as being part of the state's sovereignty, but which are *de facto* independent. They may even in political terms be externally controlled or influenced.

Often these areas, though remote from outlets to the sea, are potentially significant economically and geopolitically because of untapped mineral wealth, hydroelectric potentialities, forestry resources in a timber-short world, or most importantly because they are a strategic element in the international relations between neighbouring states. This will be dealt with in greater detail in the course of this study.

Core and Peripheral Domains and the Growth of the Nation-State

The core-periphery approach has been used by Rokkan in modern political geography in analysing the evolution of the European state.[13] Four stages in this process have been identified by Rokkan, based upon what are seen as the experiences of the states of northwestern Europe. The internal core-periphery pattern is seen by Rokkan to exist in the earliest kind of state, which is characterized by "penetration" leading to what he refers to as the "territorial state" of the absolute monarchies. Next comes the stage of nation-building characterized by standardization in religion and language. This results in a nation-state which is homogeneous in the cultural sense. The third stage is typified by participation of the citizenry through the franchise, with the final stage being the welfare state created by the redistribution springing from the nation-wide exercise of the franchise.[14]

Rokkan's perception of the essential role of culture, that is, religion and language, as the prerequisite for the formation or growth of the nation-state is useful to our understanding of conditions in the region. Such a prerequisite is not universal in Southeast Asia. The core-periphery cleavage in mainland Southeast Asia, is in itself partly a dimension of geographical, political, and social distance or estrangement from the ruling centres and its values. The rift has been accentuated by schisms which existed in many cases before the imposition of the territorially unifying but culturally fragmented and ethnically split states. In some ways the colonially-born state resembles the earlier monarchical political entity. Shared territory is the main, if not the only, common denominator linking the diverse groups, in both post-colonial and Rokkan's monarchical territorial state.

Foremost amongst the fissiparous tendencies present is ethnic separateness merging into ethnic regionalism, especially so in the case of Burma. Perennial instability leading to continued uneven economic development between core domain and the peripheries, in turn, reinforces, in the manner of a vicious circle, the underlying separateness. A post-colonial state in the region would be at a point of development somewhere between Rokkan's first (or monarchical territorial state stage) and second stage of nation-building accompanied by standardization of language and religion. Rokkan's welfare nation-state is not yet in sight.

If it is assumed that a nation-state is a political and cultural phenomenon and that in addition it must be equated with a piece of land or territory, then it follows that *ceteris paribus* homogeneity and equality, for example of opportunity or the franchise, should, in a spatial sense, pervade in equal measure all parts of the territorial holding controlled by the centre. Where sharp differentiations, territorially discernible, occur inside the territory of the aspirant "nation-state", then it can be argued that the concept of the nation-state as exemplified by European models should be applied with extreme care to the existing territorial extent of states in mainland Southeast Asia. They, in fact, enclose territorial entities which have a tendency to be disparate and even schismatic, and which are not pervaded by a single unifying *ethos*. In this sense then, many existing boundary lines serving as territorial definitions of a nation-state are, in the strategic context of power domains, not only symbolic; they can even be misleading if they are regarded as hiving off homogeneous blocks.

Core and Peripheral Domains in Strategic Analysis

The lack of concordance between the lines denoting the extent of power domains internal to a state and its international boundary lines is important and can be used as a tool of analysis in dealing with relations between adjacent states. The strategic problems of a state are compounded when the two sets of lines show a wide geographical disparity, that is when the peripheral domain is territorially large in area. The issues of preservation of "national integrity," and "national sovereignty," and the maintenance of national security can be usefully examined in the light of the extent of core and peripheral power domains.

There could arise occasions when at a given point of time the full power available to the government and which derives mostly from the population of the core — and at times only in areas around the capital — is at a considerable distance from the frontier zone of conflict or points of externally or internally generated threat. Poor communications and logistics, a common feature of the region, can exacerbate this problem. In this way the capacity of a government to subdue rebellions, to control people and resources, or to administer its territory is considerably reduced. Moreover, the rugged hinterlands are not conducive to the rapid projection of military power to meet any threat. All these come back once again to the existence of a core-periphery dichotomy. Once a peripheral domain takes shape and root, a vicious circle is formed in which the centre would find it more and more difficult to incorporate the periphery into the core, especially if there is an external interest in the maintenance of peripherality in power terms of a state's outer, border regions.

It is important to recognize that the limits of the core power domains as well as those of the peripheral domains can expand outwards under circumstances which are favourable to the state's authorities. Conversely in times of political, economic, or military stress which does not favour the popular acceptance of central rule, the limits of the core power domains can shrink inwards, even though the legal boundary lines remain intact. Expansion or contraction of the core domain at the expense of any peripheral or unaccounted domains usually remains an internal matter, while movements of the outer limits of the peripheral domain is related to the power relationship with neighbouring states. Thus for purposes of analysis, one can distinguish between the territorial limits of the majority ethnic group's share of the state's space — that is, the core domain — and the boundaries of the state which include the peripheral domains. Deutsch's concept of power domains — adapted and applied on a broader geopolitical basis and incorporating additionally spatial cores and peripheries — allows for a degree of flexibility in the analysis of the strategic problems in the region. In relation to conflict and the challenges to central authority, this multidimensional approach may explain more than concepts which emphasize one element only.

It is aggregative in nature and is based on the premise that the *nature of the state-space* with its array of geopolitical features needs to be understood in any study of post-colonial nation-states in the region. It may add to the understanding of treatments such as those emphasizing political and constitutional considerations and "ethnicity" when these should involve territorial considerations. In the case of Burma, it can also give some insight to the restraints placed on Rangoon's foreign policy and to an understanding of the internal situation in Burma.

The idea of core and peripheral power has sprung from Leach's seminal analysis of the frontiers of "Burma" or montane Southeast Asia; it incorporates Rokkan's perceptions, but owes its biggest debt to Deutsch's concept of power, while at the same time giving his power domain a spatial embodiment. This idea of core and peripheral power domain emphasizes the need to recognize the importance of the qualitative aspects of the territorial bases of power in mainland Southeast Asia, their impact on relations between neighbouring states, and their effect on the general strategic environment.

"Liberated Areas" and Power Domains

The resource base of communist "liberated areas" has been alluded to earlier. The concept of "liberated areas" in communist terminology can further be related to the concept of power domains. Communist military thinkers appear to have grasped the strategic significance of the differences between wholly controlled and partially controlled areas, for the purpose of long-term revolutionary planning. They divide the areas where they operate into *base areas*, which can be equated to a core domain, and *guerrilla zones* surrounding the base area. Control of the guerrilla zone is frequently contested by government forces, and are in fact peripheral power domains as far as the base area is concerned. Referring to its strategic hold on the easternmost parts of the Kengtung State in Burma, the BCP stated in 1978 that ". . . the 185th Military Region is located north of the Nam Loi River along the far eastern border east of Keng Tung and is separated from Laos only by the Mekong River. The base area encompasses 2,732 square kilometres and the guerrilla zone, 2,388 kilometres which also includes some areas south of the Nam Loi River. So the total area is 5,125 square kilometres."¹⁵ A process of consolidation and enlargement is envisaged through guerrilla action and described as follows: "In order to consolidate the base area, transform the guerrilla zone into a base area and expand new guerrilla zones, it is essential to expand the combat force."¹⁶ Thus the base area, namely, the party's insurgent core domain which is itself located in the outermost fringes of the government's peripheral domain is the resource base which is used to expand the geopolitical extent of power of the guerrillas.

"Popular Areas" and "The Spreading Oil Patch"

In Peninsular Malaysia, the communist guerrillas used the term "popular areas" for the territory and villages under their control and which comprised their source of recruits and supplies. The guerrillas envisaged a lengthy struggle during which their control over populated areas would slowly and steadily expand. The expansion itself would be into areas which have been carefully selected.¹⁷

In gaining control of Tonkin, the French used methods which contained the idea of an expanding power domain. Marshal Gallieni, assisted by Lyautey, laid the basis of this technique.

> With a few thousand men and modest resources they achieved amazing results in Tonkin, the most rugged of the provinces of Indo-China. They eschewed the hard-hitting mobile offensive column penetrating deep into enemy-held territory, the equivalent of air cavalry of the 1960's, in favour of slow steady expansion of a frontier of control, employing both political and military means to bring the principal populated areas under control.¹⁸

We have seen earlier how Gallieni regarded the ethnic rivalries and tensions of the Tonkin highlands as a strategic factor which could be manipulated in favour of French colonial expansionism. Later, in Morocco, the methods of the expanding pacified area used in Tonkin were further developed and were referred to as "the *Tache-d'huile* the slowly spreading oil patch, a concept which was employed with notable success by the British in the Malayan Emergency".¹⁹ These counter-insurgency successes, however, were achieved against relatively ill-armed or disorganized and divided opponents. Moreover, even in Tonkin, there was then no proximate power domain where the interests of the managers coincided with those of the insurgents.

Discarding the consecrated "Napoleonic" principles of massive manœuvre and of thrusting heavy columns deep into enemy territory, the radical strategy of creeping consolidation was adopted. Lyautey evolved the new strategic principle of avoiding as far as possible the column of armed forces and replacing it by progressive, creeping occupation. "Military occupation consists less in military operations than in organisation on the march."[20] In this doctrine, occupation of hostile territory does not begin with the actual occupation; it only starts when the organization or apparatus for occupation is ready.[21] The "spreading oil patch" connotes the steady expansion of a core domain at the expense of the peripheral domains, and involves not only the application of military power but the entire paraphernalia of government and even long-term acculturation.

The U.S. War in Vietnam

Power domains as a conceptual tool can be applied to the study of military affairs. A weakness of the Saigon authorities and their U.S. allies during the Vietnam War was that they were never able to create a stabilized power domain even around the capital city of Saigon. The highlands and the southernmost foothills of the Annamite chain extended southwards to less than 80 miles from Saigon and throughout the war were largely beyond Saigon's administrative control. For example, in 1962, the Strategic Hamlet programme was launched in a district only 27 miles north of Saigon. Military means were resorted to and the area had first of all to be seized.[22] The absence of a clear core domain was to prove a strategic asset to the opponents of the Saigon Government and its American allies. The North Vietnamese, when they intervened, seized this geo-strategic opportunity to move troops and installations close to Saigon. In fact, most of the highlands were beyond the control of the government of the Republic of South Vietnam.[23] The proximity of these highlands to all urban centres including Hue and Saigon was itself an inbuilt disadvantage for the South, which the Vietcong and the North Vietnamese used to maximum effect.

Even much of the lowlands around Saigon was peripheral to the Saigon authorities' area of control and mobilization of power. It has been estimated that in late 1967 the Vietcong controlled 3 million villagers, the South Vietnamese Government 4 million, while 6 million villagers lived in what were called contested areas.[24] Control was intermittent and defined by seasonality or even by the diurnal rhythm, with guerrillas controlling territory and collecting taxes and recruits in villages just beyond the Saigon urban sprawl. Seasonality and the diurnal rhythm of control also characterize the disputed peripheral areas of Burma and Laos, and in the case of Cambodia it features prominently in the Khmer resistance against the Vietnamese and Phnom Penh authorities after the Vietnamese invasion of 1978–79.

Needless to say, in conditions of active warfare, the extent and disposition of the various domains can change rapidly. The fundamental question is control of population. "Who controls whom?" is basic to the question of power, and in Vietnam the war was really an administrative war. It was foreseen that "the side with superior administration is likely to win".[25] The effective use and availability of administrative machinery, backed by force, to control the domestic sources of power, within the frame of politically acceptable solutions, is thus the key not only to the successful outcome of protracted wars but also in the resolution of internal power mal-distribution and instability in a state as mirrored in the elimination of its peripheral domains.

Peninsular Malaysia, Laos, and Burma

By the 1980s Peninsular Malaysia, despite its ethnic cleavages, could boast of a power domain that covers the entire country — a result of a combination of geography (there is no mountain region fringing a central plain), successful tactics countering guerrilla warfare, and the geographical distribution, in the form of intermingling, of the component ethnic groups in its population. No single potentially rebellious ethnic group occupies a piece of territory large enough from which it can defy central authority. The Iban of Sarawak in East Malayia have been acquiscent to the rule of Kuala Lumpur.

In the post-Vietnam War era, the core power domain of Laos is restricted to the confined lowlands but with Vietnamese aid the peripheral domain in the mountains is being increasingly brought under control, though the process is still far from complete, especially in northeastern Laos bordering on China and Burma.

Burma is the clearest example where the core power domain fails to coincide, and very markedly too, with the state's landward international boundaries. This could have grave impact on the strategic affairs not only of Burma itself but also the whole of mainland Southeast Asia.

Ratzel's Theory and the Organicity of Power Domains

Ratzel has stated that a nation-state is like a living organism, expanding its boundaries at the expense of weaker, lesser states of lower "culture". Boundaries in this view are in a continual state of flux over a period of time. Implied in Ratzel's thesis is that where such flux is experienced it can be accompanied by international wars.

The expansion and shrinking of power domains, as distinct from the boundaries of a state, as presented here, however, can proceed with or without involvement in external war. It is possible to go even further and postulate that in Southeast Asia there has been a historical and continuing process of expansion and shrinkage of power domains, unaccompanied by the kinds of intensive wars which marked boundary expansions in Europe, and interrupted only, and then incompletely, by the period of Western colonial rule.

In the spatial confines of a state, the changing spatial relationships between core and periphery, as seen in the expansion and contraction of either core or periphery, reflect not only shifts in the political relationship between the core and the periphery of the state concerned, mirroring its internal organization, but also indicate changes in the relationships with neighbouring states. In the same light, the expansion of core domains at the expense of peripheral domains can be seen in the growth of the imperial Chinese state or empire. In its peripheral areas, the system of indirect rule or the vassalage system was used as a convenient means of political control. John K. Fairbank has observed that, "Typically, as the area under Chinese rule extended, the tendency was for exterior vassals of one period ... to become interior vassals of another period".[26] In a reverse process, both China and Thailand experienced inward shrinkage of the peripheries when the Europeans arrived.

Strategic Utility of the Location of Core and Peripheral Domains

The actual location of a peripheral domain, usually as a belt of varying width alongside the state's international boundaries, is important. Provided that there is no challenge to the centre from the peripheral domain it means that this peripheral zone can act as a kind of buffer, or screen, preventing large-scale and continuous contact between the core domain of the lowland state and its immediate neighbour. Events which could otherwise directly affect the population of the majority ethnic, lowland core are screened off by this peripheral zone. Short of an undisguised, large-scale, and sustained invasion by the neighbouring state, the affairs of the peripheral zone can go unnoticed by the population of the lowlands or else can be deliberately ignored by the central authorities, its publicity organs, and the mass media so as to keep the population unaware of actual border conditions. This could happen when the central authorities are in a weak position and do not wish to contest border affairs involving a larger and more powerful neighbour, nor to inflame public opinion to a point where its strategic options are narrowed. Conversely peripheral tracts of limited strategic value when contested can become convenient focal points of national enthusiasm, without impairment to the affairs of the core domain.

Peripheral power domains, while a symptom of inherent internal disability in what purports to be a nation-state, can serve as useful filtering screens for the preservation of the identity of the core domain. Core domains and their inhabitants, in the final analysis, comprise the state property that really matters in the preservation of some form of political independence and cultural and social identity. The core domain of a typically lowland-centred state in the region is then the territory or sovereignty of last resort. Depending on the perceptions and policies of the centre, peripheral domains can be either strategic liabilities or buffering assets.

The dismemberment of Thai territory by the British and French in the nineteenth century came close to leaving Bangkok only its ethnic core domain. In the case of Burma and French Indochina, imperial expansion added large tracts of territory to the lowland cores which would later prove to be strategically significant peripheral domains. In Vietnam this became evident to the French and then to the Americans in the Indochina Wars from 1945 to 1975. The same problem has faced the Burmese Government since its attainment of post-war independence.

The Quality of a Core Domain

If people constitute, in the main, the basis of a power domain then their quality — in physique, health, technological knowledge, education and training, and importantly their attitudes — would be fundamental to the assessment of power even in a firmly administered core domain.

Rule by force of arms, without mobilizing the population's consent and its will to co-operate, and the imposition of unilaterally decided exactions on the resources can satisfy the accounting approach to power measurements, but will not be able to utilize the full power potential of the people, the land, and other resources to the optimum extent. Here lies a major difference between a core domain in the complete sense of the term and one which is qualitatively in itself incomplete, even though military and administrative control may be thorough. The importance of the human and cultural elements makes for variations in the quality of the domain, depending, in the main, on the quality of the population concerned, their organization, and their attitudes as expressed in the degree of agreement or motivation with respect to policies laid down by the authorities.

The degree of "power-ness" in a core domain, could vary according to the people's degree of co-operation with the central authority and the degree of commitment to, or identification with, the aims and policies of the central authorities. Thoroughness of administration is fundamental but in the end it is not enough to overcome any widespread reluctance, for example, of farmers to follow agricultural policies which are contrary to traditional practices or to the growers' self-interest.

Several methods have been used to mobilize the full power potential of agricultural areas. The factors of capital input and improved technology apart, the level of production can be raised by commitment through the instrument of the democratic process, the use of the profit motive, or by exhortations based on ideology and nationalism. The use of the instrument of consensus, achieved through long drawn-out deliberations outside of Western parliamentary democracy could also, under favourable conditions, raise the level of power available to the managers of national affairs. Repression, corvée labour, and heavy taxes have also been commonly used. Increase in power of an area can also be achieved by allowing the freer play of market forces. This has resulted in some cases, as in Thailand, in increased output through the operation of a free market in agricultural produce and the ability of Thai farmers to respond to world demand for cash crops, like tapioca (cassava) and the jute-like kenaf while at the same time not challenging the authority of Bangkok.

Where mineral and forestry resources are concerned, although they are often found in the peripheral domains, they are often, strictly speaking, not under the control of less technologically advanced people of the area, and can be exploited with capital and technological input by the central authorities if they can gain effective security in the area in question. The crucial question then is control, followed by a willingness on the part of the people.

Domain Quality, Vietnam, Thailand, and Burma

The post-1975 failure to realize the full power potential of the Socialist Republic of Vietnam's southern core domain is seen in its economic and agricultural policies which have not been able to induce the farmers of the southern deltaic area to respond with maximization of farming effort, nor to release the stipulated proportion of the harvest for the government granaries. In marked contrast, Thailand's central plain has witnessed the free play of market forces and the agricultural producers have responded by the increasing of agricultural production and by the introduction of new cash crops. However, the crucial question is whether the level of power can be maintained since the trends to landlessness and rural poverty may in the end detract from the power available to the Bangkok authorities.

In Burma's ethnic core domain, after a period of trial and error, the central authority by 1982 had increased the power it could draw on through an improved administration, improved security, and an agricultural programme with enough incentives to induce the farmers to produce more and to release more of their harvest to the buying and marketing network set up by Rangoon.

Power Domains and Regional Stability

In terms of regional order and stability, it has been pointed out that for the time being, "the major contribution that the new states of Southeast Asia can make to regional order will be to show themselves capable of overcoming an internal debility which has been their striking common characteristic since independence".[27] While the non-communist states have made considerable economic progress, after initial difficulties in the aftermath of independence, the recurrent pattern in many parts still remains one of "internal debility". The existence of core and peripheral domains is both a symptom and a cause of the continuing malaise.

The infirmity of montane boundaries in mainland Southeast Asia, the evolution of discernible divisions between core domains and peripheries, and the consequently widened opportunities for interference by stronger, contiguous states does not necessarily mean that the post-colonial states are likely to undergo a process of loss of land or territorial shrinkage in the foreseeable future. Changes in the alignments of boundary lines on a major scale are unlikely since the very existence of a state territorial unit ensures some degree of continuity and "even when . . . [it] has little organisation [and is] in fact existing only as a legal structure, as a tradition of legitimacy it remains a potential power that can be used. . . ."[28] What can be called the impetus of internationally legalized existence, together with the "state-idea"[29] upheld by the leaders and the majority population of the core domain, will ensure the continuity of the general territorial shape of the states concerned. However, it is this very continuation of incomplete political organization within fixed boundaries symptomized by the appearance of core and peripheral domains that adds substantially to the element of endemic internal instability, in some of the states of the region. Much, if not all, of this instability is confined within the territories, especially the peripheral domains, of the state.

* * *

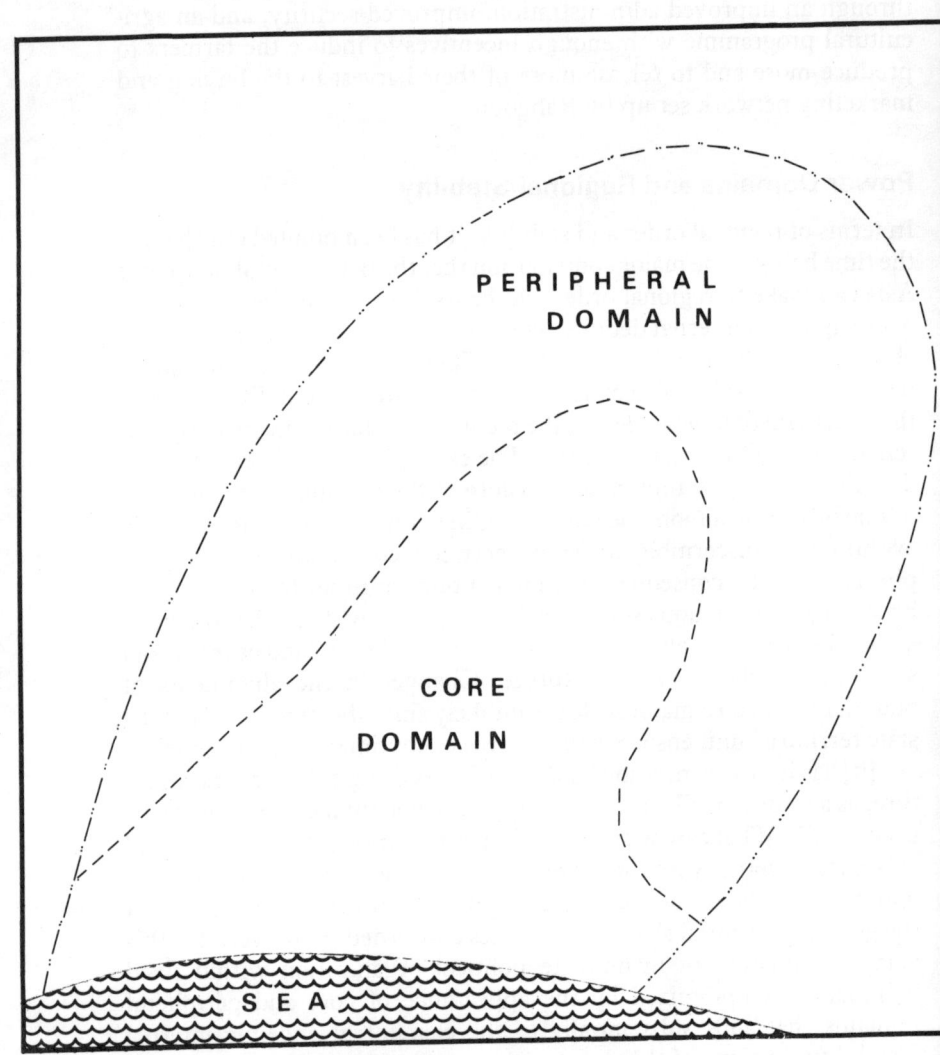

Core and Peripheral Domains

A diagram

Earlier, a definition of a power domain was put forward and the territorial basis of power as seen in mainland Southeast Asia examined. It was shown that the variations in the concentration and quality of power can be seen to occur concentrically as of cores and layered peripheries, viz. as core and peripheral power domains. These are separated by power isobars. In the peripheries or peripheral power domains there is an evident dearth of power available to the centre. Once this pattern and the utility of power isobars have been recognized, the consequences to the solidity of the territorial foundations of a post-colonial state become clearer. The instability in the peripheral domains where the sources and manifestations of state power are weak or even non-existent presents the recipients and wielders of power resident in the core domains with deep-rooted strategic problems. Core domains themselves may vary in quality and may expand or contract with time and circumstance. Where the limits of the core power domain do not coincide with the boundaries of a state, serious problems of internal instability can arise. Hence, this lack of fit introduces into the overall strategic environment of the region elements which have a direct though subtle bearing on the nature of regional stability or instability. The ideal of a strict coincidence of core domain with state boundaries has generally not been realized in the states of the region. Thus, other ideals of a modern nation-state are not attainable as long as power isobars differentiating core from periphery are discernible.

NOTES

1. This term is used by Jacques Ancel in *La Geographie des Frontieres* (Paris: Gallimard, 1938).
2. Gordon P. Means, "Cease-Fire Politics in Nagaland", *Asian Survey* 11, no. 10 (October 1971): 1015–1016.
3. Owen Lattimore, *Inner Asian Frontiers of China* (American Geographical Society of New York, 1951), pp. 482–83. The earth wall which the Moroccan Government erected to keep off the Polisario guerrillas in 1983–84 is another example of an attempt to define a power isobar and to use it for defensive military purposes. The walls erected by bull-dozers and equipped with electronic sensors enclosed almost the entire populated area but left vast tracts of desert land to the foreign-funded marauders who by 1984 were rendered impotent.
4. Means, op. cit., footnote p. 1016.
5. Derwent Whittlesey, *The Earth and the State* (New York: Henry Holt & Co., 1939), p. 597.
6. Karl W. Deutsch, "The Growth of Nations: Some Recurrent Patterns of Political and Social Integration", *World Politics* (1952–53): 168–95.

7. Chao-ting Chi, *Key Economic Areas in Chinese History* (First published London: George Allen and Unwin, 1936; reprint ed., New York: Paragon Book Reprint Corp., 1963), pp. 4–5.
8. Richard Hartshorne, "Morphology of the State Area: Significance for the State", in *Essays in Political Geography*, ed. Charles A. Fisher (London: Methuen, 1968), p. 31. See also Norman J.G. Pounds and Sue Simonds Ball, "Core Areas and the Development of the European State System", *Annals of the Association of American Geographers* 54 (1964): 24–40.
9. E.R. Leach, "The Frontiers of 'Burma'", in *Southeast Asia: The Politics of National Integration*, ed. John T. McAlister Jr., (New York: Random House, 1973), p. 324.
10. Ulrich Schweinfurth, "The Problem of Nagaland", in *Essays in Political Geography*, ed. Charles A. Fisher (London: Methuen, 1968), p. 166.
11. Chairman Thakin Ba Thein Tin, "The Entire Party! Unite and March to Achieve Victory", Political Report of the Politburo of the Central Committee of the Burma Communist Party. Submitted to the Central Committee Meeting, November 1981. Text broadcast by the Voice of the People of Burma (VOPB), 27 November 1979 to 29 January 1980, and monitored by the Foreign Broadcast Information Service (FBIS).
12. Ibid.
13. S. Rokkan, "Territories, Centres and Peripheries: toward a geoethnic-geoeconomic-geopolitical model of differentiation within Western Europe", in *Centre and Periphers: Spatial Variation in Politics*, ed. Jean Gottmann (Beverly Hills: Sage, 1980), pp. 163–204.
14. S. Rokkan, "Dimensions of State Formation and Nation-Building: a possible paradigm for research on variations within Europe", in *The Formation of Nation States in Western Europe*, ed. C. Tilley (New Jersey: Princeton University Press, 1975), pp. 318–65.
15. Thakin Ba Thein Tin, op. cit.
16. Ibid.
17. Robert Thompson, *Defeating Communist Insurgency: Experiences from Malaya and Vietnam* (London: Chatto and Windos, 1966), pp. 37–38.
18. Robert O'Neill, "Insurgency and Sub-National Violence", in *New Directions in Strategic Thinking*, ed. Robert O'Neill and D.M. Horner (London: George Allen and Unwin, 1981), p. 204.
19. Ibid.
20. Quoted by Jean Gottmann, "Bugeaud, Gallieni, Lyautey: The Development of French Colonial Warfare", in *Makers of Modern Strategy: Military Thought from Machiavelli to Hitler*, ed. Edward Mead Earle (Princeton: Princeton University Press, 1948), p. 242.
21. Gottmann, op. cit., p. 242.
22. Edgar O'Ballance, *The Wars in Vietnam 1954–1973* (New York: Hippocrene Books, 1975), p. 48.
23. Ibid. See map, p. 176.
24. J.L.S. Girling, *People's War: Conditions and Consequences in China and South East Asia* (New York: Praeger, 1969), pp. 222–23.
25. Herman Kahn, "On the Possibilities for Victory or Defeat", in *Can We Win in Vietnam?* ed. Frank E. Ambruster et al. (New York: Praeger, 1968), p. 179. See also Bernard B. Fall, *Last Reflections on a War* p. 210. Although the Saigon government had dedicated officials in some areas who worked effectively to counter the political activities of the communist cadres, the general situation was one in which the Saigon

administration was unable to muster enough personnel to offset the efforts of the communists. Milton Osborne, "Aspects of Revolutionary Warfare with particular reference to Southeast Asia", in *Strategy and Defence: Australian Essays*, ed. Desmond Ball (Sydney: George Allen and Unwin, 1982), p. 177.
26. John K. Fairbank, ed., *The Chinese World Order* (Cambridge, Mass.: Harvard University Press, 1968), p. 8.
27. Michael Leifer, *The Foreign Relations of New States* (Camberwell, Victoria: Longman, 1974), p. 109.
28. Hartshorne, op. cit., p. 30.
29. Preston E. James writes that "the state-idea is a complex of traditions, experiences, and objectives. . . . The state is created to defend and develop the state-idea". See James, "Some Fundamental Elements in the Analysis of the Viability of States", in Charles E. Fisher, ed., op. cit., p. 33.

CHAPTER

Developmental and Strategic Issues in the Frame of Core and Peripheral Domains

Concerns as diverse as developmental problems, the military situations which face communist insurgencies, and the general strategic situation of a region can be usefully examined within the broad context of the core and peripheral domain approach. For the sake of brevity this will at times be referred to as the core-periphery approach, though it has little in common with the various core-periphery theories which expound, among other things, the dependence of the periphery on the core.

Development, the Core, and the Peripheral Domains

Development, which is more often than not centre-initiated, can be usefully seen in strategic terms and in the frame of the core and the peripheries of a state. One ubiquitous and ever-present issue in the exercise of greater control and the hoped-for eventual absorption of the peripheries into the core domain is the question of providing alternatives to upland groups which are dependent on the swidden form of agriculture for their livelihood. The highland economy will be dealt with in more detail in the next chapter. However, at this stage it would be useful to examine one major aspect of the problems of the highlands. The issue of swiddening will be briefly reviewed in the perspective of development in a core-periphery environment.

Swidden Agriculture in the Context of Core and Peripheral Domains

It needs to be emphasized that the slash-and-burn hill method of agriculture has been found objectionable by all lowland-based governments, without exception.[1] This shifting agriculture is held to be the root cause

Developmental and Strategic Issues 125

of destruction of highland forests, valuable for timber and as a protective, natural mantle for the preservation of the watersheds and their soil cover. The highland swiddeners are claimed to be the cause of this undesirable deforestation. This will be dealt with in greater detail later in this study.

A constant developmental theme has been the search for viable alternatives to swiddening. In these attempts to wean the uplanders away from shifting farms, the ingrained attachment to swiddening of the highland cultural groups — swiddening being the basis of their material culture — has to be considered. However, when circumstances are exceptionally favourable and their produce can be easily sold, the Pai-Yi of Yunnan and Sichuan who fought on the Guomindang side and were resettled in the mountains of Taiwan have proved that they and their families can adapt to high altitude sedentary cultivation of cash crops.[2] Generally, however, swiddening continues to flourish and attempts to eradicate it have met with failure.

However, one of the more promising long-term efforts is to preserve the natural ecology by replacing trees of cut, burnt, and abandoned forests with other trees of a high commercial value. By replacing the natural forest with substitute plantation of forest trees, that is, a man-induced forest cover, the balance of the natural ecology of the area is restored. Much of the highlands is too steep for permanent cultivation of annual crops and is suitable only for forest growth.

A Thai Experiment in Development of the Periphery

Forest replacement has been tried in northern Thailand and takes the form of "forest villages" set up in cut-over and abandoned or degraded forest land. In this scheme, up to 100 families are resettled in one semi-permanent location known as a forest village. In the eleven years or so up to 1978, forty-seven such settlements had been set up in various parts of the country.[3]

Each family is required to plant trees in locations near the village and the annual tree-planting target for each family is a plot of 10 rai (1 rai = 0.16 hectare). "They work around different plots of land of the same size each year and back to the original plot again when the planted trees are cut and the land is cleared."[4] In return they receive wages for their work with bonuses accorded by the number of saplings that survive. The settlers are also allowed to grow and retain cash crops between the newly planted trees for up to 3 years. In addition, each family is given 5 rai for their own cultivation. Public utilities such as water supply, electricity, a school, and a clinic are provided.[5] Provision of such amenities and the movement away from food production to paid wage labour puts a strain on the financial resources even of governments which are not faced by civil war.

Obviously, this form of development incurs heavy and sustained capital expenditure with no prospect even of medium-term returns. The most valuable tree planted is teak (*tectona grandis*) and this has a cutting rotation of fully 60 years, that is, the trees are of suitable size for commercial felling only after a 60-year lapse from the planting of the seedling.

Despite the immense difficulties faced in implementing reforestation, preserving the natural ecology has become a matter of vital urgency. The magnitude of the developmental problem in mainland Southeast Asia is seen in the amounts of land estimated to have been denuded or destroyed by deforestation. Satellite photographs have indicated that in Thailand alone during the five-year period from 1973 to 1978, the amount of forest land was reduced by 46,483 square kilometres, that is, from an estimated 221,707 square kilometres or 43.2 per cent of the total area of the country to about 175,224 square kilometres or 34.2 per cent of the country. Thus in a five-year period of rapid economic growth characterized by timber extraction for export and for local use and the continuation of swiddening, 9 per cent of the total area of Thailand was deforested. This denudation amounted to more than a quarter of the country's forests.

Since most of the forest land existing prior to 1975 was suitable only for forests or tree growth (or swiddening) because of steep, easily eroded slopes, poor soils, an unreliable water supply, and poor accessibility, this kind of "crop substitution" would appear to be appropriate for the state as a whole. However, even if completed such a programme would not seem to offer a solution to the problem of an increasing population of upland minority people. Programmes of this nature also have of necessity to be subsidized by the lowland-based government. If such a programme is sustained, it would mean the allocation of scarce resources drawn from the core domain for the long-term development of the peripheries. It demonstrates the profound difficulties which are to be faced in any plans to absorb the peripheral zones and their inhabitants into the mainstream of political, social, and economic activity of the lowland-centred state.

Development in the Framework of Core and Peripheral Domain

From the viewpoint of the core and peripheral domain approach the method of tree replacement — by using solutions adapted to the natural ecology and rewarding the growers with paid labour instead of suppression — would appear to be an ideal solution to bring the peripheral zones more clearly under the control of the core power domain. Power and the patronage that accompanies it is in this manner projected from the core to the peripheries in a peaceful attempt to integrate the social order, economy, and attitudes of the peripheral uplands into the national body politic. The sheer size of the problem, however, involves high costs which only a stable, prosperous state can afford.

The outstanding problem, as in Laos and Burma, is to eliminate the existence of the outer peripheral domain or at least to reduce it to a manageable size. Ideally this needs to be done peacefully, without having to resort continually to the application of force, repression, and in the case of Laos even to massacre or "genocide", as has been reported in the Vietnamese-led campaigns against the H'mong of the upper slopes of the Phu Bai massif of Laos.

It would mean also that the hill peoples must be willing to give up their traditional agriculture and customary mode of life, while the central or lowland government must be equally willing, or have sufficient continuity in its policies, to wait for the results. It means, if the forest replacement method is used, that the lowland authorities must uninterruptedly maintain a policy for at least 60 years of allocation of scarce funds as a subsidy for hill-dwellers in new occupations as foresters until the trees begin to yield their first crops of commercially useful timber. The question can then be asked: Has this endurance and consistency been shown by lowland — centred governments so far?

The Communist Party of Thailand, Communism, and Lowland State Security

The communist-led insurgency in Thailand is to a considerable extent linked with the core-periphery or highland-lowland cleavage found in that country, as in the rest of mainland Southeast Asia. The Communist Party of Thailand (CPT) took advantage of the situation and has made extensive contact with the upland minorities; in so doing "latent conflicts were actualised . . ."[6], while new conflicts resulted from the large-scale intrusion of Thai armed forces into the hills in the 1960s and early 1970s. As with much of montane Southeast Asia, latent conflict situations existed between highlander and lowland government mainly because of the separateness of the hills from the rest of the country. This separateness was manifested, in one view, in "the exclusion of tribal peoples from the lowland political system, the inability of upland village leaders to achieve vertical mobility, and therefore some kind of a personal stake, in Thai police, military or administrative structures, and non-acceptance by Thai authorities in Bangkok of tribal land rights and agricultural methods".[7] This view regarding the desire for involvement of tribal leaderships in the Thai administration contrasts with that which states that essentially the hill peoples wanted to be left alone, but the elements making for antagonism are universal. Once the CPT had infiltrated into minority areas from bases in Laos, the nature of the Thai suppressive response proved counter-productive,[8] and this led to a further widening of the rift between lowlander and highlander. In the late 1970s and early 1980s, however, the Thai authorities appear to have taken a softer line towards the hill peoples, as distinguished from CPT personnel. This, together with a weakening of the CPT because of ideological rifts between "Maoist" and "indigenous" factions leading, at times, to mass desertions and with improved Thai military tactics, has led to a general decrease in the number of CPT-led insurgents in the hills by the mid-1980s. In December, 1980, for example, it was reported that 5,000 people, including armed insurgents and their sympathizers surrendered to the authorities. However, only 650 men, women, and children of the Karen and H'mong groups turned up for the formal surrender ceremony at Umphang airstrip, 312 km. northwest of Bangkok.[9] Significantly it was reported that "the government is also permitting the defectors to keep the public land they have been farming as outlaws, and granted them full citizenship".[10] Cash payments were made for weapons handed in. This kind of change in land policy, if maintained, would lessen the immediate causes of antagonism on the part of hill peoples, but it would still not solve the ecological and economic problems of the hills, and hence of the separateness of the highlands.

There has been a debate as to whether the communist insurrection in Thailand stems from external involvement[11] or from basic internal economic, social, and political contradictions.[12] A minority of Thai military officers acknowledged that the CPT was flourishing because of profound deficiencies in Thai society. The majority of the military establishment, however, perceived the problem in terms of criminal disruption of the social fabric or else as a kind of foreign intrusion or invasion which depended on the continued support of foreign communist elements. This group saw the solution to the problem in mainly military terms, in counter-insurgency drives and in attempts to seal the borders against infiltration.[13] Should this view prevail and the emphasis be laid on the methods of a purely military solution,[14] the chances are that there will be a further estrangement of the highlands from the lowlands.

It can be said the conventional, or at least a widely held view, is that communist parties, like the CPT, in armed opposition to state authorities of non-communist states have failed so far, and that this is evident in their being relegated to the remoter parts of the state. In reference to Maoist dogmatism and the CPT it has been said that:

> The emphasis on the armed struggle in rural areas has meant that the party's influence has been confined increasingly to the periphery of the state. The shift of the TPLA's operational headquarters to remote Tak province while perhaps providing a new link to Chinese material support via the Communist Party of Burma, illustrates the problem faced by the CPT.[15]

It should be noted, however, that seen in the framework of the core and the periphery the shift to Tak is westwards in the periphery alongside Burma, a state with relatively extensive peripheral domains and a core domain weak in relation to the peripheral domain and with considerable opposition to its government emanating from its peripheries. The area concerned is also away from the Vietnamese presence and influence to the east.

Vietnam is a much stronger lowland-core state, both in absolute terms as well as in the relationship between core and periphery. Opposition in its montane peripheries to Hanoi though existent is limited at the moment.[16] With Vietnam and its neighbour Laos unwilling to help, for the CPT or any "pro-China" or Maoist-leaning party, this means that the bases and armed forces that hitherto benefited from sanctuary in Laos or Vietnam, as during the Indochina War, would be rendered impotent. On the other hand location closer to the more open — that is, less supervised — Burma border would place the bases closer to a relatively uncontrolled space, with greater opportunities for manœuvre, into which to retreat and gather further support. There have been reports that the Burma Communist Party (BCP) has been making attempts to move southward to the Thai frontier. In this respect the mountains of northern and eastern Laos should be regarded as being part of the Vietnamese peripheries since Vietnam is the core state of "Indochina", or at least of Vietnam-Laos. Vietnam has the option of initiating and giving sponsorship to communist parties in the region which are linked to Hanoi instead of Beijing.

It is also important to note that despite current criticisms, aspects of the Maoist doctrine — namely long drawn-out guerrilla warfare — in this sense suit the wider geo-strategic interests of both the People's Republic of China (PRC) and Vietnam. The PRC's or Vietnam's strategic objectives, if the need arises, can be achieved partly through the support of the armed oppositions in peripheries inhabited by peoples inimical to lowland centre interests. Such policies if vigorously followed would further weaken a lowland authority's control of its peripheral domains. In the wider geo-strategic context, the attribution of success, or lack of it, to national communist parties merely on the basis of success in the lowland areas of the south is to ignore the process of protracted struggle which the communist parties concerned see for themselves. The guerrilla applications of Maoist doctrine also suit Vietnam and are a potential instrument in its dealings with its non-communist neighbours.

The PRC is unlikely for the present to embark on ventures into the lowlands that will completely antagonize the state authorities of the southern lowlands. Such "adventurism" would include adopting an open and outright support for urban uprisings.

Maintenance of some approximation to the *status quo*, especially in mountains bordering the PRC, appears to be paramount under present circumstances in Beijing's policy unless a lowland government adopts policies which Beijing sees as hostile to its interests. So far, the immediate ideological objectives of "liberation" do not seem to have been given any degree of sustained priority by Beijing over its southern border security, although this possibility itself acts as a form of leverage on any weak or weakened lowland state. Policies of direct intervention are clearly inimical to Beijing's wider regional and global strategic interests.

This does not imply an abandonment of these countries to Soviet-leaning governments which may come into power from the successful outcome of urban uprisings led by Moscow-oriented groups. Even if Moscow-oriented parties gain control of lowland centres they still face the basic problem of the pressure from the peripheries and will in fact inherit the geo-strategic disadvantages faced by the governments that they have ousted from the capital cities. The core-periphery dichotomy remains as an element basic to the foundations of power in mainland Southeast Asia.

In the broad frame of regional geo-strategic analysis, the PRC, as a whole, despite its being *in toto* a lowland state, is in the context of mainland Southeast Asia largely a mountain power by virtue of its extensive mountain tracts abutting on, or close to, all the southern states, except Kampuchea. Its control of the largest montane population in the strategic southern mountain marches, which reach well into the geographical confines of mainland Southeast Asia, and its relative dominance in regional power terms, point to its major role in the management of the region's strategic affairs. This role is often overlooked, as most studies of the region of mainland Southeast Asia tend to concentrate on the situations to be found in the capital cities or the lowlands of the southern states. They emphasize the coastal-oriented international connections, internal politics and capital-to-capital or government-

The Burma Communist Party

The connection between peripherality of location in relation to the centre of power and the communist resistance in Burma is clearer than in the case of Thailand. The communist insurgency in Burma is Southeast Asia's longest-lasting Marxist uprising. The Burmese communists have been rebelling since independence in 1948. In the pre-independence period, the party was at the centre of the country's nationalist movement. Gradually forced out of the country's core domain and ejected from any involvement in the mainstream of political development, by the early 1980s the party had an 8,000 to 15,000-man force which "wages a protracted insurgency along Burma's border with China, denying Rangoon effective control of potentially resource-rich areas and plaguing its attempts to forge a new basis of national unity under the government's banner of a 'Burmese Way to Socialism'."[17]

After its defeats which culminated in the destruction of its bases in the Pegu Yoma in 1975, a new BCP structure was organized in the "Northeast Military Region" adjacent to the border with the PRC. Whereas previous to 1969 the party relied on ethnic Burman manpower with its main base in the Burman heartland, by the early 1970s the BCP had become a leader of an insurgency relying on support from the ethnic minorities. The new base area in the peripheries had virtually no Burman inhabitants. By 1973 it was reported that much of the BCP force comprised men from the Wa minority.[18] There was also a significant Kachin element in the force. Significantly these ethnic groups were classified by the British administrators of the Indian empire as "martial races" because of a perceived war-like prowess. There are also Shan recruits in the fighting force. While dependence on minority manpower places limitations on the BCP's appeal to ethnic Burmans in the lowlands — Mao's views on "flightism" spring to mind — from the long-term view it ensures the continuity of the insurgency, that is, of protracted internal instability.

Proximity to the Chinese border and the PRC's reaction to the anti-Chinese riots in Rangoon in 1967 resulting in increased support, both in materials and in propaganda, strengthened the BCP to an extent that it could expand the area and scope of its operations against the government army. But with an apparent subsequent improvement in Beijing-Rangoon relations, Chinese support appears to have declined.

Reductions in Chinese aid have led to comments that the BCP might be compelled toward a policy of greater independence and self-reliance.[19] Since 1979 the BCP has indeed placed emphasis on self-reliance.[20] This would mean reliance on internal resources, both human and economic.

Any BCP attempts at self-reliance have to be seen in the light of what has been described as China's dual-track diplomacy. In order to improve relations with a southern state, the government-to-government facet of this dualistic diplomacy is given emphasis at the expense of existing party-to-party relations. At any given time, one aspect of this diplomacy will be emphasized in a long-term orchestration which will maintain a balance between satisfactory state-to-state relations while not giving up the in-built strategic assets afforded especially by friendly communist parties operating in the favourable strategic environment of the highlands. The BCP's self-reliance efforts of the early 1980s need to be seen against the long-term strategic perspectives of the PRC. In this connection it has been stated that, "Though dual track diplomacy has declined — one track is steadily being refurbished while the other track is being allowed to run down — apparently Beijing is still not willing to surrender completely its party ties in an effort to solidify its governmental relations".[21] The policy of dualism remains a powerful, flexible, and unique, diplomatic instrument in the hands of the PRC, given its geopolitical advantages. The hand of dualism is strengthened by the existence of peripheral power domains. In this respect the durability of the reformed BCP in the northeastern frontiers of Burma should be accepted as an element in any long-term analysis of the strategic situation of the region.

Furthermore, the location of bases in rugged areas east of the deep-gorged River Salween has given the communist forces an advantage in terms of defence. The Wa State which comprises the core of the communist domain, and its surrounding areas, though not rich agriculturally in terms of food production per man-acre, is suited to the growing of the opium poppy and there are signs of BCP involvement in the lucrative opium trade. This is in common with the Karen (who do not actually grow opium), Shan, and other insurgencies whose close-to-border locations enable them to accumulate cash resources by taxing illicit trade (including opium) movements.

The relationship between communist resistance on the one hand and peripherality and ethnicity on the other is also clearer in Burma than in Thailand. The communist and other, chiefly ethnic, insurgencies effectively prevent the writ of the central government from being extended to Burma's international boundaries. An alliance between the BCP, the most powerful of the insurgent groups, and the major ethnic insurgencies among the Karen, Kachin, and Shan cannot be ruled out altogether.[22] In fact, the BCP policy appears to be one which attempts to foster this application of the united front strategy. The distinction between core and peripheral domain is thus hardened.

The numerous ethnic insurgencies and war-lord groups provide a protective belt for the BCP against government military pressure. The more successful it is in its resistance against the government, the BCP could by its durability encourage defections to its ranks from other insurgencies. Finally, the anti-establishment sentiments of ethnic Burmans could result in a mollifying of majority-minority feelings and increased Burman support for the BCP[23], the ideology of which remains attractive to many Burmans including intellectuals. Furthermore, economic and political development is retarded by the diverting of scarce resources to the armed forces and internal security. With the existing Burman military capacity and expenditure the BCP is not likely to be dislodged. The war against the BCP ties down a considerable proportion of the Burmese Army. Defence spending in recent years appears to have been under-reported. It has been estimated that expenditure on defence and internal security amounts to approximately one-third of the annual budget.[24] Despite the prevailing internal dissent and insecurity Rangoon has nevertheless managed to keep its defence spending at the relatively low figure of 3.7 per cent of its GNP.[25] This is achieved by using a low-paid army, foot soldiers, minimal heavy equipment (in itself an advantage in highland warfare), the use of human porterage and mules for transport, and a generally adaptive approach to the fighting.[26] This means also that the insurgents are then often equally well-equipped and can meet the Burmese Army on not unequal terms, resulting in prolongation of the wars, which have been a constant feature of the Burmese highlands since independence. By keeping defence spending down, Burma is spared from having to adopt a war economy, but it solidifies the power isobar separating the core from peripheral domains.

The pattern in Burma fits neatly into the post-1945 framework of an infirmity of frontiers, the unsolved issue of the lack of territorial coincidence between claimed territory and the extent of central control, the linkage between ethnicity and peripherality, and finally the rise and influence of powerful new states bordering on the northern frontiers. Relegation of the BCP to the boondocks, although representing a major set-back in purely military terms for the party, is in itself symptomatic of evolving geo-strategic circumstances that have arisen in montane Southeast Asia after the withdrawal of the colonial powers and the rise of a new continental power.

Communist Insurgency and Adjacent Communist States

Although the situation with regard to Thailand has improved, in relative terms, for the lowland centre, the geo-strategic pattern indicates the potential for a revival of insurgency. This will remain so unless all borders are sealed off and unless the political, social, and economic factors underlying the dichotomy of the core and the periphery are removed.

Also, there is no guarantee that Vietnam with its ally Laos will not give aid to an ideologically reoriented CPT. In such an eventuality the former pattern of accentuated peripheral resistance to the lowland centre will be reasserted but with a different "montane" or "external" actor or helper.

The question will then arise as to which external "montane" actor — the PRC or Vietnam — will be more anxious to preserve the geo-strategic *status quo* as exemplified by the existence of independent states whose writ largely stretches only to the interior limits of the lowlands. A further question also arises: If Vietnam applies military and political pressure to its non-communist neighbours through manipulation of the core-periphery dichotomy, will the PRC not act against Vietnam or reconsider its post-1979 strategy of giving only moral aid to the indigenous communist parties?

The Influence of the Peripheries

Finally, two major facets to the core-periphery relationship should be noted. Usually it is the core or the centre which changes or influences (through military, political, or economic pressure) the periphery in directions which are in general accordance with the objectives or interests of the centre at any given time. However, peripheries can also react against the centre which dominates or attempts to dominate them politically. Owen Lattimore, using historical examples from China's northwestern frontiers, demonstrates the proposition that peripheral elements are often innovative and that experience in the periphery leads to innovation, modifying existing political institutions and territorial structures in the centre or core, or in the state as a whole.[27]

This influence can be either direct or indirect. In Burma, for example, apprehension by some military leaders of U Nu's policies toward the minorities, which were thought to be too reconciliatory and detrimental to the unity of Burma, paved the way for the military's seizure of power, led by Ne Win.

If prolonged, the unsettled conditions in the peripheries can sap the will and resources of the centre or the core. Moreover, it can also influence political events in the plains. The resistance by the Mizos against the Indian Government and its forces in the 1960s, and the secessionist Mizo platform had an effect in the adjoining plains. In 1967 it was stated, "[t]hat secessionist slogans have an appeal in the Assam lowlands as indicated by the formation last July of the Asom Rajyik Mahasabha, a political party dedicated to the thesis that the old kingdom of the Ahoms never was part of India. The failure to integrate its hill people may thus foreshadow troubles for India in the plains as well."[28]

Military and political developments in the peripheral domains can adversely affect the interests of state rulers. If these adverse effects are prolonged, they can seriously alter the political and economic situation in the core domain. At the very least they constitute a factor fundamental in the formulation of domestic and external policies of the government that holds sway over the core domain.

* * *

Developmental issues critical to the region such as those of slash-and-burn agriculture in the uplands, agricultural uplift, and reafforestation can usefully be seen in the frame of power cores and peripheral domains. In this perspective, elimination of the peripheries or in other words expansion of the core domain through developmental means, is an extremely long-term process which is itself jeopardized, in the manner of a vicious cycle, by the instability inherent in the very existence of the peripheral domains.

Similarly, armed opposition and insurgency such as those posed by the various communist parties in the non-communist states, when examined against the geo-strategic background of core and peripheral domains take on an added dimension. As in a vicious cycle, resistance against the centre or core both feeds on and nourishes the periphery which was itself previously existent, pre-dating the occurrence of the insurgencies. Relegation by military means of communist and other insurgencies to regions regarded by the centre as being comfortably beyond the pale does not strike at the roots of the problem and may indeed create and harden a geo-strategic situation, characterized by the gradual solidifying of power isobars, which in the long term could prove highly detrimental to the interests of the emergent states. Furthermore, continued hardening of the peripheral domain *vis-à-vis* the core could in itself lead to internal changes within the core domain of the post-colonial state.

NOTES

1. For an introductory sketch on hill farming see Robbins Burling, *Hill Farms and Padi Fields: Life in Mainland Southeast Asia* (Englewood Cliffs, N.J.: Prentice Hall, 1965), pp. 40–63.
2. Huang Yu-mei, "Guerrilla Veterans: Retire to a High Mountain Ranch", *Free China Review* 33, no. 1 (January 1983): 48–55.
3. Preeda Chantagul, "Forest Village: A Vehicle for Reforestation and Rural Development" (Paper delivered at the CCSEAS-ISEAS Joint International Conference, Singapore, June 1982).
4. Ibid.
5. Ibid.
6. Jeffrey Race, "The War in Northern Thailand", *Modern Asian Studies* 8, no. 1 (January 1974): 110.
7. Ibid.
8. Ibid.
9. *Singapore Monitor*, 28 December 1982.
10. Ibid.
11. Martin Stuart-Fox, "Tension within the Thai Insurgency", *Australian Outlook* 33, no. 2 (August 1979): 182–197 stressed the importance of external aid in the growth of the CPT.
12. Kevin J. Hewison, "Revolutionary Warfare in Thailand", *Australian Outlook* 34, no. 2 (August 1980): 197–208, emphasizes that while external aid could be increased or decreased, the CPT is basically rooted in Thailand's internal contradictions.
13. David Morell and Chai-Anan Samudavanija, *Political Conflict in Thailand: Reform, Reaction, Revolution* (Cambridge, Mass.: Oelgeschlager, Gunn & Hain, 1981), pp. 85–86.
14. For a description of such campaigns, and their effects on the hillmen and the CPT, see Race, op. cit.
15. Donald Weatherbee, "The Indigenisation of ASEAN Communist Parties", in typescript.
16. For a comment on resistance groups in the "Central Highlands", see *Canberra Times*, 30 May 1983.
17. Charles B. Smith, Jr., "Armed Communism in Southeast Asia: The Burmese Communist Party" (Paper presented at a Conference on "Armed Communism in Southeast Asia", Institute of Southeast Asian Studies, Singapore, November 1982). For an analysis of the BCP in the overall context of ethnic insurgencies, see Jon. A. Wiant "Insurgency in the Shan State" in *Armed Separatism in Southeast Asia*, ed. Lim Joo-Jock and Vani S. (Singapore: Institute of Southeast Asian Studies, 1984).
18. *New York Times*, 21 January 1973.
19. Justus M. van der Kroef, "Communism in Burma: Its Development and Prospects", Issues and Studies (Taipei: Institute of International Relations, March 1979).
20. *Foreign Broadcast Information Service (FBIS)*, 28 October 1981.
21. William R. Heaton, "China and Southeast Asian Communist Movements: The Decline of Dual Track Diplomacy", *Asian Survey* 22, no. 8, (August 1982): 796.
22. See *Sydney Morning Herald*, 22 April 1983.
23. Smith, Jr., op. cit.
24. See David I. Steinberg, "Burma: Ne Win After Two Decades", *Current History* 79, no. 461 (December 1980): 183 and footnote.

Developmental and Strategic Issues 137

25. Ruth Leger Sivard, *World Military and Social Expenditures 1982*, (Leasburg, Virginia: World Priorities, 1982), p. 28.
26. After the recapture of the Falklands in 1982, the British Army found that just as mules were well suited to the rough terrain of Aden and Hong Kong's New Territories, the native Falklands horse was ideally suited as a pack animal in the difficult Falklands country. A 14-mile journey which took 7 hours by Land Rover, took only 3 hours on horseback (*The Times*, 21 April 1983). The Burmese Army's adaptability in using mules — a legacy of the British Army's experience in India and Burma — adds to its manœuvrability and low costs in counter-insurgency campaigns. The Vietnamese have used both mountain ponies and human porterage in this respect. Armies which rely too heavily on modern equipment, such as motor transport and aircraft, can be at a disadvantage in this respect.
27. Owen Lattimore, "The Periphery as a Locus of Innovation", in *Centre and Periphery: Spatial Variation in Politics*, ed. Jean Gottmann (Beverly Hills, London: Sage, 1980), pp. 205–208.
28. Arthur J. Dommen, "Separatist Tendencies in Eastern India", *Asian Survey* 7, no. 10 (October 1967): 737.

CHAPTER 6

Opium in the Highland Economy, Peripherality, and Political Consolidation

The place of opium in the economy of the highlands is important to the understanding of the strategic situation in the region. Opium is often linked to the internal instability of states where it is produced in any quantity. There also appears to be widely differing attitudes of state governments to their highlands, the highland economies, and the methods of political control of the people of the highlands. These variations in attitude and policy and how they relate to power in the region are examined here.

The Highland Economies

There are many differences between the highland and lowland economies. These differences arising out of the physical environment or ecology involve not only methods of cultivation, crops grown, and the level of income of the cultivators, but also the social organizations and cultures which are based on the production of food. There then arise differences in attitudes between highlander and lowlander, particularly in the attitudes towards use of land. The core-periphery dichotomy is clearly seen in the marked differences in economic interest between highland and lowland.

The problem of swiddening, prevalent in the highlands slopes, has been alluded to earlier in this study. The ecology of the highland slopes, but not of the valley bottoms traversing in ribbon-like fashion many parts of the highlands, is such that within the limits of technology and manpower available, the only feasible type of agriculture that can sustain organized human groups is swiddening. Swiddening is also referred to as slash-and-burn or shifting agriculture. The steep slopes and the heavy rainfall usually concentrated in the wet season monsoonal period from about May to September cause accelerated erosion of cultivated fields where the invaluable topsoil is exposed. The rate of erosion is such that yields decline rapidly after the first year of cultivation. Depending on the steepness of slope and the basic fertility of the soil, as seen in the thickness of the topsoil, most fields have to be abandoned after a short period of cultivation usually between two to three years, although there have been exceptional cases where cultivation has gone on for longer. The loss in fertility reserves measured in terms of plant nutrients washed away by erosion is enormous when calculated on the basis of whole states. After cultivation the field is left to develop its own natural forest regrowth. This forest fallow can last up to a decade or more. The leaf fall from the subsequent secondary forest growth replenishes to some extent the fertility reserves locked in the topsoil.

Many factors militate against the development of *in situ* or sedentary agriculture on the mountain slopes. The whole cultural outlook of the various "tribes" or ethnic groups is focused on the annual cycle and the methods of swiddening, with dry, hill, or unirrigated paddy forming a vital part of the ritualistic aspects of swiddening. The relatively low level of agricultural technology and the lack of manpower preclude any extensive or sustained movement towards terracing of the slopes for irrigated paddy or other crops. There have been cases of Karens and Kachin among others, turning to rudimentary terracing for wet ricefields in localities where there is population pressure on land. However, in general terms, while forest land is still available, there is little incentive for swiddeners to create conditions for sedentary agriculture. The forest fallow, if undisturbed for a sufficient period of time, regenerates the fertility of the soil and in highland ecology is the most economical refertilization process in terms of capital and manpower input. In many ways, unless there is population pressure on land and the forest fallow period is subsequently shortened, thus prematurely interrupting the cycle of soil regeneration, the swiddening method is the form of food production most suited to the ecology of the highlands. Significantly, highlanders are also almost unanimous in this view. It is woven into their culture, their rituals, and their beliefs. In popular terms, it is their way of life. However, as indicated earlier, the effects of swiddening have undesirable effects on the lowlands.

Erosion of the highlands which is accelerated by the removal of the protective forest blanket by shifting cultivators is regarded as being the major case of the degradation, or even abandonment, of lowland rice fields, particularly those close to the foothills. The increased silt loads carried by the upland streams and rivers in theory has a beneficial effect on the plains below, replenishing the fertility of the lowland fields with the washed down topsoil of the hills. However, deposition of river-borne silt loads is such that the heavier particles of the load are deposited at the points where the strength or velocity of water flow is first reduced. This is at the foot of the mountains or in the narrow belt separating flat alluvial plain from sloping upland. The narrow rice-fields closest to the uplands, often already much poorer compared to the more extensive fields downstream, are, after floods, often covered by a sterile layer of sand and gravel which comprise the heaviest particles of the river's load. This together with the unevenness of river flow and frequent flooding which is also attributed to the deforestation of the watersheds cause concern to lowland agriculturalists and administrators. The thick forest with its cover of foliage, its leaf fall on the forest floor, and its mass of roots and rootlets is seen as a gigantic sponge which acts as a regulator of water supply and river flow. The highlanders are thus seen in varying degrees of antagonism as being wasteful of natural resources, as being backward, primitive, unenlightened, anti-social, and even anti-national and lawless. Differences in culture, land-use, and attitudes to land as a resource are thus yet another divisive factor in states with lowland core domains and peripheral domains in the highlands.

Attention needs to be paid to differences in economic levels between highland and lowland. The highlands are generally poorer and have little scope for raising the level of economic prosperity under existing circumstances. The generally poorer agricultural conditions in the highlands, the absence of transport facilities, the lack of a capacity in the highlands to absorb surplus agricultural produce, and general poverty work against the growth of any highland activity geared to large-scale production to meet local demands. The environment works against accumulation of wealth by lawful means.

Swiddening, Mutual Antagonisms, Cores, and Peripheries

Attempts at positive development, such as the Thai forest replacement programmes described earlier, which are attuned to the natural ecology of the region can help reduce the antagonism existing between highlanders and lowland authorities over the former's swiddening economy. The lowland view of highlanders being lawless, anti-national elements wasteful of national resources, often overlooks the fact that many of the culprits are in fact of lowland ethnic stock or are large-scale entrepreneurs who deforest the well-watered, thick-soiled, and thus most agriculturally useful lower slopes with their natural cover of large, commercially valuable trees, especially teak. Teak in mainland Southeast Asia, for example, usually grows up to only 2,000 feet above sea-level. Many highland groups, for example the H'mong, would normally avoid such low elevations. It is such well-developed forests with their high organic content in the topsoils that are most attractive to swiddeners. These lower slope cultivators are often part-time swiddeners from the lowlands who in this way supplement their income from small valley-bottom farms. Others are landless lowlanders who have no other alternative except to slash and burn the lower mountain slopes. The most valuable teak forests are in fact closest to the lowland Thai who use the mixed deciduous forest where teak grows for swiddening after the teak has been extracted by logging companies. Sometimes swiddening begins after only the larger teak trees have been removed. But the tendency is for public opinion to blame the ethnic minorities for the destruction of the nation's teak resources, for forest denudation, erosion, and consequent flooding and silting of the paddy lands downstream.[1]

The antagonism resulting from the administrations' negative view of the hill minorities gives rise to a firmness in their highland policies. These lowland attitudes and policies, crystallized usually in the activities of forest and law enforcement officers and the military, form the basis of continuing grievance and antagonism of highlander to the lowland "foreigner". This is turn forms a major plank in the platforms of revolutionary and separatist movements in the outer highland zones of mainland Southeast Asia. The negative perceptions of highlanders held by lowland officials re-accentuates their peripheral status.

The Opium Economy of the Highlands

There is one crop, however, for which the upper elevations of the highlands — normally thinly productive and hampered by difficulty of access to markets — is ideally suited. The opium poppy grows well at elevations generally above 1000 m. in Thailand. In more northerly reaches it can grow at lower levels. Opium, an annual crop, is well-suited to the swiddening cycle. It can grow on most soils of the highlands but gives the highest yields in areas where the soil is weathered from bedrock which is calcareous or limestone-like. There are numerous areas throughout mainland Southeast Asia where such soil conditions occur. The limestone outcrops which are characteristic of the scenery of Guangxi and other parts of montane South and Southwest China appear frequently southwards through the Burmese and

Vietnamese highlands and Thailand. Furthermore, where there is population pressure on land resources, the opium poppy is the crop that tolerates continued use of the same soils in a swiddening cycle with shortened periods of forest fallow.

Not only is it a crop well-suited to the region. Because of demand, it is the most lucrative crop for the villagers, like the H'mong and Yao who cultivate it. Communities which customarily grow and sell opium are invariably far more prosperous than those which do not. Indeed where a village sells its crop to big traders its average household income can be twenty-three times that of a village which grows and sells only to the local petty inter-village trade.[2] The discrepancy in wealth between opium-exporting villages and those abstaining from the crop would be even greater. What was said of the Shan plateau is true for most of the region.

> The country is too undeveloped for the opium grower to change from this crop to anything that will fetch him as much money from such a small area of ground, and the government resources are too limited to affect the change by force.[3]

Opium is easily transportable and is of high value relative to bulk or weight. This is of paramount importance in the highlands where communication lines are always rudimentary or at times non-existent. It is an important item of trade in the village economies; it is used as a form of currency in lieu of money; and it finds widespread use as medicine among hill folk as well as supplying an essential source of fats in an otherwise low-fat diet of the hill-dwellers. The prepared raw opium can be carried in bamboo baskets shouldered by men, women, or even children. In larger quantities it is moved on the backs of mountain ponies and in Burma by mules. Like the watches and clocks of pre-industrial Switzerland, high-value opium is a means whereby isolated communities of mountaineers can find a product that is exportable. Opium, moreover, can be stored for long periods without deterioration. In fact, opium appreciates in value with age; the older opium is, the higher its value.[4]

The global demand, especially in Western societies, for opium derivatives and the growing demand in regional urban centres makes raw opium produced by the highlanders a product which can be readily sold to roving merchants, opium collectors, and middlemen living in the highlands, many of whom are of Chinese origin, though in Burma Burmans also act in this capacity. The crop has been much sought after in recent years, despite the competition in the global market coming from the opium-growing regions straddling the boundaries of Iran,

Afghanistan, and Pakistan, another poor highland area of instability and ethnic unrest. Reliable world demand, suitable ecology, and a general lack of supervision in conditions of insecurity ensure the continued production of opium in montane mainland Southeast Asia.

The returns from opium-growing are high. No other crop with similar inputs of labour can ever match the relative prosperity that opium-growing brings to the village and community which grows and sells opium. However, the returns from tolls, or transit taxes on opium are even higher, while manufacture of raw opium into morphine and heroin brings in the bulk of the profits from the regional production and trade in opium and its derivatives. The sustained demand for opium gives the rare opportunity for the opium growers and the petty traders to accumulate wealth in an environment and on a scale where this is next to impossible. The degree of integration of opium-growing communities to a cash economy is seen in the practice of using a field of immature poppies as security to borrow money from opium dealers.[5]

Opium productions is by necessity and by definition also related to defiance of lowland authorities which regard swiddening as unlawful and opium growing as being the occupation of lawless elements. The lowland authorities' distaste for opium growing also springs from the anti-government activities which opium growing and the trade in opium give rise to. Opium production, valuable as it is to the highland growers, nevertheless creates a general state of instability and lawlessness in the mountains, characterized by defiance of the centre, and support of armed resistance to the government and to consequent governmental attempts to eradicate opium growing.

Since the richest gains are from the manufacture of morphine and heroin in simple makeshift laboratories and from the ensuing trade in these high value-added derivatives, the wealth of the opium economy is channelled chiefly into the hands of individuals, groups of individuals, and "political parties" which have the means or access to manufacturing processes as well as contacts via the seaports to the wider regional and global markets for their refined products. The profit from the trade is itself a factor which sustains the durability of the opium economy. To gain some idea of the profits involved, it has been pointed out that ". . . in 1969, in one area of Laos, prepared opium was selling for about 4 cents per gram. Prepared opium is obtainable . . . in the United States at 20 dollars a gram . . . any product that can be sold at a price 500 times its original value is bound to attract people to handle it."[6] The ensuing situation has given rise to banditry and warlordism. Small armies are maintained with modern infantry equipment brought from the proceeds of the sale of opium derivatives. An example of an opium-based outlaw group is that of Khun Sa who operated in the Shan plateau and in the fringes of northern Thailand under the banner of Shan nationalism.

No attempt will be made here to estimate the wealth which the various opium war-lords and insurgent groups which participate in the opium trade gain from their involvement in the opium economy. The factors are too complex, the number of times the product changes hands too numerous, and the prices paid by Mafia-like organizations regionally and abroad too well guarded. Suffice it to say that for a normally poverty-stricken region, there is enough accumulation and dispensation of wealth to enrich and strengthen militarily various war-lords and insurgent groups as well as to corrupt neighbouring lowland governments, or key individuals in the governments, as happened in South Vietnam and Laos prior to 1975.[7]

What is equally important is that the wealth from the trade arising from the rapid growth of the opium economy — a perversely successful form of development in the highlands — does in fact seep down to opium cultivators, giving them an increased purchasing power not attainable previously. This would further entrench their hesitation, apprehension of, and resistance to, lowland edicts to stamp out opium growing and to be "loyal citizens" of the state where they live.

Not all hill groups grow opium, nor do all villages of one ethnic group concentrate on opium as a cash crop. The more notable opium cultivators are the H'mong, the Yao, Lahu, Akha, and also the Wa, and some Shan and Kachin in the BCP controlled and influenced areas. These groups also constitute, apart from the Karen who do not grow opium in any significant degree, the bulk of the manpower of the insurgencies in the mountain regions.

For a crop suited to local conditions and cultivated without any more difficulty than the other main crops of the swiddening cycle, the opium culture has brought in considerable wealth to the cultivators; in other words, development in this perverse form has benefited those at the grass-roots level, at least in terms of cash income. It has been estimated that since 1949 opium has become a major cash crop of the region, and thus a mounting problem for lowland authorities, for example in Thailand and Burma. But it has also brought in a new level of prosperity for many highland groups. An indication of the amount of wealth flowing into the mountain zone, is given by the estimate of an annual production of about 700 tons from the highlands, mainly the "Golden Triangle" stretching from northern Thailand through the Shan plateau to the Kachin State of Burma. The Triangle also includes parts of Laos. At an approximate farm gate price of US$100 per kilo of raw opium, an estimated income of US$70,000,000 flowed to the growers alone in 1983. Another source states that morphine base in 1983 sold at more than US$1,500 per kilo within the region.[8] Much higher profits then would accrue from the transportation, taxing, and refinement to morphine and then to heroin. Since a high proportion of the raw opium of the highlands is refined into morphine base, and some into heroin, the actual flow of wealth into the region as payment for opium exports would be far higher than US$70 million per year. However, only a small proportion of total sales, namely the receipts from the sales of raw opium, actually gets into the hands of the growers. The much higher receipts from sales of morphine base and heroin enrich the various insurgent groups, the apolitical outlaws, and their leaders. Of the total crop value, the growers in Thailand account for 15 per cent, those in Laos 10 to 15 per cent, while growers in Burma receive as much as 75 per cent. The potential strength of the BCP, which has deviated from its previous policy of avoiding involvement in the opium economy since the decline or cessation of PRC material aid in the early 1980s is thus underlined.

McAlister has used a similar approach in estimating the volume of wealth or power accruing from opium production in north Vietnam during the First Indochina War. This can be measured in terms of incomes from direct cash sales or in the context of increased armaments and firepower, the guns having been bartered for raw opium. In 1947, H'mong producers in north Vietnam had available 38 tons for export. This was valued at 400 million piastres or about US$16 million at 1957 value. The rice crop and exports for all Indochina in 1948 had increased greatly over 1947 and yet with a 233,000 ton export in 1948 could fetch a value of only 452 million piastres. The magnitude which the opium economy can attain is also shown in the barter trade in Cao Bang in 1949. In that year the Vietnamese could obtain a light machine gun and 500 rounds of ammunition smuggled in from China for 6 kilograms of raw opium. Four kilograms of opium fetched an automatic rifle and 500 rounds, while a rifle and 500 rounds were traded for 2.5 kilograms of opium. If the Vietminh could theoretically control the total North Vietnam opium trade, then it could equip six regular divisions through opium barter alone.[9] Though this was never attained by the Vietminh, it is an indication of the power which can be generated by the opium economy.

The opium economy enables minorities dissatisfied with lowland rule, lowland direction of their agricultural methods, or oppressive chieftains inclined to banditry, to buy firearms and thus give themselves a measure of protection against intruders. Whereas they were more docile, unarmed (except for flintlocks and crossbows), and hence powerless previously, the opium crop enables them to arm themselves, sometimes with modern automatic rifles. With an increasing number of arms available in the region, the threats to instability grow, while at the same time the unsettled conditions and the sporadic and infrequent presence of government troops are conducive to organized dissident groups gaining added fire-power and achieving a certain degree of freedom of action.

Opium is the only feasible source of wealth and hence of power in the highlands. Those who control the opium economy are able to tap a considerable source of power. Well-equipped, well-trained men, even in limited numbers and with the help of friendly locals, would pose a serious problem to any lowland army operating in the rugged mountains. Previously this source of power was utilized, if not monopolized, by the opium war-lords of whom Khun Sa was among the latest and better-known, and by the French and U.S. undercover operators in the Vietnam Wars. Communist parties, because of their ideological stance and the accompanying puritanical reasons, have generally eschewed any part in the growing or in the trafficking of opium. To this degree, the communist parties except for the Vietminh have not benefited in the past from the source of wealth and power which is best attuned to the ecology of the highlands. That they were able to maintain this policy was because of the availability of across-the-border aid from either Vietnam or the PRC. However, with the increased cordiality of state-to-state relations with Beijing and the southern lowland state of Burma, the BCP has found its supply of aid from China dwindling. To offset this loss, the BCP had begun by the early 1980s to participate in the opium economy.

With its sources of production widely scattered and scarcely detectable in an unsettled, rebellious, and inaccessible region, the opium economy is a strategic factor that would be difficult to eliminate. This difficulty of eradication, compounded by the mobile or shifting nature of its swiddening base, adds to the power of insurgent groups which benefit from it. Conversely, in a symbiotic relationship the power of the insurgent groups such as the BCP and some of the Shan rebellions would serve to give some measure of protection to the opium economy from external interference from those whose objective is to destroy it and thus to cut away at the roots the source of power of the insurgencies. Unfortunately, in the cultural mosaic of the highlands, anti-opium and anti-insurgency campaigners become inextricably mixed up with ethnic suppression or allegedly ethnic elimination campaigns. One result of these campaigns would be to provide motives for ethnic insurgencies to join forces with well-organized ideological insurgencies, such as that of the BCP, further strengthening the dichotomy between core and periphery.

When foreign governments, faced by a domestic drug problem, donate cash, expertise, and equipment for the suppression of opium-growing, a situation is created wherein the equipment, particularly helicopters, is used for anti-insurgency operations instead. With the accompanying undertones of ethnic suppression, more reason is given to the leaders of ethnic rebellions to consider co-operating with credible resistances, like that of the BCP.

Without opium and without external aid — an unlikely scenario — the minority and ideologically-based insurgencies would find themselves hard put to repel governmental military pressures or indeed to survive at all. Without opium but with external aid — again an unlikely eventuality — ethnic insurgencies would be sorely pressed, whilst communist or more precisely those willing to align themselves with PRC or Vietnamese interests and especially if they are based close to the borders, would be able to survive and fight a protracted war from "liberated" base areas. In a third kind of scenario — that is with both opium and with limited external aid — turbulent conditions of instability in the montane region would persist and the peripheries would be hardened in relation to the core domains. Of the three scenarios, so far enlisted, this last one is the most likely. Finally without external aid, except for declamatory messages of moral support, but with the resources of the opium economy available to them, both ethnic and ideological insurgencies would be able to resist governmental campaigns to eliminate them and would be able to survive in peripheral domains which would be likely to retain their peripherality but which, however, would be unlikely to threaten the authorities and their apparatus in the core domains. These last two kinds of scenarios, that is with opium present as a strategic factor, are closest to that obtaining in the period after 1979 when the global and wider regional interests of the PRC influenced its position towards the communist parties of Burma and Thailand.

However, there is no guarantee that the situation will not move rapidly back to that of the third kind of scenario, when both opium wealth and external aid combine to give impetus to yet another wave of heightened instability in the region. Nor is there any guarantee that despite its protestations, Vietnam will not take the opportunity to fill the aid vacuum left by the PRC and thus play a greater role in the unrest in the more westerly portions of the montane zone to which Dien Bien Phu serves as a gateway. Dien Bien Phu is a firm Vietnamese foothold in the Tai-speaking upland regions and is a base from which to exercise its armed power in regions of the upper Mekong and westwards and beyond. A declining Chinese power or a waning Chinese interest in the highlands would encourage the Vietnamese to extend their influence westwards. Much of what China can do in the montane northern frontiers of Southeast Asia can be achieved, albeit on a smaller scale, by the Vietnamese who have fewer global interests to dilute their aims or to divert them from their regional goals.

Finally, it can be said that existence of an opium economy with its connotations of dissent and of insufficiency of central control is as much a symptom of peripherality as it is a major cause of the geopolitical and strategic condition of peripherality. The existence of an opium economy in the peripheries of a state renders such a state more vulnerable to external intervention.

Differing Attitudes and Policies to Highland Economies and Highland Resource Potential

Lowland governments — many of whom are concerned with more immediately pressing and visible problems concerning power, leadership, and other developments in the capital areas and lowlands — tend to have widely differing attitudes and policies towards the highlands even though these highlands constitute a substantial proportion of the area of their states. These policies towards the highlands and attitudes range from what can be termed negative to positive.

Negatively, some lowland governments tend to view the highlands and their inhabitants as part of the national possessions which have to be integrated into the body politic by any means, including force if necessary. Aspirations of the highlanders are not taken into account, or else are merely secondary to the overriding objective of inclusion in the aspiring lowland-based nation state.

The problem of the highland economies is seen in the non-communist states as one which requires little attention compared to the lowlands. There is also a general disinterest on the part of the state governments in the highland economies. While at times there may not be active antagonism to the highlanders, the attitude is one of benign neglect of the highlands and the highland economy, although sporadic and much-publicized efforts may be made to establish agricultural centres and schools in areas nearer the towns in the plains. The highland village-type economy, however, still remains largely separate from the state economy.

A positive policy towards the highlands and their economies would consist of a sustained attempt to weld the lowland and highland economies into a single economy, with the highlands playing an essential role in supplying raw materials to the lowlands, accompanied by attempts to utilize any comparative advantage offered by the highland environment.

The contrast in attitudes coincides with the state ideology. The communist countries of the PRC and Vietnam tend to look positively at the highland components of their state economies. This no doubt is facilitated by the authoritarian nature of the state and the kinds of opportunities accorded by central planning. Laos, however, still emerging from the effects of the Indochina Wars, is an exception, where the problem of the backward highland economy is nowhere near solution. In contrast to the PRC and Vietnam, the non-communist countries of Burma and Thailand show a relative indifference to the economic potential of the highlands. In Burma, the problems of internal strife preclude any major policy attempt to the improvement of the highland economies. In Thailand, as in Burma, the outlook has been geared to economic development in the plains and especially in the areas near the capital city. The highlands are both peripheral in space as well as in the minds of most planners, faced as they are by seemingly more urgent problems in the capital and in the lowlands where the bulk of the state population resides. The policy options available to planners in states where internal strife prevails are narrowed and this should be taken into account when examining the variations in attitude and policy to highland development.

On the premise that economic uplift is the basis for overall political and developmental progress, it can be said that while there is little or no highland improvement in Burma, Thailand, and Laos, there are firm indications that both China and Vietnam have made serious attempts to consolidate their highland economies by giving them a specific role in the overall state economies. However, evidence of an improvement in the actual standard of living in the highlands of the PRC and Vietnam is still lacking. The PRC and Vietnam have quite successfully prohibited the cultivation of opium in their respective territories except where opium is needed as raw material for the local pharmaceutical industries and where, as in Vietnam, it is an item of export. In Vietnam's case, it is for the pharmaceutical industries of the COMECON (Council for Mutual Economic Assistance) countries. China is generally regarded as having successfully eradicated the opium economy of the uplands of Yunnan which used to grow a large crop annually. However, on the related problem of swiddening, it has been reported that although slash-and-burn agriculture has been declared illegal in China, in some cases it is still practised.[10]

If the opium economy is to be destroyed in the convergent interests of insurgency control, drug eradication, and the social health of the Western world, then it would be imperative that not only a viable alternative in terms of crop substitution and alternative agricultural technologies be found, but that these projects of highland uplift be integrated into the overall economies of the states concerned, and be under firm governmental control. The task would, of course, be made more difficult where insurgencies, victualled by the opium trade, persist and where economic conditions in the lowlands, more immediately visible to policy-makers and populace alike, are in need of all available resources for their improvement.

In the non-communist states there is apart from investment in exploitative or extractive industries such as timber extraction and mining, little developmental effort in the highlands. The highland belt produces precious and semi-precious stones and is also in the stanniferous, or tin-bearing, belt which stretches from Yunnan to Peninsular Malaysia. Wolfram and other heavy metal ores are often associated with any tin deposits that can be found.

In these countries, namely the states other than China and Vietnam, there is the occasional trade at a localized level between highland and lowland, with each largely functioning in its own economic milieu. Comparative advantage encourages local barter, exchange, or sale of highland produce for goods brought in from, or produced in, the lowlands. In northeast India and in the Chittagong hill tracts of Bangladesh there has developed a sizeable and sustained trade in the market garden and orchard produce of the highlands. The lowlands are unsuitable for the production of high quality, temperate, or mediterranean-type fruits and vegetables. In northeast India and Bangladesh, potatoes and vegetables are an important item of export from the highlands. Potatoes provide lowland consumers with a valuable bulk item in their diet, especially when there are shortages of grain which can be of frequent occurrence. Onions and ginger, both spices needed in the methods of food preparation in the lowlands, move from highlands to lowlands, while fruits, especially citrus fruits but including lychees, an exotic fruit from China, find a ready sale in nearby lowland market towns and even in the cities. In northern India and northern Bangladesh the Khasis and Garos are conspicuous in this highland export trade. The Shan highlands supply the Burmese markets with tea, tobacco, and *thanatpet* (cigar wrapping leaf), coffee, oranges, cabbages, garlic, indigo, wheat, temperate fruits, cotton, and vegetables of temperate origin.[11]

In return for the hill produce, lowland traders bring iron-ware and implements, textiles and clothing, salt, edible oils, and other consumer goods to the hills. Where consumer goods have been in short supply, considerable amounts of low-priced manufactures for the consumer market have moved in from across the frontiers from China into northern India and northern Burma, causing some concern for the Indian authorities. The distribution and sale of lowland-derived goods, especially of ironware, textiles, and salt by itinerant traders, is a common feature of the entire montane zone. In Burma and Thailand it is largely in the hands of Chinese traders. More recently, after the upheavals caused by the Chinese revolution, these traders have been based in the southern states themselves. This minimal trade suffices to meet the economic needs of the highlands.

Considerable numbers of cattle are also driven down from upland villages to be sold as draught animals and for meat in the lowlands. There is little organization in this livestock trade, but it does indicate the kind of trade and economic integration, based on comparative advantages of the different regions, which non-communist countries could adopt. The trade in draught cattle is the best example of the highlands being able to produce goods which are vital to the agricultural economy of the lowlands. Generally, however, trade between lowland core and upland periphery is minimal.

In contrast, China and Vietnam show a radically different approach to their highland territories. Their attitude can best be described as being positive. In terms of the relevant economic resources of the highlands, their immediate potential for exploitation and the needs of the main, that is lowland economy, both China and Vietnam have lost little opportunity to utilize the highlands. These highland resources are generally seen by both Hanoi and Beijing from the viewpoint of appropriate technology.

In China, the economic resources and potential of the highlands is considerable. With the exception of Hainan Island and southern Guangdong, parts of these highlands have some of China's warmest climates. In sheltered valleys and in southward-facing slopes protected from the dry, cold season winds that blow in from the interior and exposed to the full force of the rain-bearing winds of the hot season monsoon, temperatures, rainfall, and general conditions of natural ecology approach the conditions of insular Southeast Asia where the world's main sources of plantation-grown tropical cash crops are to be found. In southern Yunnan, for example, as in Hainan Island, rubber is being grown. Sugar and oilseeds are major crops of the more favoured parts of the southern highlands. The need for integration into the national economy is emphasized by the fact that these are among the few areas in the PRC that can grow vegetable raw materials of fully tropical origin and therefore intensive efforts are being made to utilize this advantage to the maximum.

On the question of rubber growing in Yunnan, it was reported in the context of Sino-Vietnamese border clashes that Chinese artillery counter-attacks against Vietnamese positions had taken place in April 1983 because of Vietnamese provocations which included the killing of Chinese border inhabitants working in the fields and the infiltration of agents into Chinese territory who set fire to 600 hectares of woods, bamboo groves, and rubber trees.[12]

Land suited to the production of tropical crops is of high value to the Chinese economy. In southwestern Yunnan alone there are between 120 and 130 fertile and level river flatlands and intermontane basins with hot, tropical climates, ample water for irrigation, and considerable potential for agricultural development. Population densities are very low compared to the more settled parts of China. In southwestern Yunnan alone, "Unexploited, agriculturally usable land amounts to some 2,000,000 hectares."[13] The economic potential of the frontier zones still remains considerable. Much of this basin land is ideally suited to the growing of sugar-cane. Sugar is a scarce commodity in the PRC and much of it has to be imported.

Apart from the specialization in tropical industrial and food crops in the more sheltered locations, the southern highlands have been given another role in the process of integration into China's national economy. This is the growing of medicinal herbs and traditional drugs for the vast market of more than a billion people who rely very little on modern or Western medical treatment. The south and the southern highlands have traditionally been a major source of medicinal barks, fruit, and rare herbs for curative or invigorative uses. The hill minorities, including the H'mong, are noted and valued for their skill in the recognition of herbal plants. Hill-dwelling Hans, like the Hakka, are also respected by the lowlanders for their knowledge of herbal medicines. For example, much of the treatment given to wounded and sick MCP (Malayan Communist Party) guerrillas by their comrades in their war against the British was herbal, locally gathered by forest-fringe dwelling Chinese who were to a large extent Hakka.

In an effort to eliminate wasteful swiddening, to elevate the standard of living in the highlands, to give the former swiddeners fixed habitations or villages that can be more easily administered, and finally to utilize more fully the economic potential of the highland's natural ecology, the southern and southwestern highlands of China have seen the rise of medicinal herb cultivation, often on a large plantation-like scale and with modern agronomic methods. Attempts have been made to make the vegetation of the more sheltered highlands more useful by re-creating the three tiers of the natural rain forest, using economically useful timber, oil-bearing and fruiting trees for the upper two levels and resorting to shade-loving medicinal herbs, like the *Rauwolfia Serpentina* used by both Western and Chinese pharmacology for control of hypertension, as a cultivated undergrowth.

Tea, coffee in the southern parts, and soya beans are crops which are also suitable to the environment and which are being encouraged. While China's tea production is large, its population and consuming capacity are even larger. Tea appears to be in short supply. Visitors to Beijing University, for example, have reported that during mealtimes students and staff drank hot water instead of chinese tea. The tea shrub is indigenous to montane Southeast Asia and its cultivation has reached its highest expression in durable, soil-conserving cash crop production in the British-initiated tea plantations of the Assam hills. Mulberry also grows vigorously in the highlands, and in the PRC sericulture is an important industry with potential for further growth. Both tea and silkworms are potential crops in the uplands not only in China but all the other states as well.

The variations in climatic condition deriving from altitudinal differences in the mountainous areas make it possible to grow crops of tropical, subtropical, and temperate origin. Besides those already mentioned, other crops valued in China but not well-known outside the country include lotus seeds for food, various flours made from edible roots such as the lily root, dried bamboo shoots for human consumption, and bamboo paper. Other highland products are tea-seeds for the tea industry, tobacco, hemp, cinnamon, mushrooms, tea oil, tung seeds, and tung oil. Timber, another product of the highlands, is regarded as a valuable resource in a country which is chronically short of timber and wood. Many highland products not generally known outside China are found useful and even valuable by the Sinic culture.

In an expanding economy like China's, where basic consumer needs for seeming essentials like tea are barely met, the resources and resource potential of a tropical and subtropical environment like the country's southwest and south are likely to see accelerated development, both for economic and strategic reasons.

The Vietnamese, as with many other aspects of their Sinic-derived culture, including agriculture, have parallelled Chinese management methods of the highlands. In terms of the natural resources the Vietnamese authorities regard their highlands — as the Chinese do theirs — as resource-rich areas, or rather as regions where products not found in abundance in the crowded lowlands are with some effort readily available. With the added effects of devastation by the Vietnam War bombings by the United States, the Vietnamese, especially rural Vietnamese, remain what the French scholar Pierre Gourou termed a "vegetable civilisation". Little metal, or even ceramics, pottery, or material of animal origin is used in the rural economy and maximum use is made of vegetable products for housing construction, implements, bridges, clothing and household, farming utensils, food, and footwear. This reliance on locally available raw material and the ability to maximize the use of even small quantities of iron or steel was a war-time asset and a major factor in the strategic resilience of North Vietnam in the face of what was dramatically reported as a sustained U.S. air campaign to "bomb them back to the Stone Ages".

In this framework of the prevailing cultural attitude to natural resources, the highlands are regarded as a source of useful vegetational products, notably bamboo. The northern Vietnamese uplands have to a large extent been denuded of tall timber trees and the resulting regrowths are to a large extent composed of bamboo. The adaptability of bamboo to the relatively infertile conditions of overworked and abandoned swidden fields is a feature common throughout montane southwest Asia from the Chin Hills in Burma through to China and Vietnam. Bamboo is useful, if not indispensable, for housing and bridge construction in both China and Vietnam and also in many parts of the other countries. In the construction industry, for example, it is indispensable as scaffolding. Household furniture, implements, and farming equipment are made from bamboo stems or woven from split bamboo. Bamboo also makes a low-grade paper pulp. Bamboo is floated in rafts down from the uplands to the population centres of the Tonkim delta; where intensive rice cultivation leaves little room for trees, bamboo groves or grazing land. It could be said that without bamboo, the economies of Vietnam and South China would be adversely affected to a serious extent. Bamboo helps to bridge the economic gap between highlands and lowlands in South China and North Vietnam.

In contrast to the lowlands, the highlands of North Vietnam also contain large tracts of grazing land, which are of high grade by tropical standards. The grasslands of the mountains are seen as yet another resource, complementing the economy of the lowlands which is dependent on draught buffalo and cattle for the cultivation of rice. Annually, in North Vietnam, considerable numbers of cattle and water buffalo are herded down to the lowlands, where there is a chronic shortage of draught animals due to lack of grazing land and the high mortality rate. Cattle and even water buffalo do not appear to breed well in the rice-growing lowlands. The annual deficit of draught animals has to be replenished by movements in from the highlands, where the minorities breed them, owning herds of large size by Southeast Asian standards.

In 1967, about 1.7 million water buffalo were in use as draught animals in the lowlands of North Vietnam. While the delta had 37 per cent of the arable land, it had only 17 per cent of the animals. The highlands with only 21.3 per cent of the arable land had fully 40 per cent of the animals. About 20,000 head were moved from the mountains to the delta each year in the early 1960s.[14] By the end of 1965, the highlands though sparsely populated had half of all the water buffaloes in all of North Vietnam despite the fact that arable land, but not grazing land, is highly restricted in the highlands.[15]

Furthermore, to underline the Vietnamese and Chinese perception of maximization in the exploitation of available resources, in part dictated by population pressure on land resources, even the wild foliage of the uplands is seen as a economic resource. The Vietnamese use green manure from wild foliage to a greater extent than do their historic agricultural tutors, the Chinese. For North Vietnam it is claimed that "the highlands are rich in fertilizers — dung, green composts, lime — which under the old regime were rarely used".[16] The Sinic culture is not prone to livestock raising, but the high, grassy mountains have been found by the Chinese in recent years to be well suited for the production of beef and milk, especially when pastures are improved using rye-grass and white clover seed from Australia and New Zealand.[17]

Highland Utilization and Policies in the Strategic Context

The differences in the treatment of the highlands extend beyond the formulation of policies towards the restructuring of essentially subsistence level economies. The differences go deeper than mere policies. The policies themselves are tangible manifestations of differences in basic outlook. The post-colonial era saw upheavals in China, Burma, India, Laos, Vietnam, and to a much lesser extent in Thailand. Thus, all countries including northeastern India were affected by the changes wrought by power re-alignments, rising ethnic militancy, the appearance of ideological rebellion, and the creation of new states with policies motivated by and large by newly re-discovered forces of ethnic nationalism. The non-communist states generally ignored the highlands as in the case of Thailand. In Burma in circumstances of persistent civil strife there have been attempts to forge a form of national unity, first through mainly political means based on the federal idea, then later through both political and military means to achieve a unitary state. In contrast, the new communist states firstly China and then North Vietnam, were able to take control of the entire extent of their territories by means of force or persuasion. In China, the presence of Han agriculturists in the highlands aided the process of establishing control. In their policies regarding the issue of minority problems these two countries show the most significant attempts at consolidation of power and the absorption of hitherto peripheral zones into the national body politic. It is the principle of limited autonomy for minorities and the implementation of this policy which has enabled Vietnam and particularly China to consolidate their frontiers without resort to large-scale force. The forward approach reflected in the attitudes to resources of the highland economy is also apparent in the manner of political settlement of the problems of ethnicity, underdevelopment, and separateness of the highlands from the plains.

While the Chinese appear to abstain from mass population movements of Han cultivators into the minority areas, the Vietnamese in contrast regard their highlands as relatively open spaces which needed rapid economic development through the injection of large numbers of Kinh or ethnic Vietnamese. This was carried out even before the North Vietnamese victory of 1975. It is worth quoting at some length from Vietnamese sources in this respect.

> The successes recorded in economic construction in the mountain regions are closely linked to the widespread migration of lowlanders to these regions, to take part in their economic and cultural development. In order to boost the exploitation of natural resources for socialist industrialisation, which will benefit the highlanders as well as the whole nation, more than 830,000 inhabitants of the lowlands, responding to appeal of the Party and Government, have settled in the highlands. . . .[18]

Most of these appear to have taken up agricultural pursuits, rather than in industries, thus competing directly with the minorities on the land. Since 1975, more rapid and even larger shifts of Kinh population have taken place in both the northern and southern highlands, where there have been significant increases in population.[19] As far back as 1954, Ngo Dinh Diem had followed a similar policy of ethnic extension and encroachment by settling 100,000 ethnic Vietnamese in the richer parts of Montagnard highlands of the south, displacing 25,000 tribal people.[20] In the early 1980s, this movement appears to have been enlarged and accelerated. In the first nine months of 1983 alone, in a long-term programme of population shift, 97,000 persons from the more densely populated parts of Vietnam were resettled in "new economic zones", to work in state-owned agricultural plantations.[21] The "new economic zones" tend to cluster in the hilly edges of the inland mountain belt.

In Vietnam, population movement westwards into the highlands appears to be a strategic instrument which strengthens its position in the montane zone and which projects its power deeper into the western portions of mainland Southeast Asia. The aim is fourfold. Firstly it is defensive, that is, bringing the effective defence forward into the frontiers. Secondly, as has been noted, it projects Vietnam's power, as exemplified by loyal Kinh farmers settled on the land, well into the highland zone. Thirdly, it is an instrument for rapid development of the economic potential of the highlands, at the same time relieving population pressure on cultivatable land in the lowlands. Finally, in the framework of the core-periphery analysis, it is an attempt, together with the setting up of autonomous areas, to eliminate the historical dichotomy between lowland core power domain and the peripheral highlands. At this point, it would be useful to note that Hanoi has regarded, before the punitive campaign by China in 1979, its western flank as being particularly vulnerable.

The mass movement of Kinh into the northern highlands ultimately means that the highlands will to a large extent be Vietnamized, with the ensuing disappearance of the ethnic divide and the highland-lowland strategic dichotomy. In this sense, the programme of Kinh movement in the highlands and the policy of autonomy for the highland minorities is mutually contradictory. Such an organized and officially encouraged Vietnamese move westwards into the highlands would resemble the much longer Han penetration southwards over many centuries. The Han movement was however largely unorganized. It was a process of Han farmers in search of cultivable valley land, involving not only intermarriage but also sinization of the indigenous cultures of the south. The Vietnamese movement would also differ from the Chinese military settlements of Tibet and the northwest, an historical as well as contemporary technique of Chinese western frontier control and management, in which units of the regular army are given land on which to grow food crops for their own sustenance in remote, relatively inaccessible areas, and are required to perform their military duties at the same time. The settlement of Vietnamese in the highlands can be seen, however, as an attempt at expansion of Vietnam's core domain to Vietnam's outermost territorial limits established by their former French rulers. Implementation of such settlements could lead to resentment on the part of the highland minorities and this could be exploited by a hostile China.

Autonomous Minorities and the Consolidation of the Peripheries: PRC and Vietnam

As alluded to earlier, the main instrument used in an absorptive process, in the course of which the frontiers of both the PRC and Vietnam were consolidated and brought under the firm control of the centre, was based on the policy of "minority autonomy". Autonomous territorial tracts were set up in which the minorities, under the leadership of communist party cadres, and regional leaders, many of whom were of minority stock and under central committee control, were given a measure of local self-government. These local leaders were given some degree of autonomy in the running of domestic affairs of the area within their jurisdiction. Needless to say, all local initiatives had to be within the context of the principles of communist central planning.

In China development of minority scripts and alphabets was given priority and was rapidly carried out through the help of linguistics experts from the lowlands. Education in the minority languages, alongside education in standard Chinese, was encouraged.[22] Economic development took the form of the implementation of socialized agricultural endeavour, typified in the commune or co-operative. Local self-reliance, at least on the Chinese side was encouraged, and alongside the co-operative system, small local industries such as metal-working and the making of farm implements was also regarded as an ideal objective. There were attempts at agricultural improvement, and the introduction of new crops and intensive, sedentary methods of agriculture.

In Vietnam, too, minority literacy has been encouraged. While the Vietnamese have undoubtedly made considerable progress in the political integration of their minority areas, the larger size and economic potential of the Chinese minority areas have given rise to more spectacular results. The Xhuang autonomous region in China's Guangxi province is held up as a major success in political consolidation achieved through the willingness of the Han people, particularly those of Guangxi, to make concessions to other ethnic groups in the PRC, and to eliminate or subdue "great Han chauvinism". It is in the Xhuang autonomous region that some major industrial developments have taken place, for example, an agricultural tractor factory which produced 4,500 tractors in 1977.[23] Further west in China, there are many other smaller autonomous areas, but the size of the autonomous Xhuang alongside the Vietnamese border, demonstrates by mere juxtapositioning, the relative paucity of economic development in the adjoining Vietnamese Tay Bac (Northwest) Autonomous Region and the Viet Bac (North) Autonomous Region.

With the PRC, the basis for minority autonomy is embedded in its Constitution. Article 3 declares that the People's Republic of China is "a unified, multinational state" in which all nationals are equal. Areas in which the minorities are dominant numerically are to be given autonomy within the national framework. National minorities are represented in both their local people's congresses, and in the National People's Congress. In the National People's Congress, representation of minorities is considerably more than the proportional entitlement.[24]

In Vietnam, the same kind of attention is given to its minorities, as shown in the Amended Constitution of 1960, Article 3 of which declares that the Democratic Republic of Vietnam is "a unified multinational state". The right to retain or reform their cultures and languages is reserved for the minorities. The Constitution also states that "autonomous zones may be established in areas where people of national minorities live in compact communities". It goes on further to assert that "such autonomous zones are integral and inalienable parts of the Democratic Republic of Vietnam", and that "[t]he State will strive to help the national minorities attain the general economic and cultural level within the shortest possible time". No mention is made of the possibility of massive Kinh migration into the minority areas in order to "help . . . attain the general economic and cultural level within the shortest possible time".

Active steps have been taken to ensure minority co-operation by the granting of localized autonomy. In 1955, the Tai Meo Autonomous Region, the first of its kind in Vietnam, was founded. It embraced the three provinces of Son La, Lai Chau, and Nghia Lo. It covered fully one-fifth of the total area of North Vietnam. The population in the mid-1960s was estimated to be 500,000 belonging to 25 different ethnic groups, of which the numerically dominant ones were the Tai and the Miao. However, the name was later changed into that of the Tay Bac (Northwest) Autonomous Region. The other autonomous region the Viet Bac Autonomous Region came into being in 1956 and comprised the six Northeastern provinces: Lang Son, Cao Bang, Ha Giang, Tuyen Quang, Bac Can, and Thai Nguyen. Bac Can and Thai Nguyen were later merged to form the single province of Bac Thai. The Viet Bac Autonomous Region has a population totalling more than 1,500,000, with 14 different ethnic groups, the most numerous being the Tay or Tho and the Nung.

In China the policy of regional autonomy was applied especially to minorities that formed distinct and separate communities. The mosaic of Han and non-Han peoples, in Yunnan for example, meant that some of these autonomous units were very small in area and population. Regional autonomy was based on the principle that minority communities which constituted major concentrations of population or which occupied large areas should be given some degree of local control of community affairs. Where two or more fairly sizeable minorities shared a single cohesive area the device resorted to was one of coalition governments.

> As early as 1951, autonomy for minorities at township, district and then county level was established in Yunnan and Quangxi. The county (hsien) was used as the basic unit of development in the PRC. Only at the county level was there an administrative seat, and even in the highlands, this would have a concentration, however small, of Han Chinese who were, in the final analysis, the only reliable foundation of control of the South China frontier regions.[25]

This Han population of the highlands, even though scattered, afforded the PRC an advantage which the southern states, including Vietnam, did not have and which it utilized in the consolidation of its far south.

Autonomous counties and prefectures were set up in both Yunnan and Guangxi in the 1950s, with attention being given to the frontier areas near to the international boundary. These areas had priority over minority-inhabited regions which lay deeper in the territory of the PRC. This priority and emphasis on the hardening of the perimeter should be noted. In contrast to Yunnan where minorities occurred in relatively small and scattered locations and were moreover often intermingled with Han habitation, the situation in Guangxi was less complex. The relatively uncomplicated composition and geographical distribution of ethnic minorities in Guangxi enabled the authorities to complete the major work of setting up autonomous areas in the two years of 1952 and 1953. The Xhuang, a Tai-speaking people, totalled 5.4 million during that period and had an identifiable common language, territory, economy, and culture which were regarded as the necessary characteristics of a nation. There are striking similarities in speech and customs between the Xhuang of Guangxi and the people in the Viet Bac Autonomous Region, who are however much smaller in numbers. This linguistic and cultural straddling of the boundaries is a recurrent and pervasive feature of the ethnic distribution in the montane zone and particularly between China and its southern neighbours. The West Guangxi Xhuang autonomous area was established in 1952. By 1958, this autonomous area had been elevated and expanded into the provincial level Xhuang Autonomous Region. The number of Xhuang had increased and by 1981, it was reported that there were 12,090,000 in China.[26]

Three other areas given local autonomy were the autonomous area in the almost wholly Tai-inhabited Xishuangpanna which retained the traditional units of the Tai region for the new administrative purposes. The Tais and Ching-p'o's (Kachin) in Yunnan adjoining the Burma border were also organized into an autonomous area. In the tracts between the Salween and Mekong Rivers the Wa and Lahu, both groups firmly represented in Burma as well, were organized, alongside others, into an autonomous area. This general area is also known as the "Chinese Shan States" by external observers because of the resemblance in many ways to the Shan States of Burma.

The whole process involved the accelerated training of minority cadres to work among their own people. Preparatory work was usually done by outsiders in teams which involved suitable individuals of chosen areas who had been previously selected for training in an urban area. In sensitive areas the Chinese Communist Party (CCP) made use of existing social and political institutions. They relied on traditional leaders and avoided mass campaigns. Political indoctrination was provided for the Buddhist clergy in Tai areas, an indication of an awareness of the local cultural environment and ethnic sensitivities.

Very significantly, the process also involved the transfer of resources from Han to the poorer non-Han areas. While in Han areas, the emphasis on communist reform in the initial stages was on the redistribution of wealth, including land, in the minority areas, the CCP's chief concern was to ensure the solidarity between Han and the non-Han minorities. Stable ethnic relations between Han and non-Han was central to the political control of the southern frontiers.

To this end there was a transfer of wealth from state reserves to minority areas. Funds and materials for the development of the minority areas come not from the surplus of the minority areas, but in the form of a subsidy from the Han-populated lowlands.

> This policy of state assistance to national minority areas was especially important to frontier regions having ties with the external world. Gifts of grain, seed and tools were a regular feature of the preparatory work that preceded the establishment of autonomous areas both in Yunnan and Kwangsi. State-controlled commerce, manipulated so as to benefit national minority areas, was used for the same purpose.[27]

The major responsibility of the local government of an autonomous area is, with Han Chinese help, "to develop the economy of the area so as to give substance to the people's newly acquired political rights and to contribute to the progress of the national economy".[28] Developmental and budgetary policies, besides the political, were instrumental in the integration of the periphery into the core.

The CCP approach in its moves to strengthen central control of the minority-inhabited frontier areas was to diffuse communist ideology with a sensitivity to local conditions, loyalties, and customs. This is most clearly seen in the de-emphasis of mass movement in areas prone to unrest and the adoption of united front tactics which utilized the traditional local political élite, in order to bring the followers of these traditional leaders more firmly under central control.

Both China and Vietnam have paid serious attention to the political and economic problems of their highlands. In both cases, the strategic value of the highlands and their inhabitants was impressed on the state leaderships by the experiences gained during times of war. The Democratic Republic of Vietnam (DRV) or North Vietnamese took pains to develop an effective working relationship with some of their minority groups. The seriousness of intent was ". . . reflected in the fact that in the process Pham Van Dong is reported to have learnt fluent Tay and Vo Nguyen Giap mastered both Tay and Yao".[29] It will be recalled that Liu Bocheng and other CCP leaders learnt Luoluo and other minority tongues from the time of the Long March. The attitude of the Chinese and Vietnamese leaderships is unique in the attention they give to the highlands and their inhabitants.

The establishment of autonomous tracts — be they "Regions", prefectures, or counties — by both China and Vietnam, in the latter case only in the north, has within the context of authoritarian systems helped to bring their respective core domains closer to their boundary-defined territorial limits. While Vietnam is thus defensively in a better position with regard to the proximate PRC power and is able to project its own power into Laos, the PRC's core domains abut directly on Burma, Laos, and Vietnam. This puts the PRC in a firm position in its relations with these southern states. With regard to Thailand, although after 1980 the PRC did withdraw from the strategic road which they built through northwestern Laos to the Mekong at the Thai border, China has been able to maintain a pervading influence on the Vietnam-Thailand relationship through its ability to apply direct as well as indirect pressure on Vietnam. Direct pressure is applied on the mountainous common border, while indirect pressure is applied through aid to the Cambodian resistance forces and encouragement of Thailand's efforts to confront Vietnam over Vietnamese intrusions into Thai territory in the course of anti-Cambodian resistance operations.

In summary, it can be said that before the 1950s, Yunnan and southern Guangxi were indeed peripheral to China's power domain. Consolidation was achieved first through the use of force, in order to expel forces owing allegiance to local war-lords or to the Guomindang. It was cemented by the political device of minority autonomy within the framework of undisputed national sovereignty. Consolidation of PRC power in the southern frontier lands was also strengthened infrastructurally by the construction of new roads and the improvement of existing ones. As early as 1953 it was reported that the old Burma Road had been fully hard-surfaced and made into an important strategic highway.[30] Other notable highways included that which reached from the border with Laos to the banks of the Mekong. Although the Laotian section was later handed over to the Laotian authorities, the metalled highway to the Laotian border itself constitutes a strategic asset for the PRC. It has been noted that the modern history of communications in China had been one which featured foreign penetration into China. However, with the Burma Road of World War II, it was the Chinese themselves who built the first modern line of communications pushing outward to foreign frontiers.[31] This process was re-activated with the PRC's political consolidation of the highlands in the 1950s. Finally, the forced Chinese retreat into China's peripheries during World War II had given the first impetus for the consolidation of the southern frontiers and for a significant, further movement of Han people and skills into montane mainland Southeast Asia.

By thus strengthening its southern frontiers the PRC has made its forward southerly regions an integral part of the power configuration in mainland Southeast Asia. This has been especially evident in the post-1975 situation, when the accumulation of power to Vietnam after its unification indicated a Vietnamese predominance in the eastern portion of mainland Southeast Asia. The PRC attempted first of all to support the Kampuchean state against Vietnam. With the failure of this move, the PRC was then able to resort to using its consolidated southern frontier tracts to exert continuing pressure on Vietnam, beginning with the punitive campaign of early 1979. Thus Vietnam's diversion of resources to its northern frontier has meant a limitation of options with regard to its westward policies.

PRC pressure southwards was facilitated by the thorough control of its own "autonomous" minority areas. This was done by extending through peaceful, chiefly political, means, the limits of its core domain to its outermost boundaries. A positive approach to the integration of the highland economy has also helped.

For its southern borderlands as a whole, the PRC's lack of sophisticated weaponry is, unlike its position on its inner Asian frontiers, not a drawback. The strategic environment ensures that in circumstances of infiltration and low-key warfare, men and organization are more important than the highly sophisticated weaponry which is generally regarded as the PRC's chief weakness. The asymmetrical power configuration thus created between the PRC and those southern states, burdened by peripheral domains, is in this matter of weaponry and technology again emphasized.

* * *

Opium is the cash crop *par excellence* in the mountains. In the normally impoverished highlands, its cultivation brings with it unprecedented material wealth. It is the only product of the highlands which is supported by a collecting, processing, and marketing infrastructure with regional and global ramifications. The wealth accumulated through growing, processing, and marketing, together with the ease of arms purchases, creates an endemic or perhaps even permanent instability in the region.

Opium is grown almost entirely in those states with uncontrolled or uncontrollable peripheries. Opium and the swiddening cycle associated with it are generally regarded as synonymous with the wasteful use of land resources by lowland governments, who are however helpless in preventing it as they do not have absolute control of the upland peripheries. Opium is symbiotic with dissent and adds to the peripherality of the highlands. There appears to be a vicious cycle in which lack of control leads to increased opium production, engendering more armed dissent thus paving the way for the further weakening of control. Moreover, opium is very much woven into the way of life of many highland groups, some of which are regarded as being the most martial of the mountaineers.

In sharp contrast to the negative attitude towards the highlands and the highland economies on the part of the non-communist states, the PRC and Vietnam appear to have taken steps to utilize more fully the economic potential of their highlands, the products of which are often sought after in the lowland markets.

China and Vietnam have managed to eradicate illegal opium growing in their territories. Progress in the direction has been part of a general movement involving concrete policies in the political and economic development of their uplands, strengthening control of their peripheries. The major political instrument used in consolidating the minority areas has been the granting of regional or local autonomy.

The extension of their core power to their boundary limits means that these two states are in immediate or potential positions from which they can utilize, if the need arises, the peripheral looseness and vulnerabilities of their neighbours for their own policy ends. Economic, and particularly political, reorganization of the highland territories of these two states add to their power in the montane region, relative to the other comparatively unorganized states.

NOTES

1. C.L.J. Van der Meer, *Rural Development in Northern Thailand: An Interpretation and Analysis* (Groningen: Rijksuniversiteit te Groningen, 1981), pp. 84–85.
2. Anthony R. Walker, "The Production and Use of Opium in the Northern Thai Uplands: An Introduction", *Contemporary Southeast Asia* 2, no. 2 (September 1980): 147.
3. Sao Saimong Mangrai, *The Shan States and the British Annexation*, Data Paper No. 57, Southeast Asia Program (Ithaca: Cornell University, 1965), p. 7.
4. David Feingold, "Opium and Politics in Laos", in *Laos: War and Revolution*, ed. Nina S. Adams and Alfred W. McCoy (New York: Harper and Row, 1970), p. 326.
5. Walker, op. cit.
6. Feingold, op. cit., p. 326.
7. See Alfred W. McCoy, *The Politics of Heroin in Southeast Asia* (New York: Harper and Row, 1972), pp. 149–217.
8. The price of US$100 per kilo of raw opium was given by a senior Thai anti-narcotics official. Jon A. Wiant, "Insurgency in the Shan State", in *Armed Separatist Movements in Southeast Asia*, ed. Lim Joo-Jock (Singapore: Institute of Southeast Asian Studies, 1984) gives the figures of US$30–50 a kilo for raw opium and more than US$1,500 per kilo for morphine base. Obviously prices for raw opium, like any other agricultural commodity, fluctuate according to weather conditions, quality, and quantity of supply and of demand.
9. John T. McAlister, Jr., "Mountain Minorities and the Vietminh: A Key to the Indochina War", in *Southeast Asian Tribes, Minorities and Nations* vol. II, ed. Peter Kundstadter (New Jersey: Princeton University Press, 1967), pp. 821–22.
10. J.A.C. Mackie, "China Report", in *Southeast Asian Studies in China: A Report*, ed. Wang Gungwu et al. (Canberra: Research School of Pacific Studies, Australian National University, 1981), p. 18.
11. Sao Saimong Mangrai, op. cit., p. 7.
12. Xinhua News Agency, 17 April 1983.
13. Herold J. Wiens, *China's March Toward the Tropics* (Hamden, Conn.: Shoe String Press, 1954), pp. 330–31.
14. Jon M. Van Dyke, *North Vietnam's Strategy for Survival* (Palo Alto, California: Pacific Books, 1972), pp. 174–75.
15. Quang Canh, "Economic Transformation of the Highlands" in Nguyen *Mountain Regions and National Minorities in the D.R. of Vietnam*, Vietnamese Studies, No. 15, ed. Nguyen Khac Vien, 1968), p. 99.

16. Quang Canh, op. cit., p. 100.
17. *China Reconstructs* 3, no. 11 (1982): 17–18.
18. Quang Canh, op. cit., pp. 106–107.
19. There is one view that attributes this increase partly to natural increase in the population of the minorities. Stewart E. Fraser "Vietnam's 1980 Census: Current Position and Future Outlook", *Contemporary Southeast Asia* 3, no. 3 (Dec. 1981): 227.
20. J. Price Gittinger, *Terminal Report of J. Price Gittinger*, U.S. Operations Mission to Vietnam, Saigon, 1957, p. 27.
21. Vietnam News Agency, 2 October 1983.
22. See Mackie, op. cit., p. 19.
23. *China Reconstructs* 27, no. 5 (1978): 33.
24. Constitution of the People's Republic of China (PRC) in *Documents of the First Session of the First National Congress of the PRC* (Beijing, 1955).
25. George V.H. Moseley, III, *The Consolidation of the South China Frontier* (Berkeley: University of California Press, 1973), p. 49.
26. James C. Fox, "An Anthropologist's View", in Wang Gungwu et al., eds. op. cit., p. 69.
27. Moseley, III, op. cit., p. 78.
28. Moseley, III, op. cit., p. 79.
29. George McT. Kahin, "Minorities in the Democratic Republic of Vietnam", *Asian Survey* 12, no. 7 (July 1972): 586.
30. *Washington Post*, 27 December 1953.
31. Owen Lattimore, "Yunnan, Pivot of Southeast Asia", *Foreign Affairs*, April 1943, p. 481.

CHAPTER 9

Geo-Power, National Power, and Regional Stability

This chapter examines the linkage between various facets of power and the way the aggregate environment — geographical, political, socio-cultural, and economic — influences the exercise of power. Some state to state relations are then interpreted in this context and with reference to regional stability.

The Highlands in the Context of Power

Incorporation of intractable peripheral zones, which in aggregate constitute a high proportion of the state's territorial area, constitutes a source of detractive power sapping the lowland core domain's strength in military as well as economic or developmental terms. By incorporating large tracts of mountainous territory an expanded lowland or valley state would be faced with formidable problems of control and administration and maintenance of territorial sovereignty. The net result of these efforts at implementing territoriality, attempting the elimination of the peripheral power domains and protection of the boundaries is that the lowland state is lessened in relative power terms compared to its neighbours. Kautilya is quoted as commenting on this condition in the Indic sub-continent of his time.

> ... the king shall avoid taking possession of any country which is liable to the inroads of enemies and wild tribes and which is harassed by frequent visitations of famine and pestilence.[1]

In the contemporary environment of mainland Southeast Asia, formidable problems can still arise when lowland-based cultures or states expand into inhospitable frontier territory, which are liable to the depradations of hostile ethnic minorities, vulnerable to the inroads of enemies, and the poverty of which would ultimately be a drain on the state exchequer in developmental terms.

It can perhaps be perceived at this stage, that the nature of the relationship between core domain and highland peripheries could be a crucial factor determining whether highland belts which they legally possess through inheritance and which are contiguous to other states will constitute a source of strength or weakness to the centre. Though it may increase the geographical area of the state greatly, it may not add significantly to the power of the state.

Territorial size has to be seen in the total geo-strategic context. Size of territory alone may give a distorted view of a state's power. Nor by pushing the boundaries as far away as possible from the capital city is the security of the state as a whole necessarily increased. In fact, internal insecurity inviting external involvement may be increased. The incorporation of part of the central massif within a state's boundaries may be directly related to the degree of power, or powerlessness, possessed by the state. It can either be a source of strength or weakness to the state concerned.

Some Further Definitions of Power: "Reward Power" and "Coercive Power"

Power has been customarily measured in terms of national attributes such as size of population, size of territory, economic capability measured in various ways, level of technology possessed, inventories of natural resources, military strength, and the quality or will of the nation to pursue national strategies.[2] For example, Cline uses a list of such attributes, weighted, in creating comparative national indices of power. "Critical Mass" incorporating the sum of population and territory is used as one factor in the assessment of national power. This kind of approach is based on attributes internal to the state and is much used by students of strategic affairs.

Scholars investigating social power have identified various types of power, some of which are particularly relevant to the problems under discussion. These forms of social power include "reward power" and "coercive power".[3] It has been further observed that these categories of power, stated as they were originally in societal terms, nevertheless have considerable relevance to strategic studies and to the study of international power.[4]

A certain definable category of power resides in that dimension of power which enables the holder of power to reward another actor in the international stage. It is, however, dependent on a situation in which there is "consensus and the will to voluntary cooperation".[5] It should be emphasized that reward power is essentially a feature of exchange transactions.[6] Elaborating on this, Chong states that "'reward power' in fact involves interdependence or mutual dependence — the supplier of the reward is as dependent on the recipient as the latter is to the former. Both actors in the relationship are rewarded and are, in this sense, dependent on the other for his reward. Hence, 'reward power' is likely to prove attractive to both the involved actors".[7]

Reward power involves a subtle distinction in the categorization of power. It implies that not only the large and the powerful can reward the small and the weak, but that even the weak can possess forms of power which can be applied to further their interests. It further reminds us again that in assessments of power, the question of linkage between its various aspects is basic. Thus, coercive power (to be dealt with later) cannot be isolated from reward power and vice versa.[8] The two should always be considered together in studying any given situation.

Reward power, as will be shown later, is evident in the state-to-state relations in mainland Southeast Asia. So is coercive power, which in part at least grows out of reward power. Regular fulfilling of another's needs can result to a greater or lesser degree in dependence on the rewarder. Unilateral withdrawal of rewarding — since rewarding involves mutuality of interests — no doubt hurts the interests of both actors, yet it becomes a persuasive weapon in the hands of the actor who needs the other less than the other needs him. In this sense, the idea of power balance can be brought in and need not come into conflict with power translated in terms of reward and interdependence in the fulfilling of needs. The balance would tip in favour of that actor who is in a position to dispense — or from another perspective needs the rewards or return from rewards less than the other — with the rewards given by the other. Conversely, the actor who has come to need the rewards of the other crucially has the balance tilted potentially against him.

Rewards need not be limited to things substantial or tangible such as trade, aid, and investment, though these are the items which are very important and are most often apparent in the exchange transactions. Rewards and rewarding can be found in the form of policy postures which show mutual regard for each other's interests in any one particular field or fields. Thus in the context of Southeast Asia a southern state, by being non-aligned and refusing bases to maritime powers or superpowers hostile to China, would be following a policy which takes China's security interests into consideration. In this transaction China is the receiver of a reward. A lesser state can be in a position to reward a larger state. Recognition of the mutual power to reward in inter-state relations would again indicate that dependencies are often in themselves reciprocal in nature. However, as indicated earlier, this reciprocity is seldom evenly balanced.

It has been noted that reward power cannot be viewed in isolation from the closely related aspect of power referred to as "coercive power". Military power — a widely accepted indicator of a nation's strength in international relations and reflecting its inventory of leadership or management expertise, industrial resources, human resources, economic power, and other tangible items — is the simplest and an integral part of the power to coerce. It provides a major though clearly not the only dimension to coercive power. Among strategic thinkers, however, there is a tendency to equate military power with coercive power.[9]

Application of military force or the threat of it, although an important element of coercive power, is not synonymous with the latter. Coercive power should not be confused with coercion in the more popular usage of the term. For example, withdrawal of rewards is a part of coercive power. Conversely withdrawal of coercion or the threat of coercion constitutes a form of reward.

Significantly, all aspects of coercive power involving force can be used alongside or simultaneously with the power to withdraw or withhold rewards. The military aspect of coercive power is yet another reminder that power, including the power to coerce and to reward, is more often than not unevenly distributed.

Exercise of Power and the Montane Zone

How then do the attributes of the montane zone relate to national power? In the montane belt, the PRC (and Vietnam, too) can exert significant coercive pressure on a neighbouring state without incurring high costs. This kind of pressure would involve activity falling far short of conventional warfare or invasion using conventional armies. This state-against-state pressure is realizable mainly because of the characteristics including unguarded or indeed unguardable terrain, internal tension, and ethnic discontent in the montane region, all of which are expressed in the influence of power domains peripheral to the core of a state. Any policy of pressure in this region is sometimes, ironically enough, aided in a very positive manner by the internal policies of the governments of lowland states under pressure.

Weaker lowland states theoretically have the option of coalition among themselves and with others to enhance their power in order to counter the more organized and more powerful, in the manner of the classic balance of power approach to strategic issues. This would mean, however, that their internal organization and their military forces would have to possess the strength, "resilience", and durability to withstand protracted conflict well beyond their core power domains. In such contested mountain zones, foreign-inspired infiltration, and even larger-scale encroachment, would not be in unfamiliar and hostile country, or even on "neutral" ground. Indeed, in some cases, the lowland forces although theoretically defending a territorial sovereignty derived from a colonially inspired legacy would in fact be operating in peripheral or even hostile country. Lack of support from the local population for an army can mean its ultimate defeat as seen in the protracted civil wars in both China and Vietnam. Mao, for example, had pointed out during the Chinese revolution that a province garrisoned by troops from other provinces constituted a strategic liability to the central government, for such troops tended to be less involved than if they were local troops, they lacked enthusiasm, and importantly were unfamiliar with local conditions.[10]

Depending on a state's policy towards China and just as importantly towards its own wedge of the dividing massif, this mountain belt can be an attribute which either increases or decreases its national power. Even with the most amicable of relations with its montane neighbours, a considerable part of a state's military and developmental budget is often diverted to the "pacification" of its mountainous possessions. Such a turbulent state of affairs further impels the lowland state to adopt a policy of deference to the security interests of more powerful neighbours.

If there is a situation of hostile relations existing between a lowland state and China, for example, the lowland state's resources would be absorbed and its power would be reduced, both in absolute terms and in relation to other neighbouring states', through military pressure, exerted in the form of irregular warfare. Warfare waged in the areas, removed from the rival state's core domain, can be prolonged without necessarily leading to full-scale war.

A capability and a willingness to deploy resources to exert pressure, heavy at times and withdrawn at others, in order to advance its policy objectives towards states to its south has been demonstrated by China in its dealings with Vietnam since 1979, and to a much lesser extent with Burma. Similarly Vietnam could use its geo-strategic advantages in this respect in any attempt to influence events in Laos, in northern Thailand or even in Burma.

Hypothetically speaking such situations could doubtless also evolve in the strategic environment of one large, powerful state sharing common borders with a fragmented group of smaller, "balkanized" states, being separated from them not by a broad mountain belt but instead by international boundaries traversing cultivated or industrialized and heavily populated plains; or, in a simpler situation with two states sharing a common boundary through populated, developed lowlands. In such instances, however, the risk of the escalation of conflict would appear to be greater since it would be easier to move troops to points of foreign intrusion. This would be coupled with the need or desire to protect the "sacred homeland", that is, the core domain. The small-scale border fighting between Kampuchea and Vietnamese troops in 1978, which rapidly escalated into full-scale war is one recent example of such a conflagration. If there is no internal disorder in the target states involved, the temptation to use small-scale conflict in such situations as a means of political leverage would in consequence be considerably decreased.

Like the sea, the mountain belt affords within limitations a strategically "neutral" arena where projection of power, albeit often clandestine, can take place to coerce an opponent or to support a friend. As with the sea, temporary loss of control of a montane tract or distant bases, is in the strategic circumstances of Southeast Asia not as damaging as loss of control of parts of the core domain or in the case of naval warfare loss of home bases. Like the sea, too, it separates the core domains of neighbouring states thus reducing, but not eliminating, the risk of direct large-scale warfare.

Ceteris paribus, the mountain belt separating the lowland cores of the mainland states of Southeast Asia enhances, in the manner described above, the power of the stronger or the well-managed state and can subtract from the power of the weaker or the inefficiently managed state. Securing the loyalty of the mountain-dwelling people and having possession and control of large tracts of mountain region which is contiguous to similar terrain in smaller states, aids a more organized power in its efforts to lessen the power of those less organized states which adopt policies hostile to it. Conversely, a weaker or less organized state can — by following policies not considered inimical to the interests of the stronger state and through the systemic exchange with the stronger state — increase its own power relative to other neighbouring states which are often actual or potential rivals or even adversaries. This point is important since policy-makers in the southern lowland capitals could see their lowland neighbours — whose core domains are only thinly separated from their own — and not China as more immediate threats to their security. Vietnam's posture towards China is an exception, though even this may change in the course of time. In the context of power rivalry between neighbouring southern lowland states, a southern state's needs for China's non-action in these circumstances is increased. It would be to the advantage of a southern state if PRC hostility were to be directed against its lowland neighbours. Since the colonial intrusions, the near elimination of the attractions of China's civilization could mean that as far as its attitudes to the southern states are concerned the temptation is increased for China to use its geo-strategic advantages in the region in pursuit of its overall objectives towards the south. Geo-strategic advantages have replaced China's old advantage of a "morally superior civilisation".

Rewarding of a stronger state by desisting from actions which are seen to be against the latter's security interests (and being rewarded in return by amicable relations) and the indefensibility of the peripheral domains are not mutually irreconcilable. In fact, the former springs from the latter, and is in terms of the old adage, making a virtue out of necessity. It has, however, been interpreted as a dilemma facing lowland states. "It is one thing to bend diplomatically with the external political wind, it is another to seal off the soft exterior of an easily penetrated state."[11] It is precisely the strategic porosity of the frontier-straddling montane zone that gives mainland Southeast Asia a unique strategic environment in which possibly new forms of state-to-state relationships are evolving. One feature which is emerging and that has not previously been studied as such, is the indication that state-to-state dealings appear to take on a measure of the traditional means of settling matters of mutual concern, that is, the methods based on hierarchical relationships.[12] Vietnam and its two smaller neighbours of the old French Indochina is one such emerging example, while China is another, but larger example of a coercing and rewarding regional hierarch. The conflictual situation that has existed since 1979 springs directly from the confrontation between China and what it terms the "the little hegemony" painstakingly built up by Vietnam.

In the case of Burma it has been observed that the principle around which all Rangoon's "foreign policy considerations always clustered was the relationship with China. In the two decades since independence, every Rangoon government has worried over its long frontier with China, which is indefensible without major military aid. Past colonial leaders reached the same conclusion as did all but the most bellicose of pre-colonial monarchs. That conclusion was that Chinese hegemony should be acknowledged so that China would leave Burma alone."[13] The frequent, unpublicized visits to Beijing of Burmese leaders before as well as after the 1967 crisis in relations between Maoist China and Burma are indicative of the continuation of this policy. In fact, despite the bitterness of the invective, the rift emanating from both sides but especially from Beijing did not change the cautious Burmese policy of not provoking China in international affairs as opposed to Burmese domestic affairs. It has been pointed out that "in [an] important aspect of the Burmese situation, the deterioration of its relations with Peking did not seem to have too great an impact on Burma's foreign policy. Rangoon showed no inclination to alter its policy of rigid neutralism and 'isolationism' in international affairs."[14] This refusal to align itself with any of China's superpower rivals has been central to Rangoon's policy of not provoking Beijing on major strategic issues.

Finally, the combination of strategic elements to be found, sometimes uniquely, in the mountainous regions of mainland Southeast Asia have to be considered seriously in any attempt to understand the causes of instability in the region as a whole. The location and the geographical spread of the montane zone, the political, economic, and social conditions within it, and its linkage with the peripheral power domains of lowland states, give it a pervasive role in the power relationships of the region. The existence of the northern massif of mainland Southeast Asia straddling the "symbolic" boundaries of several states constitutes in itself an element of considerable significance in the regional power configuration. It constitutes a major influence on the direction in which future state-to-state relations in this region will flow. The mountain zone *per se* constitutes an element basic to the power equation of the region.

The PRC and its Southern Borders: Inducement and Coercion

With its experience of foreign, "barbarian" incursions, China has traditionally regarded its interior border lands with high concern. While the north and northwest have historically been zones of invasion by the mobile military power of steppe-based, horse-rearing, nomadic cultures, its southern border lands have been in quite a different category. The historically more recent sensitivity to developments in the southern mountainous borderlands stem not from threats arising from indigenous sources of power within the southern border regions, but from external maritime-borne penetration of this frontier which took place during the colonial era as well as during the Japanese occupation of the southern states in 1942, the subsequent turmoil which took place after World War II and especially during the Indochina Wars, and the support given by the USSR to Vietnam which began from 1978–79.

The French competed with the British in seeking a back door to

China from the south. After acquiring the Tonkin region, France won the race against the British by building a communication line to Guangxi, and thus into the south-western interior of China. It was a limited penetration — the French-built railway line then led only as far as Nanning in Guangxi. This was, for the period before World War II, the only modern route which led from the interior of the Chinese montane zone to a seaport. Subsequently, routes were opened up from Yunnan to British-controlled Burma. The war against Japan, the opening of the Burma Road and the Ledo Road, and the subsequent Japanese occupation of the countries south of the montane zone which led to the closure of the Burma Boad in 1942, China's last remaining link to the sea, emphasized the strategic value to China of the security of the southern border lands.

The geo-strategic pattern obtaining during the Japanese invasion of China was one in which the Guomindang and Chinese Communist Party forces occupied China's peripheral power domain, while as far as resources, particularly agricultural resources, were concerned, the Japanese were able to take over almost the entire core domain with the exception of the Sichuan or Red River basin. An analysis of the nature of the war front made during the Japanese invasion states: "When the Chinese were driven back from Hankow at the end of 1938, they lost the last important industrial area in the country. Since then the Chinese have held a fairly stable front which corresponded with the topography, or contours of the terrain. The Chinese held the uplands where guerilla type resistance ensured their survival in the face of technologically superior Japanese forces."[15] Can it be said that this experience has given the PRC a clearer understanding of the strategic importance of peripheral zones?

Both Imperial China and Nationalist China — in its commitment to the defence of Burma in 1941 and 1942 — as well as Communist China can be said to regard with concern any developments in the south which would threaten its security. In comparison with past inner Asian "barbarian" threats and present Soviet deployments along the western and northwestern border, this concern for the south is muted. To counter unwelcome developments in the south in the past, pressure or influence was through "moral superiority" or an occasional campaign. However, the present situation shows that the intermix of ideology, problems of ethnicity, and the lack of concordance between southern core power domains and the extent of their territorial possessions means that the PRC's power to influence events to its immediate south is enhanced, compared to its imperial predecessors. The evolution and refinements in the techniques of guerrilla warfare, the honing of the techniques, and application to political situations, of low-key protracted war, coupled with the widespread unrest in the highlands has meant that modern China has the means to exert or withdraw pressure of a kind not available to Imperial China in its dealings with the southern states, even though the PRC, or the CCP, may no longer possess the moral authority of the Imperial Court in Beijing.

The Chinese strategic outlook embraces, among other things, seven forms of warfare. These are main ground force operations, small unit border operations, coastal defence operations, co-ordinated air and sea operations, linear defence which is the protection of airspace and territory, nuclear deterrence, and finally people's war. Each form had different and distinctive needs with regard to organizational effort, training, tactics, and the type as well as the level of sophistication of military technology.[16] With such a varied array of methods and preparedness, PRC strategists are able to meet most of the likely problems facing their country. In addition, such a range of methods of warfare gives them options to deal with the diverse security situations likely to arise along its border.

In the environment of mountainous areas, such as that of northern mainland Southeast Asia, small unit operations as distinct from support of insurgencies are the mode of military activity suited to existing political conditions. It has been stated that:

> small unit border operations . . . have frequently demonstrated considerable value. . . . They testify to the commitment of Chinese forces, frequently to remote, highly inaccessible locations. They provide a ready military instrument for limited, low-level military engagements which can be linked to diplomatic efforts. . . . Inasmuch as their technological needs are modest, they cost little to maintain. Given that they reduce the prospects for undetected intrusion and interference by various adversaries, their worth seems clearly justified.[17]

Some of the dissenting ethnic groups of the south have shown considerable stamina and aptitude in small unit operations in difficult terrain, as was discovered by the United States in the Vietnam War.

However, this physical capacity to influence has to be seen additionally in the context of exchange transactions, and reward and coercive power. The Chinese policy towards the south has been described as a "carrot and stick" policy.[18] This description, implying both reward and coercion, of the PRC's handling of the southern rim states, largely holds true. However, even with the nature of the mountain frontier zone maximizing the coercive and reward power of the PRC, the observer cannot but feel that the "carrot and stick" description also implies a one-sidedness in the inevitable train of exchanges which characterizes state-to-state relations. For, in fact, the PRC is the recipient of a reward, or "carrot", when any southern state does not, for example, allow the use of airfields or ports by a maritime power hostile to China.

Indeed, with regard to China-Burma relations, the reward for China given in exchange for a relatively calm status quo on the frontier — that is, any insurgent-induced instability being restricted to low-key fighting that the Burmese Army, even though it cannot eradicate the instability, can keep within tolerable bounds — is a constant posture, backed up by publicly-made assurances that Burma does not, and does not intend to, adhere to any policies inimical to China's security interests. Burma maintains its strict neutrality. "One component of Burma's policy thus involved respect for China's strategic interests by not permitting any use of Burmese territory that could be conceived as a threat to China."[19] In 1968, for example, Burma declined to join twelve other Asian states in the setting up of a five-year work plan for the Asian Highway joining Western Europe to Singapore and which was to be built under the auspices of the United Nations Development Programme. The report that Burma "was wary of offending China which has dubbed the highway an imperialist plan to encircle China",[20] would not contradict a geopolitical assessment that such an international highway would run close to China's southwestern border and through a region of instability adjacent to China. It has also been observed that the government controlled press in Rangoon has constantly reiterated the theme that Burma would not join any Asian regional security bloc.[21] Indeed, despite the quarrel with Beijing and the intensified BCP activity on the border, Rangoon took pains to reaffirm its positive form of neutralism and its strict adherence to neutrality. Despite the temptations of seeking massive U.S. or Soviet aid, as done by India in 1962, General Ne Win made it clear to both Burmese as well as Chinese that:

> We are fighting with our own might. We do not depend on others. As said before, we must be on our own. We will then fight with what we have. In short we will never give up our neutral policy despite all these happenings and even if others want war.[22]

In this context, even limited military assistance from the United States was not continued, even though it would have been useful and attractive to the hard-pressed Burmese Armed Forces which lacked access to more modern forms of military technology. U.S. military assistance was stopped after 1969. The Rangoon government rejected an offer from the United States to "renew its modest aid program in military equipment including the proferred sale at bargain rates of surplus trucks and other transport facilities from South Vietnam".[23] All this can be construed as a firm assurance of the limitation of the quarrel by not internationalizing it. It was a signal to China that Burma, in the face of China's coercive power, was ready to proffer a reward for a lessening, or withdrawal, or even a non-increase of Chinese-aided insurgent pressure in the highlands. By the early 1980s this pattern in PRC-Burma relations still held good.

The use of the ideas of coercive power and reward power in a geostrategic framework would pay more attention to the mutuality of the relationships existing between the PRC and the individual southern rim states. Doubtless the balance is weighted in China's favour. Nevertheless a reward given, or the inducement of a possible reward, ensures that the giver or holder of the reward power also benefits from a reciprocally beneficial action, or non-action, which benefits the giver's policies or security interests.

Briefly, the coercive power of the PRC is amplified if the core domains of southern states are relatively weak in relation to their total state territory, that is where peripheral domains remain large and uncontrolled. This would also apply on a smaller scale to Vietnam in its relations with its landward neighbours to the west. In this manner the peripheries of lowland-centred states are embedded as much in the strategic issues of the overall montane region as they are in the internal affairs of the individual states.

Coercive Power and Military Action

Coercion in its simplest and crudest form can be applied through the use of escalating force to the level of "limited war". On the other hand, lowering the level of conflict or pain inflicted or withdrawing it for limited periods would be an inverted variant of reward power, applied strategically. This "negative" aspect of reward power can, as mentioned earlier, be used in conjunction with the more positive aspects of reward power such as financial loans and grants, aid in developmental projects, and the raising of the level of mutual trade. Instead of a straightforward policy of hostility or belligerency to achieve the aims of the stronger state, a two-faceted policy as described above can be used. This policy can in turn be orchestrated with the more familiar aspects of the "dual track" policy of differentiating between state-to-state and party-to-party relations.

Coercive power can also be brought into play even when both sides are more evenly balanced as was the case with Thailand and Laos which had Vietnam's support on Thailand's northeastern frontier in the period 1975–76. Support of across-the-border resistance groups, by the provision of sanctuaries, training facilities, supplies and arms, is a technique used in the mountainous borderlands. Thus, in the wake of the Pathet Lao's assumption of power in Laos in 1975, both Thailand and Laos used this method in attempting to strengthen their positions against one another. There have been indications that on occasion, insurgent groups operating into a neighbouring country from bases in unpopulated peripheries have been tolerated, ignored, or even encouraged, if these groups were ideologically not hostile to the "host" country. Such groups provided strategic buffers and could serve as forward screens to give advance warning of hostile movements. For example, Shan ethnic insurgents who could provide intelligence of communist movements in the areas adjacent to Thailand were tolerated by the local Thai authorities.

The mutuality of the application of this form of low-cost application of coercive power is seen in the area straddling northeast Thailand and neighbouring Laotian territory. In the period from 1975 to 1976, ". . . the reciprocal nature of the relationship between the support of Laos for the CPT and of Thailand for Laotian rebels should not be underestimated. Each country maintains an indirect and inexpensive means of harassing the other, which neither side seemed willing to relinquish unless the other did likewise. The result was incessant low-intensity warfare on the border. . . ."[24] In this kind of situation, the side with a weaker peripheral domain would be more likely to be coerced than its protagonist.

Coercion and Persuasion

It is important that strategies relying on the multi-faceted applications of coercive power need to be differentiated (although there are similarities) from the type of strategy exemplified in Beaufre's "Strategy of Persuasion" which can be described as a strategy of psychological attrition. In this the state using this strategy becomes increasingly threatening in pursuit of its objectives, at first by political, economic, and psychological methods, followed where necessary by covert military actions supporting the overall psychological attrition. This could also involve small operations to seize limited objectives, at which stage it becomes a "strategy of *fait accompli*".[25]

Strategies using, among other forms of power, coercive as well as reward power since the two go hand in hand, are much broader in application and can involve a much longer time-span, with advantage to the unswerving user. It can be said that threatening postures and actions and the application of military force occupy a much smaller place in an overall strategy of coercion (and of reward) than in strategies of persuasion which extend by necessity into the presentation of a *fait accompli* to the state under pressure. The many strategic options available to a state with firmly consolidated peripheries enable it to adopt policies which go well beyond mere psychological attrition.

Geopolitics of the Vietnamese Position

The PRC with its relatively well-organized highland minorities is in a firm position to use this coercive aspect of its total potential power. Vietnam, too, has created an advantageous position for itself in this respect. Vietnam has, as in many cases, consistently imitated Chinese techniques, historically as well as more recently, and is thus also in a position to exploit its strategic mountain regions, provided there is no massive PRC opposition, in the furthering of its long-term securing of national interests.

Imitation by Vietnamese of Chinese methods has historically taken the form of the adoption of agricultural systems, the traditional culture, the written script before the French introduced Romanization, and the sinic culture's accompanying technology. More recently this has been shown, though arguably, in the adoption of protracted guerrilla warfare by the Vietnamese. Both countries now show similarities in their policies towards controlling and winning over the mountain minorities.

With access to the strategically susceptible or "soft" mountain zones of east-central Burma, Laos, and through Laos, Thailand, and with its USSR-supported military strength and communication facilities such as helicopters and large manpower resources of its dense lowland population, Vietnam is also in a position to deploy coercive power directly on its neighbours. Vietnam has already done this to Laos. With a long and almost common indefensible mountain border there are few options left for the Lao leadership. Vietnam is able to control the weak and territorially restricted lowland power domain of Laos in this manner, using its dominance of the separating highlands.

The conditions in Laos make it a suitable base area for the projection of Vietnamese power. It has to be recognized that a scenario could arise in which there is foreign-aided Vietnamese coercion of Burma and Thailand. This would extend the influence of any Vietnamese-Soviet partnership, tacitly or by treaty, westwards along the axis of the montane zone into parts of Southeast Asia where Vietnam or the Soviet Union has never had any presence or influence before. This penetration would bring Russo-Vietnamese power to points close to India which has come increasingly to depend on arms aid and arms technology from the

USSR. Vietnam has several distinct advantages in this respect. It has forward military bases of considerable capacity in the montane zone especially the installations and garrison sited in the plain of Dien Bien Phu which is well within the minority-inhabited highlands and which is also close to the Laotian border.

Spread as they are over almost the entire montane zone, the Tai-inhabited lands are apportioned between Burma, China, Thailand, Laos, and Vietnam. The Vietnamese portion has as its centre Dien Bien Phu, the legendary centre of dispersion of all Tai peoples and kingdoms. From Dien Bien Phu routes lead into the lowlands of Laos. With this foothold in Tai-inhabited territory, Vietnam is a power of importance in the montane zone since ". . . because of its location Dien Bien Phu is the gateway to the lands of Tai-speaking peoples in South-east Asia, which stretch across the states of Burma, Thailand and Laos, as well as southern China".[26] The victory of the Vietminh over the French colonial forces and the incorporation of Dien Bien Phu and the surrounding uplands into the main body of land under Vietminh control "established the Vietnamese Communists as a power among the Tai-speaking peoples. It identified them with traditional goals of driving to the Mekong and acquiring a hegemony over the peoples to the west."[27]

Since 1976, an active road construction programme westwards from Vietnamese ports has linked the Vietnamese coast through Laos to the Mekong lowlands. There is a motorable road crossing the dividing highlands and joining the Vietnamese port of Danang to Savannakhet. Improvement of an existing road was carried out by the Vietnamese prior to 1980. By 1980, an estimated one-fifth of the external trade of Laos, a land-locked state, was passing through Danang[28] by-passing the traditional outlet through Bangkok. In 1982 Vietnamese road-builders completed two major highways in northern Laos. The 90 km Highway Six connects the Vietnamese coast with the northern Laotian province of Houa Phan. The 130 km Highway Seven links the Vietnamese port of Vinh, southeast of Hanoi, to the Laotian city of Phonsavan in the north of the country.[29]

Vietnam also has control of much of northern Laos, even though some resistance groups are actively supporting anti-Vietnamese policies and are encouraged in this respect by China. The H'mong of Laos, strongly anti-Vietnamese, had by the early 1980s been largely neutralized or eliminated by Vietnamese offensive action which included the alleged use of chemical warfare.

By the early 1980s too, the Soviet Union had been able to enter into close relationship with an otherwise Vietnamese-dominated Laos and having provided economic aid and advisers has been rewarded through being allowed to build radar facilities in Laos, ostensibly for the surveillance of Chinese air movements and missile tests.

The Soviet Union's disadvantages in this zone are, however, considerable. Not only is the mountain region far removed from the direct influence of Soviet naval power, but Russians and troops of other Warsaw Pact countries such as East Germany and even Cubans would be easily recognized as being complete foreigners if deployed in the region. Here the preponderant and proximate land or continental power of China would in the long term be of crucial consideration in the outcome of a long-drawn conflict or period of instability.

Limited Hostile Action in the Montane Zone

The term "limited hostile action" as given here, falls short of limited war with its connotations of conventional warfare. The physical, political, and cultural environment of the mountainous geo-strategic region is an arena providing conditions where limited action can be used as a means of furthering national interests through the projection of coercive power. It is recognized, of course, that limited action can also be used to coerce, a neighbouring state across a lowland border. In such cases, however, where direct military force is applied, the risk of the enlargement of the series of limited actions into a larger conflagration would be much greater. This is especially so if the action involves areas close to main urban and industrial centres or the core power domains of one or both states. When hostilities, even though low-key and limited, impinge upon or reach into the geographical limits of one actor's core power domain, its defensive reaction would more likely be stronger.

On the other hand when such actions are limited both in scale and duration and in geographical extent, and are restricted to the fringing mountains or peripheral domains, the risk of escalation is lessened, though not eliminated. The continuous low-key hostilities may even in fact become "habitual" in the sense that the authorities of the weaker state give it low priority.

It can be argued further that military manœuvres alone, that is, a display of force held close to the boundaries of the weaker state, can also have the same desired coercive effect. However it must be emphasized that military manœuvres, or even the classic intimidatory method of the stationing of large numbers or massing of troops with their equipment close to the borders, would carry its economic costs. Costs of sustained manœuvres can be as high as costs of actual campaigns. Furthermore, in the montane area under study the terrain inhibits the stationing and supply of large numbers of troops for long periods. A strategy involving display of force and massing of troops may also invite hasty decisions of a weaker state to form alliances by treaty or by tacit understanding with a third state.

Should a situation of massive military threat trigger off an armed conflict, the internal and international consequences of it would be likely to be much graver than the staving off of mere guerrilla-type irregular actions. This would be especially so if the fluid, often locally indecisive guerrilla-type actions take place in zones far away from the power domain of the defending state. Such low-key and intermittent hostilities would not then appear to be threatening to the security of the centre.

The use of power to further national interests and as applied through the technique of limited action finds a special adaptation in the environment of mainland Southeast Asia's montane zone. Geopolitical and cultural basics thus indicate the existence of a distinct strategic and military environment in the region.

The Concept of Geo-Power

The proposition can now be put forward here that in the power relationships existing between nations there sometimes occurs a discernible element which can be most conveniently termed as geo-power. Under favourable conditions geo-power can be one additional aspect of total national power. It enhances the power of one state in relation to other states. It should be seen as a synthesis of many of the traditional elements of power as listed by political geographers, namely, size and shape of territory and boundaries, population, ethnic composition, national characteristics, natural resources, access to sea or to other friendly states, and the position and location of territory possessed in relation to other states. The American naval historian, Mahan, was one of the earliest to see this traditionally accepted connection between geography and power.

In its simplest form any description of the geographical sources of power can be categorized as the aggregate of all the elements of geography which go toward constituting, or more precisely adding to, the traditional elements of power. It can be said that this approach although placing some emphasis on the geographical basis of national power is by no means deterministic. What is postulated here is that where conditions are conducive to the application of geo-power — and conditions may change with changing political and technological circumstances — it can aid in furthering national interests.

The concept of geo-power as presented here goes beyond the traditional view of geography in its relation to power though geography is fundamental to it. The coherence of political and economic organization is integral to it. The concept of geo-power while still dependent to a large extent on the traditional elements such as position, size, shape, population, resources, and so on proceeds further and its pith lies in the idea that where conditions for the existence of geo-power are identifiable, the analyst is able to point to additional options in a state's policies towards its neighbours. In this sense, geo-power is essentially the power of a combination of favourable geopolitical advantages and options. Geo-power does not stand alone. It is just one facet of a state's overall power potential though often unrecognized as such.

Geo-power through its relationship with coercive power and reward power which are themselves elements or facets of aggregate power adds an extra dimension to the power of a state which possesses it. With a minimum of effort, that is, with a minimum of expenditure of resources, it increases the power available to a state relative to its neighbour. Unlike the military or industrial aspects of national power, geo-power, like national will, is largely intangible. The potential of geo-power can be realized if it is harnessed in tandem with appropriate diplomacy, and political or military pressure. When geo-power is thus harnessed, it places a state's neighbour or adversary at a relative disadvantage. Geo-power particularly enhances military power. The relative aggregate power of one state which harnesses geo-power to its own ends is then increased while that of its protagonist, which does not or cannot, is decreased.

It needs to be repeated that geo-power is constituted of many elements, some of which are fixed such as terrain and climate, some of which are man-made, like boundaries, while yet others are even less tangible and may change over a period of time due to many reasons including the policies of the centre of a state. Such less tangible factors include the level of loyalty, reliability, or dissent and the existence of peripheral power domains in any one state in a zone where the exercise of geo-power is latent. Geo-power can be tapped both by rival states as well as competing forces within states.

★ ★ ★

Mere size of territory is no indication of the level of national power. The level of power available to nations in the region and with peripheral domains is inextricably linked to the conditions in their highland possessions. The strategic circumstances of the region appear to be conducive to the exercise of various forms of power, such as the "coercive" and the related "reward" power. When taken in the context of other considerations, such as the military, these aspects of power can be used in the analysis of the strategic issues facing the region. Burma's post-war policies, for example, can to a considerable extent be explained by the complex of factors involving weak peripheries which make the centre open to coercion and reward. Moreover, the strategic environment of the peripheries lends itself to obtrusive, low-key and long drawn-out warfare which tends to be "unnoticed". This is in itself an adjunct of the coercion-reward combination. In this environment, large-scale warfare can be seen as an anomaly.

The environment of the montane zone tends to add to the power of the stronger and detracts from the power of the weaker or less-organized. In other words, a territorial share of the strategic massif is a liability to a weak state. At the same time it makes the strong state even more dominant. The environment of the region thus widens the differential power gap between strong and weak states or more precisely, states weakened by the condition of peripheral power domains.

The environment of the region gives emphasis to a form of power which can be best described as geo-power. Geo-power is available to a state which taps the power accruing from a combination of favourable geopolitical vantages. This combination of factors includes space, location, terrain, culture, population, and economic and political policies and circumstances.

Through the exercise of various forms of power first discerned in societal analysis and which are enhanced by the environment of the central massif, modern China has to some extent with minimal expenditure of effort and resources regained its historical position as regional hierarch, though this has been challenged by Vietnam's "little hegemony".

NOTES

1. Kautilya, *Arthashastra*, translated by R. Shamasastry, 8th edition, (Mysore: Sri Raghuveer Printing Press, 1951), p. 54, quoted in R. Solomon, "Boundary Concepts and Practices in Southeast Asia", *World Politics* 23, no. 1 (October 1970): 1–16.
2. See for example, Ray S. Cline, *World Power Assessment: A Calculus of Strategic Drift* (Boulder, Col.: Westview Press, 1975).
3. John R.P. French, Jr. and Bertram Raven, "The Bases of Social Power", in *Studies in Social Power*, ed. Dorwin Cartwright (Ann Arbor: University of Michigan, 1959), pp. 150–67.

4. Chong Li Choy, "International Development and International Dependence: A Study of Aid and Social Development" (D. Soc. Sc. thesis, University of Bielefeld, 1977, University Microfilms International, Ann Arbor, 1977).
5. Talcott Parsons, "On the Concept of Political Power", in *Political Power: A Reader in Theory and Research*, ed. R. Bell et al. (New York: The Free Press, 1969), p. 251.
6. Peter Blau, "Differentiation of Power", in Bell et al., eds., op. cit., p. 293.
7. Chong, op. cit., p. 62.
8. Historically, the bestowment or the prospect of bestowment of the benefits of Chinese civilization on the southern minority groups served as an element in the reward power wielded by the Chinese over the less advanced minorities while the withdrawal of this prospect could serve as a form of coercive power. Thus the Chuang were largely sinicized, and to a lesser extent the H'mongs and Yao.
9. See, for example, Thomas P. Rona, *Our Changing Geopolitical Premises* (New Brunswick: Transaction Books, 1982), pp. 191–234.
10. J.L.S. Girling, *People's War: Conditions and Consequences in China and South East Asia* (New York: Praeger, 1969), p. 76.
11. Michael Leifer, "Post Mortem on the Third Indochina War", *The World Today* 35, no. 6 (June 1979): 256.
12. See Matthew M. Gardner, Jr., "The Heritage of South Asian Borders", *SAIS Review* 13, no. 2 (Winter 1969): 28–29.
13. John H. Badgley, "Burma's China Crisis: The Choices Ahead", *Asian Survey* 7, no. 11 (November 1967): 758.
14. Robert A. Holmes, "China-Burma Relations Since the Rift", *Asian Survey* 12, no. 8 (August 1972): 691.
15. Owen Lattimore, "Yunnan, Pivot of Southeast Asia", *Foreign Affairs*, April 1943, p. 483.
16. Jonathan D. Pollack, "China as a Military Power", in *Military Power and Policy in Asian States*, ed. O. Marwah and J.D. Pollack (Boulder, Colorado: Westview Press, 1980).
17. Jonathan D. Pollack, "The Evolution of Chinese Strategic Thought", in *New Directions in Strategic Thinking*, ed. Robert O'Neill and D.M. Horner (London: George Allen and Unwin, 1981), p. 144.
18. David Mozingo, "Communist China: Its Southern Border Lands", *SAIS Review* 12, no. 2 (Winter 1968): 43–54.
19. Holmes, op. cit.
20. *Asian Recorder* 14, no. 6 5–11 February 1968): 8155.
21. Holmes, op. cit., p. 691.
22. Rangoon Domestic Service, 1 March 1968, quoted by Holmes, op. cit., p. 692.
23. John F. Cady, *The United States and Burma* (Cambridge, Mass.: Harvard University Press, 1976), pp. 269–70.
24. Tim Huxley, *Indochina and Insurgency in the Asean States 1975–1981*, Working Paper No 67 (Canberra: The Strategic and Defence Studies Centre, Australian National University, January 1983), pp. 14–15.
25. Andre Beaufre, *Strategy for Tomorrow* (London: McDonald James, 1974).
26. John T. McAlister, Jr., "Mountain Minorities and the Vietminh: A Key to the Indochina Way", in *Southeast Asian Tribes, Minorities and Nations*, ed. Peter Kundstadter (New Jersey: Princeton University Press, 1967), p. 834.
27. Ibid.
28. *Bangkok Post*, 26 November 1980.
29. Vietnam News Agency, 20 December 1982, also *Straits Times* (Singapore), 21 December 1982.

CHAPTER *10*

The Post-1975 Power Situation in "Indochina"

The post-1975 situation in the portion of mainland Southeast Asia known formerly as French Indochina shows the extent of the influence of the disposition of power domains on the power configuration existing among the states in the region.

Strategic Implication of Vietnam's Core Domains

Within Vietnam, the chief feature of the post-1975 situation was the establishment of the Kinh-based power domain that stretched from the Tonkin lowlands to the frontiers of North Vietnam. The consolidation of Hanoi's power was seen in the weakening if not the virtual disappearance of any peripheral stretches where previously Hanoi's control was not effective. It should be noted, however, that this consolidation does not appear to be complete. In the far north, enough of an earlier peripherality remains for the PRC to infiltrate into Vietnamese-held areas. In the south, although the Mekong deltaic region is wholly under Hanoi's control, the highlands (known during the Vietnamese War as the Central Highlands of South Vietnam) were even by 1983 not entirely free from insurgent activity. Control of the highlands is, however, more thorough than what the U.S. forces and the Saigon government ever achieved. The existence of this post-1975 insurgency, involving relatively small numbers of Montagnards, anti-Vietnamese Laotians, and the Khmer Rouge is made possible because of the incompleteness of Vietnamese control over adjacent Cambodian territory and the presence of Khmer Rouge bases in north and northeast Cambodia.

Although Hanoi's control over the southern deltaic zone enables it to establish a core domain in the south, there are variations between the northern and southern cores of Hanoi's power. Control over the north is more thorough in terms of the people's response to planning, agricultural and other edicts. In the south, this control is less complete, and since 1975 there have been periods of passive resistance to measures by the government designed at implementing socialization of agriculture and the abolition of private agricultural production. The south has agricultural yields per person or man-hour which are considerably higher in the north. Yields per crop of rice also tend to be higher in the south than in the north. However, yields per year would tend to be higher in the north where as many as three crops of rice are grown each year, compared to one crop in the southern region. Domain quality varies therefore between north and south, both in terms of degree of control and the productivity of the natural environment. Despite tighter political control of the northern core, its denser population per unit area of land and its generally poorer soils have meant that the north has remained a food-deficit area, in food grains as well as in sources of protein.[1] Dependence on the rice-crop of the south, and the importance of communications to the southern delta, is thus underlined. French geographers have in the past characterized Vietnam as consisting of two bags of rice — the discontinuous north and south — slung at both sides of a bamboo pole.

For all practical purposes, however, Hanoi's control over its northern and southern domains is thorough enough to enable it to deal with neighbouring states, either in a directly aggressive manner or with a western-style "sovereign" stance that would not tolerate any detectable intrusion into its territory. The core-periphery dichotomy has been very blurred in North Vietnam since 1975, though since the Chinese incursion of 1979 signs have appeared that Hanoi's control over its geographically peripheral regions in the north and northwest has begun to flag. In the south the lowland portion of the deltaic terrain enabled the core domain to be easily extended to the Cambodian boundary line. The juxtaposition of the Cambodian and the southern Vietnamese power domains in the Mekong lowland sector areas resulted in a situation unusual in mainland Southeast Asia, namely the adjacency of two core domains unbuffered by peripheral domains. This facilitated direct large-scale and historically continuous conflict. "The cultural frontier between Cambodia and Vietnam seems . . . to be the sharpest in Southeast Asia. . . . If you moved from one village to the next, you found complete changes in such very basic things, besides the language of course, as hairstyle, clothing, food, architecture . . . kitchen utensils, alphabet, educational systems, agricultural techniques, treatment of the dead, foreign relations, attitudes towards history . . . make up an almost complete set of oppositions. . . ."[2] In the context of ethnic antipathy — the Cambodians were said to be joyful in *Kap Yuon* or "killing

Vietnamese"[3] — and power rivalries, the scene was well set for a major conflict after the retreat of the Americans.

Establishment of the twin power domains of Vietnam, the concomitant continuity of control, and the mobilization of resources which this control yielded, gave Vietnam the impetus and capacity to attempt to accomplish its dominance over eastern mainland Southeast Asia, through political leadership of the old French Indochina, mooted by Hanoi in the proposed mechanism of a Vietnamese-led Indochina grouping — the "small-time hegemony" which was repugnant to Beijing.

An initial step to the establishment of any kind of Indochina federation would be to eliminate the governmental structure and the leadership of Democratic Kampuchea which was relying heavily on PRC support and which was spurning the concept of federation. The proximity, in fact the juxtapositioning, of Vietnam's southern domain to a weaker Cambodia facilitated the Vietnamese military thrust of early 1979 into the Cambodian plains, the subsequent occupation of most of the Cambodian lowlands, and the installation of the Heng Samrin regime. It also made easier attempts to dominate the Cambodian core domain. The proximity of Vietnam's southern core to a Cambodia equipped with arms supplied by the PRC, had made settlements and installations well within the southern Vietnamese ethnic heartland vulnerable to assault by Cambodian forces operating at night and in small units. Border fighting had preceded the 1979 Vietnamese campaign into Cambodia.

Although Cambodia is situated well south of the geo-strategic region of montane mainland Southeast Asia, the Vietnamese war there shows some of the salient features of the persistence of the core-periphery situation characteristic of the main mountainous region to the north.

Vietnam in Cambodia

Military occupation by Vietnam of most of the Cambodian lowlands meant in fact the occupation, but not necessarily the complete control, of the Cambodian core domain. The Cambodian resistance was thus relegated to the hilly, mountainous forested peripheries and along the Thai border across which cuts the Aranyaprathet corridor leading to Thailand. While Vietnamese control over the rich, eastern portion of Cambodia was facilitated by Vietnam's proximity, the situation has been different in the westerly, northern, and north-western rims of the Cambodian plain. Control was rendered more difficult by sheer distance, the poor condition of roads and the partially repaired or unrepaired bridges. This was compounded by vulnerability to attack by small guerrilla units moving under cover of darkness or during the rainy season, and the shortage of local food supplies. This last shortcoming made Vietnamese reliance on logistical lines even more crucial. For the massing of men and supplies for the annually recurring dry-season offensives against Khmer resistance bases, Soviet or Soviet-supplied transport aircraft had to be used to fly from bases in Vietnam to airfields in the Battambang and Sisophon areas.

In the first three years following the Vietnamese invasion of Cambodia, the conflict very rapidly reached a condition of stalemate after the rapid Vietnamese victory which led to the occupation of the urban centres and to control of all vital routes. The situation of military stalemate, would in the Maoist sense give rise to conditions conducive to protracted war. Deteriorating domestic conditions in Vietnam, especially in its economy, were related to a shift to a more defensive posture. After three successive dry-season offensives to wipe out Khmer resistance bases in the west, the emphasis by 1981 was on urban security and the safeguarding of all main routes leading to Phnom Penh. However, the Khmer resistance does not appear to have the necessary strength or the guerrilla infrastructure in the central plains to take full advantage of the Vietnamese emphasis on defence and security, though in the dry season of early 1984 successful guerrilla activity was carried deep into Cambodia with successes scored in large-scale raids on military installations and airfields in western Cambodia, notably the towns of Battambang and Siem Riep, as well as a marked recrudescence of guerrilla initiatives in central and even eastern Cambodia.

With each rainy season, areas under Vietnamese control shrink, as exemplified by repeated withdrawals from logistics bases and newly captured territory near the Thai border. The pattern is one of a fluctuating core domain under Vietnamese control with the contraction most marked during the wet monsoon.

Compared to 1980, the area under Vietnamese control in 1981 was actually reduced. Examination of the territorial extent of Vietnamese control shows that it extends over nearly all of the Mekong plains adjoining the Vietnamese border, including the Phnom Penh area. It also includes both banks of the Tonle Sap and the rice-producing plains of western Cambodia which have Battambang and Sisiphon as their urban centres. The Vietnamese also occupy a tongue of territory leading from Phnom Penh to the coastal seaport of Kompong Som. In addition the Vietnamese control narrow strips of territory along all main routes as well as an isolated pocket in the north and adjoining the southwestern tip of Laos, around the junction town of Choam Khsant. The spatial pattern of Vietnamese control coincides with all significant urban centres, their immediate environs, and all major routes. Large tracts remain contested territory which separate the Vietnamese-held areas from those controlled by the Khmer resistance, mainly the Khmer Rouge. The contested territory is at its narrowest in the sector of the Aranyaprathet corridor. Areas controlled by the Khmer resistance are mainly in the fringes in the west, northwest, north, and northeast. There is also a sizeable Khmer resistance area in the Cardamon mountains in the southwest.[4]

This pattern of division of areas under rival control in Cambodia is reminiscent of the division between core, peripheral, and extraneous power domains. In times of war, especially of protracted guerrilla war, in the conditions of Southeast Asia, the core-periphery dichotomy emerges and assumes vivid proportions. Vietnam — whatever the reasons for doing so, on moral grounds or for sheer conquest — by attempting to dominate Cambodia has in actual fact subjected most of the Cambodian core domain to military occupation and has in the process created yet another classic-style, hostile peripheral power domain that has the advantage of access to external aid and sanctuary, challenging its hold on Cambodia, which it has yet to subdue. The emergence of resistance-held peripheral domains which re-expand with each rainy season after loss of territory to Vietnamese dry-season offensives, points to a long drawn-out war which the Vietnamese would have to face. This would in turn increase the susceptibility of Vietnam to any future application by the PRC of geo-power on Vietnam's northern marches. There are signs, however, that the Vietnamese are utilizing the strategic nature of the military stalemate to their own advantage by a large-scale movement of ethnic Kinh, or Vietnamese, as agricultural settlers, riverine fishermen, and artisans into the Cambodian core domain, thus changing its character by a process of ethnic dilution. By early 1984, 600,000 Kinh were to be granted Cambodian citizenship by the Heng Samrin regime. This is one kind of attempt to upgrade the quality of the Cambodian core domain. To the Vietnamese, the subjugated Khmer lands are essentially a low-grade domain. Kinh settlement in Cambodia can be interpreted in this context as being aimed at raising the quality of power available to the Vietnamese authorities in Cambodia. From the Khmer viewpoint this Vietnamese policy can only lead to a weakening of the Khmer core power domain.

The extension of Vietnamese military power into the far west of Cambodia brings Vietnamese security interests into conflict with those of Thailand. One of the ironies of the Third Indochina War has been that large concentrations of Khmer resistance forces occur not in the more easily defended mountains of the north and northeast — although there are significant Khmer Rouge forces operating in those regions — but in the accessible and less defensible areas in, and adjacent to, the boundary at the Aranyaprathet corridor leading to Thailand. The relatively level and open nature of the terrain of the corridor and its relatively sparse vegetation cover make it suitable ground for the use of heavy equipment by the Vietnamese, including tanks and self-propelled artillery during the dry season. While forested rocky outcrops like Phnom Chat and Phnom Malai have enabled the Khmer Rouge to set up substantial bases, the restricted extent of these isolated hill ranges and their closeness to flat areas with firm well-drained subsoils make them extremely vulnerable to the consequences of Vietnamese road-building encroachment.

Any attempt by the Vietnamese to eradicate these close-to-the-border bases would mean that large-scale fighting would spill over — as has happened each dry season — into Thai-defended territory. The Thai Army has shown the will to resist Vietnamese incursions and to repel Vietnamese units operating ostensibly in hot pursuit of Khmer guerrillas. Extended over relatively long supply lines after its rapid advance through Cambodia, Vietnamese military power has been confronted by Thai military forces with the advantage of being based on Thailand's own core domain. Ethnicity and proximity to domestic bases are in Thailand's favour. The main army camps and supplies dumps in and around the Bangkok area are only several hours away if the main highways are used. The raising of Thai village defence corps to be used as a military instrument serving as a warning screen against Vietnamese advances and to detect and resist small units of intruding Vietnamese troops is a sign that the Vietnamese Army is on the threshold of the Thai ethnic domain. Moreover, Vietnamese supply lines would need to traverse long stretches of alien country. However, the terrain of the Aranyaprathet corridor — but not of the rest of the Thai-Cambodian border consisting of rugged country and of sharp escarpments the crests of which are Thai territory — favours the Vietnamese, should an advance be carried out by the latter.

In terms of equipment, especially armour, artillery, and air support, the Vietnamese are also superior to the Thai Army. Should the Thai Army rely entirely on conventional tactics in a scenario of a sustained Vietnamese attack into Thailand, it will face an experienced army and army leadership down to platoon level, familiar with both conventional and irregular tactics. The training of Thai army troops and that of their officers, together with U.S.-type doctrines on the deployment of armour and air support, are factors that will influence the Thai Army in adopting U.S.-style tactics in their defence, as well as in counter-attack. These methods proved to be of limited effectiveness against the Vietnamese during U.S. involvement in the Vietnam War. The experience of Thai irregular forces operating against the Pathet Lao in Laos during the Vietnam War, provided their value is recognized, will be invaluable in dealing with Vietnamese penetrations into Thailand. In a scenario of a Vietnamese-initiated armed conflict with Thailand, any Thai predispositions militating against the use of irregular warfare on Thai territory, or which reject the notion of the involvement of the Thai population in such forms of warfare, and inflexibility in co-operation with the Khmer resistance within Cambodia could help tilt the balance in Vietnam's favour. A state defending its own core domain has strategic and tactical advantages, even though material damage to its economic infrastructure has to be taken into account. The participation of the local populace, whether in terms of people's war, the Yugoslavian total defence concept, or the Indonesian ideas on popular involvement in territorial defence can be a decided military advantage. It can be said that core domains, in terms of people's war, are favourable operational areas. In this sense, the existence of part of the Thai core domain close to vital Khmer resistance bases (which would be highly vulnerable otherwise) is a strategic boon to the anti-Vietnamese forces, and strengthens the Khmer-held peripheral domains in relation to the Vietnamese-held plains. It is interesting to note that the Chinese PLA with its expertise in mountain warfare, as demonstrated in Korea, the Himalayas, and less markedly in north Vietnam, and its awareness of the efficacy of people's war, stopped short of the lowland core domains of Vietnam in 1979 and of India in 1962.

Vietnam and Laos

The mountains dividing the Vietnamese coastal plains from the Mekong valley lowlands of Laos have in the past functioned as a screen to preserve some measure of Lao separateness from Vietnam. The withdrawal of the French power, which had frozen Vietnamese westward ambitions and had kept out Vietnamese agricultural settlement from the Laotian plains, and Hanoi's victory in the Vietnam War have meant that any externally imposed barrier against a westward extension of Vietnamese power has been removed. The sheer size of the Vietnamese population in comparison to the number of ethnic Lao, the co-operative attitude of the Laotian Government to Vietnam after 1975, and the construction of all-weather roads crossing the mountains from Vietnamese seaports to the Mekong have re-emphasized the weakness and vulnerability of the Laotian core domain. Should unrest be evident, the Laotian peripheral zones can be attacked by the Vietnamese and their Laotian supporters, from both east and west. By 1980 it was estimated that 60,000 Vietnamese troops were garrisoned in Laos.

With continuing co-operation between Hanoi and Vientiane, and sustained Vietnamese-led anti-insurgency operations, the Laotian peripheries are likely to diminish, except significantly in the areas bordering on the PRC. Vietnamese troops have been reported as having kept their distance from the PRC-Laos boundary. The weakness of the Laotian state in comparison to Thailand is offset by the post-1975 Laotian-Vietnamese co-operation in political, economic, and security fields. Laos used to be a field of contention between Thailand and Vietnam, but since 1975 the resources of Laos would be within that of a Vietnamese-led and -dominated grouping of states.

However, it can be noted that should the leaderships in Vientiane and Phnom Penh and more particularly popular feeling in Laos and Cambodia turn against Vietnam, then Hanoi would be confronted with a situation in which inheritance of the mantle of French rule over all of Indochina would also involve the burden of pacification and control of peripheral domains, vulnerable to external interference, a condition already discernible in parts of Cambodia and Laos.

China in "Indochina"

The power situation in the Vietnam-Laos-Cambodia-Thailand quadrilateral although weighing against Thailand cannot, however, be viewed in isolation. Here it would be relevant to add that notions of regionality depend on intellectually imposed delimitations of a selected region. In the case of the wider "Indochina" that is the Vietnam-Laos-Cambodia-Thailand quadrilateral, it has to be viewed against what are generally termed "external" interests. These are the USSR, the United States, and the PRC. The interests of the Association of Southeast Asian Nations (ASEAN), or rather the interests of the various component states of ASEAN, are also highly relevant. ASEAN, however, is usually regarded as being part of the region and hence its interests are seen as not being external in character. Such perceptions of regionality and of the limits of Southeast Asia have to be taken into account in analysing the situation in post-1975 "Indochina". Without doubt, Vietnam is the dominant power within the old French Indochina. Moreover, within the Vietnam-Laos-Cambodia-Thailand quadrilateral, Vietnam, with its strengthened position in Laos and its destruction of the anti-Vietnamese Khmer Rouge conventional army, can also be regarded as the strongest military power. However, any conclusions on Vietnam's eventual paramountcy in this zone would necessarily rest on the premise that the wider Indochina or mainland Southeast Asia is an enclosed region, where "external" actors have limited choice of action. While this may be correct for the United States and the USSR and even for ASEAN as a whole, it does not apply to the PRC, should Beijing perceive the expansion of Vietnamese interests to China's south as a destabilizing factor, inimical to China's interests. The long, northern frontier belt of this region and the proximity of the PRC as a fully resident state in the strategic montane zone would indicate that definitions of regionality need to be applied flexibly. It also points to the kind of patterns of power that are likely to evolve in "Indochina" and its surrounding region — that is, in mainland Southeast Asia.

Vietnam, with aid from the USSR, would be or would have been the dominant power in mainland Southeast Asia if not for the large-scale but time-limited PRC intervention in northern Vietnam in February-March 1979. Though brief, this punitive campaign involved relatively large numbers of troops on the part of both protagonists. It demonstrated the PRC's will and capacity to go beyond mere rhetoric. This proven PRC capacity to intervene will be an important factor in determining the extent of Vietnam's influence beyond its own boundaries. From early 1979 on, any threat from Beijing has to be taken seriously by Hanoi, and hence cannot but play an important role in the latter's decision-making with regard to military objectives in "Indochina" and also in the allocations of scarce economic resources. Posed as a direct military challenge to Vietnam, the Chinese moves have swung the pendulum away from a total and undisputed Vietnamese hegemony in Indochina. The Chinese strategy was made possible because of the adjacency of Yunnan and Guangxi provinces and because of the grain of the country. The rivers, valleys, and ridge lines in the northwestern sector of Vietnam's northern front facilitated the Chinese advance during the punitive war, while the Chinese capture of Langson in the northeastern sector brought the People's Liberation Army (PLA) close to the centres of production in Tonkin. This advance was made all the more telling from the fact that the vanguard of the PLA, after the fall of Langson 130 km. north of Hanoi, held a vital junction south of Langson close to the Tonkin plains and well clear of the labyrinth of dry gorges. The narrow winding valleys of this area are enclosed by limestone cliffs which characterize the Langson landscape. Such terrain constitutes Vietnam's natural line of defence in depth which controls the northern approaches to Hanoi and Haiphong. In this area, imperial Chinese and French colonial forces have at different points of history met defeat at the hands of the defending Vietnamese.

That Guangxi and Yunnan are part of Southeast Asia's northern mountain marches has made them strategically advantageous to the PLA's punitive campaign in yet another way. Troops from these two southern provinces constituted a high proportion of the Chinese forces that took part in the campaign. This source of manpower was acclimatized to terrain, vegetation, and temperature and rainfall conditions, while some of the specialist personnel from China's northern provinces who manned the armoured and artillery components of the invading force were not. In this sense the southern mountain provinces and Hainan Island constitute "Tropical China in Southeast Asia".

Application of coercive power in the highland environment can be at low cost to the user. When it fails to yield results, then a heightened form of coercion through large-scale military activity can supplant it. Such application of large-scale military means of coercion is what can be termed coercion of the last resort. While low-key coercion is done at low cost, it takes time to produce results. It is essentially a long-term strategem and can be a semi-permanent feature of relations between states. Large-scale attacks on the other hand, though involving much higher costs and political and military risks, have the effect of distracting the protagonist more immediately from undiluted attention to its objectives in other areas. This rapid creation of a crucial second front for Vietnam threatening its industrial and economic centres was made possible by the proximity of the two rival core domains. This has consequences for Hanoi's entire range of economic and military planning, especially in view of the PRC's propensity to follow up threats with direct action. If Hanoi's planners were to work on the assumption that Beijing's hostility is long lasting, and if the issues of Vietnamese withdrawal from Cambodia and Cambodian independence remain unsolved, then Vietnam would need to be in a constant state of military preparedness, of the level of an alert, for an indefinite period with all its consequences on economic development.

Faced by such a situation, the existence of Vietnam's twin power domains, joined only by a single, lengthy, and inadequate rail link is a strategic disadvantage for Vietnam. This vulnerability of Vietnam to interdiction of its vital sea-borne links between the north and the south would be relevant to any consideration of the reasons as to why Vietnam allowed the USSR fleet to use the bases in Camranh Bay and Danang. The naval strength of the Soviet Union protects the political link between Vietnam's northern and southern cores. Maritime states or groupings of maritime states like ASEAN would need to consider this when hoping for a Soviet naval withdrawal from Southeast Asia and a "loosening" of the Hanoi-Moscow linkage. Another strategic weakness inherent in Vietnam's geopolitical situation lies in the fact that both its core domains are close to rival or potentially rival core domains of neighbouring states, namely the PRC and Cambodia. It is significant that the two major conventional armed conflicts in Southeast Asia after 1945 have both involved core domains in close proximity to one another. Vietnam was involved in both wars.

Significantly again, the third area where power domains meet also involves Vietnam — at the highly sensitive Aranyaprathet sector of the Thai-Cambodian border. The narrow belt separating the north Vietnam core from the Chinese power domain has characteristically been a historic zone of conflict and battle between imperial China and its erstwhile vassal Vietnam. The conflict lies deep in the Kinh psyche and in this area has been romanticized in modern Vietnamese historical literature.[5] The proximity of the Chinese core power domain is a geo-strategic factor which holds Vietnam, especially north Vietnam's core domain, in a state of strategic thraldom.

It is necessary here to distinguish between mountainous frontier zones which are wholly peripheral in terms of power and mountainous frontiers which are only partially peripheral in nature. The latter is largely the case with the frontier tracts of north Vietnam, even though since 1979 the PRC has shown its capacity to unsettle the Vietnamese peripheries. However, even if frontier tracts are not peripheral in power terms they are nonetheless distant from the centres of lowland population and industrial production and moreover are inhabited by minority peoples, not by those of the main ethnic group. Peripherality not in terms of power but in distance and ethnicity is relevant to a state's perception of ultimate threat to its existence. An attack in such a geographically and ethnically peripheral area, especially if accompanied by the attacker's declaration of a limited duration of hostilities, and which stops short of the densely populated plains, serves more as a reminder of a possible repetition of future attacks than as open-ended war to which no swift end is in sight. Significantly, despite Vietnamese threats to counter-attack, they did not follow or harass the PLA when it carried out its announced withdrawal on schedule. This form of limited war involving the stated objective to punish, a declared time limit to the hostilities, restriction to land fighting in the hills, and the avoidance of causing any damage or disturbance in the main ethnic core is the kind of armed coercion ideally tuned to the geo-strategic environment of mainland Southeast Asia. It was also used by the PLA in India's northern frontier in 1962.

China and Vietnam's Northern Peripheries

It has been stated that two important principles in Chinese strategic thinking are *assertion* and *demonstration*. These are of necessity linked. The goal of strategic assertion involves ". . . the readiness to use force quickly and decisively . . .", and is a valuable tool in Chinese strategic planning.[6] The principle of *demonstration* involves military efforts that are aimed at gaining political effect. They would necessitate a conscious decision to escalate hostilities in areas where there is no immediate danger of a conflagration into general war, even though local tensions may persist. The 1979 campaign by the PRC in northern Vietnam is an excellent example of military demonstration largely, but not solely, for political purposes.

> By intervening on a very considerable scale, one establishes a clear precedent for the willingness to use force on subsequent occasions. The specific calculations seem clear: attack in strength: achieve specific tactical objectives (these can obviously vary widely); and cease military activity as soon as practicable, but not in a way to suggest that one's forces might never return. In the attack against Vietnam, the Chinese suffered very considerable casualties, but they also exacted an extremely heavy toll against Vietnam. By launching a limited invasion in defiance of Soviet treaty obligations to Vietnam, the Chinese demonstrated that even in the face of severe risk the PRC would be heard from and respected within the Southeast Asian region.[7]

It is, however, in the longer term that the effects of this demonstration of the willingness and the capacity to use force on a considerable scale in the face of risks would be important to Chinese objectives in mainland Southeast Asia. The withdrawal of PLA divisions from Vietnam did not affect Chinese strength in the border where considerable numbers remained in nearby locations. Vietnam was thereby compelled to redeploy its best units to the far northern frontier. With a far larger army, the PRC is better able to afford to spare troops on a longterm basis than is Vietnam, which in the face of periodic threats of a "second lesson", is compelled to take seriously any such threatening statements and movement of PLA troops and to place many of its élite forces in positions facing China. These élite forces are thus tied down and would not be available for action in other places. The economic cost to Hanoi would also be considerable.

The 1979 Chinese military intervention "has increased the price which Vietnam has been obliged to pay for the sake of asserting a special relationship with its smaller neighbours in Indo-china".[8] The price, it must be added, is to be paid over a protracted period. Part of the price is in the diversion of resources to put the country on a continuous war-footing. Vietnam has had to increase its army through conscription to between 1,023,000 and 1,200,000 men in 1978 alone.[9]

Vietnam's armed involvement in Cambodia and its continued and possibly prolonged watch on the northern frontier does not mean that the PRC has no other ways, or areas, in which to exert further pressure on Hanoi. The physical and cultural conditions of Vietnam's, and Laos', northern boundaries with China make it difficult, if not impossible, to prevent infiltration by a determined opponent. This is apparent in admissions by the Vietnamese that the "tribal" frontier areas bordering on China have been subject to Chinese pressure. It has been stated that

> The tribal people in the northeast border areas have experienced a number of ordeals and complicated developments in their struggle against the Chinese reactionaries in defence of our national sovereignty and the country's border security.[10]

The PRC was alleged to have launched an espionage campaign, psychological war, and "a war of economic sabotage".[11] The tactics used were said to be "nibbling land, shelling and firing . . ." and sending "spies, reconnaisance agents and henchmen across the border into our hamlets and villages in order to collect intelligence information, spread false rumours and incite the people to riot. This they have done in an effort to disrupt our political, economic and social security and our social order, and to disrupt our production and livelihood."[12] The tone of urgency in the *Nhan Dan* article indicated that the border regions have after the Chinese campaign of 1979 been in a state of some instability.

Apparently, the "provocations" go much deeper than mere border skirmishes and raiding or fact-gathering parties. The Chinese it was alleged . . . "have sown divisions among the tribal people and the cadres of the public security force, army, party and administration. . . ."[13] Deviant cadres and party members in the border areas are recruited by the Chinese to set up an underground "double-dealing administration in the service of their war of invasion and subversion. . . ."[14] The nature, scale, and extent of alleged Chinese attempts to destabilize the Vietnamese peripheries reflects all the main elements of the montane region which in the past have been synonymous with the instability and dissent characteristic of the condition of peripherality. Thus it is claimed that: "For a long time the Chinese reactionaries have been infiltrating thousands of their hoodlums, ruffians, cadres, and soldiers disguised as civilians into our territory where they live among our tribal people and operate clandestinely in *all highland villages and hamlets of our northern border regions*" [italics added].[15] The scale and extent of Chinese penetration of Vietnam's far north is indicative of the cross-boundary affinities of language, culture, and outlook shared by minorities on both sides of the boundary, and which the PRC appeared to be utilizing in its campaign of peripheral attrition against Hanoi. Civic action and economic aid to the impoverished minorities by the PRC supports the general encroachment and takes the form of sending "seeds, breeding animals, fertilizer, physicians and even road and bridge engineers across the border to help our tribal people...."[16] The ability to do this on a significant scale is again a pointer to the extent of Chinese influence and penetration of the borderlands since 1979, or perhaps even earlier. The Chinese use of the factors of border-straddling language, ethnicity, kinship ties, and common tribal sympathies is shown in Hanoi's complaint that:

> Among the thousands of Chinese reactionaries who have crossed the border into Bao Lac District, Cao Bang Province, there is one Chinese army colonel who wears tribal Vietnamese clothes and speaks the local dialect. He has also brought his son along and plans to marry him to a tribal girl in order to establish a legal, long-range operational base.[17]

Not only have thousands been moved into one frontier district alone, but active guerrilla warfare appears to have taken place in both the political and military spheres. For it is stated that the Chinese

> have instigated and lured our tribal people into opposing the local public security agents and troops to plunder our people and then distort our party policy, separating the people from the armed forces. They have ... intercepted our public security force and army combatants and cadres ... and robbed them of their weapons. This has created suspicion among the tribal people and undermined their confidence in the regional armed forces.[18]

Despite subsequent claims of a total Vietnamese determination to expose and wipe out the "Chinese reactionary elements" ensconced in the frontier areas, the post-1979 conditions in the borderlands display basic features of a strategic environment reminiscent of the unstable frontiers to be found throughout montane Southeast Asia. The Vietnamese complaints mirror in microcosm the problems of loose borders, dissent, the difficulties of detecting intruders and the border-straddling kinship ties that characterize the turbulence, actual and latent, in the region. That such a situation could arise, despite a rather tight Vietnamese military and political control, is again an indication of the deep-rooted nature of the elements that make up the montane frontier environment and which seem to have survived Vietnamese reorganization of their borderlands. Indeed, in July 1983 the situation had deteriorated, or at least had not improved, to the extent that the Vietnamese stated to the effect that China continued to:

> Send spies, commandos and secret agents to gather intelligence, carry out acts of sabotage and psychological warfare and build bases and even armed forces to be used as an internal force in combination with an eventual second large-scale aggression.[19]

A direct accusation was made in October of the same year, when the Vietnamese Foreign Minister, Nguyen Co Thach, said that the Chinese authorities were training "ten of thousands of mercenaries" in camps in the southern Chinese island of Hainan and in regions north of the Vietnamese frontier.[20]

While this could happen in Vietnam, it is not inconceivable that Chinese penetration of Laos is even more extensive and persuasive. By comparison to Vietnam's northern frontiers, the Laotian areas bordering China are poorly organized from the viewpoint of central control, and minority dissidence is stronger than in Vietnam's north.

Dissatisfaction over the ubiquitous Vietnamese presence in Laos sows the seeds of an anti-Vietnamese reaction among lowland Lao and highland minorities alike. The training of selected refugees in guerrilla warfare both from the minority groups and the Lao for eventual reinfiltration into Laos and the training and stiffening of pro-Chinese minorities within Laos, together with the encouragement of defectors from the Pathet Lao to join in anti-Vietnamese activities, provide China with yet one more arena for pressuring Vietnam's already stretched resources.[21] The ethnic groups of northern Laos have their traditional contacts with larger communities of kinsmen in Yunnan rather than with Hanoi or Vientiane. Chinese cadres have been working for years with the ethnic groups in the area of the Chinese road-making projects in northern Laos, while thousands of the tribals have fled to China. The Chinese have recruited able-bodied men of the minorities from refugee camps in Thailand.[22] An amorphous third front of low-key warfare in north-western and northern Laos remains a possibility that Hanoi's decision-makers must no doubt take account of in their long-range planning.

On their part the Chinese have made numerous complaints over Vietnamese commando-type intrusions into Yunnan and Guangxi which resulted in loss of life and property.

The unequal power relationship between China and Vietnam now weighs heavily on Hanoi's planning processes, because:

For a hundred years, the French provided a countervailing force in relations with China that the Vietnamese had never had.[23]

The unevenness of this power relationship has been further aggravated by Hanoi's decision to acquire militarily the peripheral zones of northwestern and northern Laos. For in so doing the Vietnamese have added the burden of a peripheral domain to themselves. They have not been able to heed Kautilya's injunction to desist from holding territory which is wild and inhospitable, inhabited by hostile tribes and open to the incursions of a powerful foe. Yet not to have done so would have exposed their landward flank to the Chinese. This is yet one more Vietnamese dilemma.

By thus spreading resources over two fronts in Cambodia and in the northern frontiers, and with the possibility of a third front in northwestern Laos, Vietnam has extended its power which has been prevented from focusing on or obtaining dominance in southern mainland Southeast Asia through compelling Thailand to subordinate its interests to those of Hanoi. The often repeated intention of the PRC to come to Thailand's aid in case of a Vietnamese attack on Thailand has been taken seriously by both Hanoi and Bangkok in the post-1979 period and was in itself a considerable factor in the power equation existing in Southeast Asia. This form of support for Thailand and limited material support for the Khmer resistance, though it has not compelled the Vietnamese to evacuate Cambodia, is nevertheless a form of encirclement of Vietnam and a constriction of its present or potential ambitions especially with regard to the creation of a *de facto* Vietnamese-dominated "federation" of the states of Vietnam, Laos, and Cambodia. This distraction on two and possibly three fronts is the major dilemma faced by Hanoi.

Increasing reliance by Hanoi on Soviet support to counter PRC pressure and the USSR's use of naval and air bases in the harbour-rich coast of southern Vietnam which bulges strategically into the South China Sea heightens the perceptions of maritime powers, like the United States, of a Soviet threat in the region. What is often overlooked is the fact that the physical separation of Vietnam's two core domains renders it vulnerable to naval interdiction of communications between north and south. In view of China's growing naval and considerable aerial capacity, the Soviet naval presence on and off the Vietnamese coastline would not be unwelcome to Vietnam. It is likely then that the Soviet use of bases in Vietnam, with the accompanying increased power projective capability in Southeast Asia would continue for some time to come, at least until such a time as the Sino-Soviet rift is healed.

Wider Implications of the Sino-Vietnam Conflict

The post-1975 mood in the United States was one of avoidance of large-scale involvement in land-wars in East and Southeast Asia. The debate in the late 1970s and early 1980s in the United States was on the relative merits of using coastal rim and insular states in a coalition form of defence or alternatively of relying for the major part on naval supremacy alone.[24] In simplified terms, one school of thought in the U.S. would acknowledge Soviet superiority in the Eurasian land mass and would hence rely on maritime supremacy, stressing exploitation of the element that the United States can most readily dominate, viz. the seas. The other school would rely instead on conventional defence effort *via* collective effort with the rim states.[25]

Vietnam has put itself forward as a front-line state of Southeast Asia, acting as a strong bulwark against Chinese "aggression and southward expansion". Its propaganda and even its supposedly scholarly research attempts to depict the Vietnamese as "indigenous Southeast Asians" who among other things developed such distinctly Southeast Asian art forms as the Dongson drums. In the 1980s, with China's slow approach to superpower status of the second degree, this Vietnamese-disseminated perception of a threatening China may gain widening concurrence in the non-communist states of the region. With Soviet aid, Vietnam shows by its seemingly resolute behaviour towards China that in this perception it is indeed acting as a bulwark, or at least as a reliable buffer. In this kind of situation, there may be external compellants for Thailand to loosen its tacit security co-operation with the PRC, or even to break off its links with China altogether. China is a firmly resident power in northern mainland Southeast Asia and is by the circumstances of the geo-power generated in the strategic overarching massif the only state which has the ability to influence or restrain Vietnam, without having to resort constantly to large-scale war. Such attempts to remove Thailand from its "dependency" on China would ignore the intermeshing of China's power with the southern states' affairs in the zones of their peripheral highlands. They would also help to improve the chances for a Soviet-supported Vietnam to gain paramountcy in the southern parts of mainland Southeast Asia.

That the PRC is not antagonistic to the U.S. naval presence in Southeast Asia is significant, for the U.S. Navy can be regarded as the only potential counter-balance to an increasingly powerful Soviet Navy with its global capabilities. Any preoccupation with naval-supported off-shore, or coastal coalition, defence systems in the region of Southeast Asia would also need to recognize that the PRC is a resident coastal state of the region with a long coastline on the South China Sea, which can be regarded as the core sea of Southeast Asia, where the maritime claims and interests of every Southeast Asian state meet.[26] In this context, the growing naval presence of the USSR in the region is as much a potential threat to PRC security as it is to those of non-communist states like the ASEAN grouping. Likewise, a relative dearth of Soviet and Vietnamese power in the interior highlands means that the PRC is less constricted in the pursuance of what it regards as its legitimate security interests in its southern border regions. The attitude of China to the highlands on its south would remain a factor fundamental to the stability of the Southeast Asian region.

★ ★ ★

Divergences of attitudes and policy follow on the differing perceptions of China as a threat to the region. Vietnam's propaganda and diplomacy constantly reiterate the theme that China is the threat to a "non-Chinese Southeast Asia" of which Vietnam is an integral part. This perception is widely shared in the insular states of the region. Indeed, it can be argued that an issue central to the thinking of the regional grouping, ASEAN, is posed in the question: How should China be handled? China can be treated either as a foe, with uncompromising lines drawn to define the extent to which it is regarded as an extraneous power to be kept out of the region or in a working relationship of accommodation in which it is recognized as having certain legitimate security interests in the region to its south. How to respond to the new-found power of China is the emotionally tempered hinge of ASEAN unity.

Maritime powers of any ideological persuasion which plan for either a coalition of coastal states or the purely maritime defence of the insular arc of Southeast Asia or the buttressing of Vietnam, based on the premise of naval supremacy, would need to consider the relative immunity of Chinese power, resting to a large extent on the successful tapping of available geo-power, in northern mainland Southeast Asia, to the projection of naval power, either Soviet or American. This element of immunity to projection of naval power — in itself comprising one more characteristic of geo-power as found in the region — ensconced deep in the hinterlands of Southeast Asia would then be crucial to the region. This is because the PRC's perception of its security interests to its south would be a factor working either for or against stability in mainland Southeast Asia.

It should be noted here that despite past, mainly Maoist, rhetoric and political stances which obscured the issue, China has maintained an essentially defensive military posture.[27] In Korea, in the Himalayas, and in "Indochina" its moves have been basically reactive to externally generated stimuli of real or perceived security threats to its borders. It has been observed that the PRC is concerned more with denying its superpower rivals' control of the region rather than with occupation of lands to its south.[28]

The geo-strategic nature of the PRC's southern borderlands provides an arena *par excellence* for the exercise of counter-balancing moves by Beijing to offset hostile actions farther afield and to which the PRC has no direct answer. In this context, the presence of the Chinese core power domain merging southwards into the mountains of the wider Indochina and maximizing, for the PRC, the available geo-power of the boundary-straddling massif cannot be easily dismissed in any contemplation by maritime powers of moves in both continental and insular Southeast Asia which are designed to meet either the power of the Soviet-Vietnam combination which emerged in the post-1975 situation or the perceived threat of China itself.

NOTES

1. See Adam Fforde, "Problems of Agricultural Development in North Vietnam" (Paper presented to seminar on "Vietnam, Indochina and Southeast Asia", Institute of Social Studies, The Hague, Netherlands Sept/Oct 1980.)
2. David Chandler, "Kampuchea-Vietnam: The Roots of Strife", in *The Vietnam-Kampuchea-China Conflicts*, ed. Malcolm Salmon (Canberra: Australian National University, 1979), pp. 1, 2.
3. Ibid.
4. See *Asian Security 1982* (Tokyo: Research Institute for Peace and Security, 1982), pp. 117–19, and map on p. 118.
5. Dennis Duncanson, "China's Vietnam War: New and Old Strategic Imperatives", *The World Today* 35, no. 6 (June 1979): 244.
6. Jonathan D. Pollack, "The Evolution of Chinese Strategic Thought", in *New Directions in Strategic Thinking*, ed. Robert O'Neill and D.M. Horner (London: George Allen & Unwin, 1981), p. 149.
7. Pollack, op. cit., p. 149.
8. Michael Leifer, "Post Mortem on the Third Indochina War", *The World Today* 35, no. 6 (June 1979): 253.
9. Masashi Nishihara, "The Sino-Vietnamese War of 1979: Only the First Round?", *Southeast Asian Affairs 1980* (Singapore: Institute of Southeast Asian Studies, 1980), p. 70.
10. *Nhan Dan* (Hanoi), 29 September 1981.
11. Ibid.
12. Ibid.

13. Ibid.
14. Ibid.
15. Ibid. The tendency by Hanoi to portray a condition as being worse than it really is in order to make a point has to be kept in mind when making evaluations. With internal problems this tactic is referred to as *kiem thao* or criticism and self-criticism. *Indochina Chronology* 11, no. 2 (April-June 1983): 12–13. However, Hanoi's complaints have been consistent over a number of years to warrant the view that its frontiers with China remain unsettled. Its hyperbole may not be unjustified.
16. Ibid.
17. Ibid.
18. Ibid.
19. *The Age* (Melbourne), 26 July 1983 quoting *Nhan Dan*, undated.
20. *Straits Times* (Singapore), 15 October 1983.
21. See Martin Stuart-Fox, "Laos in China's Anti-Vietnam Strategy", *Asia Pacific Community*, no. 11 (Winter 1982), pp. 83–104.
22. Martin Stuart-Fox, "Laos: The Vietnamese Connection", *Southeast Asian Affairs 1980* (Singapore: Institute of Southeast Asian Studies, 1980), p. 206.
23. Wang Gungwu, "China-Vietnam: Nostalgia for, Rejection of, the Past", in Salmon, op. cit., p. 47.
24. Robert W. Komer, "Maritime Strategy vs. Coalition Defense", *Foreign Affairs*, Summer 1981, pp. 1124–1143.
25. Komer, op. cit.
26. See Lim Joo-Jock, "The South China Sea: Changing Strategic Perspectives", in *Southeast Asian Seas: Frontiers for Development*, ed. Chia Lin Sien and Colin MacAndrews (Singapore: McGraw-Hill, 1981).
27. Arthur Huck, *The Security of China: Chinese Approaches to Problems of War and Strategy* (London: Chatto and Windus for the Institute of Strategic Studies, 1971), p. 93.
28. Michael Yahuda in Lecture to Institute of Strategic and International Studies, Kuala Lumpur, September 1984. See *Sunday Monitor* (Singapore), 9 September 1984.

Conclusion: Southeast Asia and China

For purposes of strategic analysis regions need not necessarily be comprised only of groupings of states, with the outer limits of the region defined by the international boundary lines of the various component states. Boundary definitions of states also have their limitations in strategic analysis. This study has attempted to demonstrate the constrictive nature of conventional definitions of regions and of state boundaries. It indicates the utility of the notion of a geo-strategic region as a tool for analysis.

The concept of a geo-strategic region which has common "unifying" elements that give it a homogeneity and which contrast with those of surrounding territories is useful in viewing strategic problems. Reliance on boundary definitions of states and of regions alone would tend to channel analysis in terms of relations between state A and state B and to view others, such as state C, as being external to a particular region. Hence state C occupies a position and a role implicitly different from those of "internal" states, namely A and B. This study has instead used the montane zone of mainland Southeast Asia as a basic geo-strategic unit of analysis. In doing so, the approach basic to the thrust of the analysis gives perspectives which can cut across boundaries both national and regional.

While recognizing the legitimacy and the undoubtedly important role of international boundary lines, the study indicates that not only should the strategic relations between states in the region be seen in the context of the boundary-defined actor states themselves but also that the boundaries *per se* could usefully be examined in the wider environment of the enveloping geo-strategic region. The changing role of bi-national boundaries, with the attached symbolic aspects of their function, is indicative of the problems facing some states and of the way these states have behaved when faced with problematic situations on their frontiers.

Western-style linear boundaries appear as legal superimpositions on the spatially wider base of the traditional "Asian" concept of frontiers, boundaries and boundary functions. At various times, the phenomenon arises in which both approaches, Western and "Asian", are tacitly followed and implicitly acknowledged as being functionally appropriate.

Boundaries need to be seen against the backdrop of the geo-ethnic dispositions and inter-ethnic competition in which minority groups in the highlands play an important part. In fact, ethnic relations are central to the division between highland and lowlands which in some ways is as significant a dividing line as some interstate boundaries.

The phenomenon of the highland-lowland dichotomy appears to be persistent in time and in space. The existence of a schism within states indicated areally by the power isobars which for the most part are an expression of this same dichotomy poses the question of the influence of this schism on the power potential of states where such cleavages are apparent. Power can be variously defined and measured. Power can, for example, be examined in the context of territory. Here territory has been seen as the unifying base for all forms of power, and is expressed in the concept of territorial power domains. Furthermore a power domain can be divided into the core domain and into varying degrees of peripheral domains, reflecting gradations, or the contours, of a state's "powerness" in its own territory. The existence of the phenomena of peripheral domains is a symptom of a state's condition of internal malaise and is also an indicator which helps explain its external behaviour in relation to other states. Peripherality of parts of a state's possessions arise partly because of historical or current geo-strategic orientations which influence a state's leadership to be more occupied with certain compass directions than with others.

The newer states in striving to attain the ideal of a European-type nation-state often use territoriality as a means of integration but do not as a rule achieve territorial homogeneity. At best they obtain legal ownership over tracts of land. These attempts at territoriality to overcome spatially identifiable primordialisms create political shatter-belts or broad seams of weakness within the geographical limits of aspirant nation-states. These internal fractures can reduce the power of states in absolute terms as well as weaken them in relation to others. They also considerably reduce the strategic options open to the leaders of these states. To treat states invariably as territorially homogeneous blocks would add further impediments to strategic assessments.

The broad pattern emerges of a central montane zone partitioned into

Conclusion: Southeast Asia and China

the territories of different states and fringed by the power peripheries of what are otherwise essentially lowland-centric states. Seen thus, the montane zone is not only central geopolitically in the matter of state-to-state relations in mainland Southeast Asia but is also central to the manner in which these relations are operated. For here, in the central massif the weak and unconsolidated peripheral domains of several states abut on those which are stronger, thus creating a distinct geo-strategic environment.

The existence, as shown by power or political isobars, of core and peripheral domains in a state has yet another strategic connotation. It means that a state with sizeable uncontrolled or undercontrolled peripheries is open to outside interference. The centre's administrative apparatus may be absent altogether in some portions of its peripheries. Such a state is administratively and hence politically incomplete. There would be severe limitations to its sovereignty in its peripheral domains. Such handicaps would mean that the influence of an external actor with politically consolidated mountain tracts could be felt to a considerable degree in the peripheral zones of a state with these spatially defined hindrances to its territorial sovereignty. Within the geo-strategic region the occurrence of territories of varying degrees of hardness in power terms and the location of soft peripheral domains have a direct bearing on the mode of the exercise of power between states.

Where weak peripheral domains are adversely affected by more powerful external sources of power, then bi-national boundaries, already symbolic in terms of unauthorized movement of men and materials, need to be examined in the light of the extent of what can be called zones of power permeation. The north to south permeation of China's power goes beyond its southern boundary lines into the weakest parts of neighbouring peripheral domains, while the direction of Vietnam's east-west power permeation clearly ignores the Laotian-Vietnam boundary line. The post-1975 conflictual situation can be seen against the background of the meeting of the Chinese and Vietnamese zones of power permeation.

There is an ebb and flow in these zones of power permeation depending on changes in the internal organization of states and the international strategic and political environment. They further underline the symbolism of Western-style boundaries in the montane zone. The strategic significance of the power isobars within a state is, therefore, not confined to the state itself. It is intimately connected with the power relationships between states which share common borders in the highlands of this region. Power permeation affects peripheral domains but skirts core domains of affected states.

Vietnam has tried to redress the imbalance in its power relationship with China, by strengthening its border regions, that is by trying to eradicate its internal power isobars, and by cultivating a relationship with the USSR. However, as indicated by Vietnamese pronouncements, the northern highlands of Tonkin still remain a zone liable to power permeation from the PRC.

The general pattern is that even without active intervention peripheral domains subtract from the owner state's power while actually adding, in relative terms, to a better organized neighbour's power. This kind of geo-strategic setting is conducive to the exercise of coercive as well as reward power. Coercive power to be applied need not in this region entail sophisticated weaponry. This is another reminder of environmental propensity to influence warfare, power projection, and dealings between states.

The highlands of south and southwestern China make the PRC a major factor in a power equation which affects the whole of Southeast Asia, including its archipelagic portion. The PRC's political consolidation of its previously peripheral zones in mainland Southeast Asia makes the southern provinces of Guangxi and Yunnan — particularly the latter — a seat of PRC power protruding southwards into "Southeast Asia". Having eradicated its own belts of lower powerness, the southern provinces of the PRC comprise a broad tongue of the Chinese core domain wedged into mainland Southeast Asia. Fringed as it is for the most part by the fractured peripheral domains of relatively small southern states, the capacity for the PRC to project power and influence into mainland Southeast Asia is considerably enhanced. In this sense, the power relationships between China and its southern neighbours, by their very nature and their compass, make the southern and southwestern provinces of China inextricably a part of the strategic environment of the mainland or continental Southeast Asia.

Possession of the island of Hainan and of the Paracels, together with its claims to the Spratley Islands, compels China to take an active interest in the maritime affairs of Southeast Asia. Its long, harbour-rich littoral fronting the South China Sea was the basis of prolonged historical contacts with insular Southeast Asia. Geo-strategically this makes China a regional maritime state by virtue of location, residency, and interests. The South China Sea is the central sea of Southeast Asia for its shores are shared by every Southeast Asian state with the exception of Laos and Burma. Claims of extended maritime jurisdiction have resulted in the South China Sea being the arena where the interests of all coastal states meet and often overlap in a physical convergence of conflicting interests. The maritime nature of China-in-Southeast Asia together with the strategic advantages it holds in the mountains deep in continental Southeast Asia mean that China is no longer an external actor, in the same category as the United States and the USSR, in the affairs of Southeast Asia. With the mountains of the mainland largely immune to the projection of naval power, China maintains the strategic flexibility of being able to exercise the weight of its presence in two mutually exclusive strategic regions. PRC power for the present is more heavily felt in the mountains. The seas and the uplands provide China with the prerequisites for the adoption of a flexibly dualistic strategic approach in the solution of security issues to its south.

In the mountain zone, the territorially-expressed sovereignties of all the states of mainland Southeast Asia meet with the exception of Cambodia. The geo-strategic environment of this region has an effect on states which have a territorial share in it. At one time or another all states have found their mountainous possessions to be problematic, especially when it came to absorption, subjugation, or integration, as the case may be, into the main body politic of the state.

Yunnan has been described by Owen Lattimore as the "pivot on which events in Southeast Asia are likely to turn after the war".* The position of PRC power and influence can be expressed in terms of the seepage southwards of elements of its power. Just as political or power isobars differentiate between the areas of firm power and weakened power of a state, so can these power isobars denote the areas beyond boundary lines where PRC power is felt southwards in gradually lessening gradations. While historically, the northern and northwestern frontiers were fluid and were zones of contention between China and the mainly nomadic tribes, the south received relatively little attention. With the drawing of a Western-style boundary in the north, northwest, and west, China now has for the first time a line, so far stable, which clearly delineates its own territories** and hence defines its spatial relations with the USSR.

In contrast, the situation in the southwest and south is markedly different. The geo-strategic environment has as one of its aspects a fluidity which favours the more organized at the expense of the less organized. Its unique nature generates latent geo-power, strengthens the better administered and weakens further the poorly administered

---

*Owen Lattimore, "Yunnan, Pivot of Southeast Asia", *Foreign Affairs*, April 1943, p. 493.
**Wang Gungwu in commentary on D. McMillen, "Chinese Perspectives on International Security" (Paper presented at Conference on "Asian Perspectives on International Security" held at the ANU, Canberra, in April 1983).

and less organized states. The historical influence China had beyond its borders in the south is likely to be reasserted not through the previous dominance of sheer cultural superiority, but through utilization of the factors of geo-power in the areas of its southern borderlands. The broad tracts of the geostrategic massif, like the sea, provides an arena where power can be projected without incurring the risk of full-scale war. This exercise of power can be achieved with minimal cost.

The strategic nature of the montane region allows for such excursions of power to take place in conditions of peace, or more correctly of non-war. This condition of subdued conflict is seen in the low-key hostilities, mostly of strife internal to states, in remote areas which has been a feature of the montane region ever since World War II. If stability is equated with an absence of war or of large-scale fighting, then the region appears to show a peculiar equilibrium in which there is overall stability in the relationships between states. This larger stability encompasses the lesser instabilities which occur at village, local, or district level and in which hostilities can often be fierce. These lesser instabilities are largely within the territories of states, while the larger stability characterizes the region as a whole with the notable exception, once again, of the easternmost portion of the region, that is the Sino-Vietnam border region. There the power based on the parent, Sinic culture faces a smaller Sinic-derived state, which has rejected the notion that China is reverting to its historical role as the regional hierarch. The proximity of the Chinese core domain to Vietnam's has had the effect of exacerbating friction. However, it does not mean that this condition of mutual hostility is a permanent feature of Sino-Vietnam relations. When there has been friendship and cooperation, the juxtaposition or their core domain allows for an intimate relationship, the benefits of which were demonstrated to Vietnam during the Vietnam War and which proved to be crucial to the Vietnamese war effort, especially when it involved the question of what Zhou Enlai referred to as "reliable rear areas".

Geo-strategic characteristics have given rise to the feature of a larger stability containing the lesser instabilities. Upholding of this larger over-arching regional stability depends to a vital degree on China's perception of the emergence of security threats to its south. The lesser, localized turmoil contained by the greater equilibrium is to some extent in the interests of the PRC. The potential for widespread regional instability, however, remains considerable. The national weaknesses as portrayed by extensive peripheral domains and unguarded boundaries allows scope for either one- or two-way interventions. The foundation of the greater stability thus rests largely on the behaviour of the dominant power in the montane zone and its desire for, and emphasis on, smooth inter-state relations rather than ideological linkages with dissidents in the smaller states.

Essentially, territorial power is intimately linked to the ways by which states attempt to manage their highland possessions. The states which share the montane zone between themselves have proceeded along different lines in their attempts — either through territoriality, human contact or the granting of local autonomy — at incorporating their peripheral domains into their lowland-based cores. By their different reactions to the strategic features of the montane zone, the various states, more often than not hampered by traditional geo-strategic orientatious have either added to, or depleted their national power. Those states which have successfully tapped the available sources of geo-power have a strategic advantage over their neighbours which have neglected, or have been unable, to realise the power potential latent in the combination of geo-strategic factors of the region. The negative facet of this latency becomes apparent when in the evolving strategic environment outer territorial belts of depleted indispensability begin to coincide with occurrences of increasing ethnic unreliability within states.

Thus there is a picture of a mountainous belt where territorial power domains of greatly varying quality meet and overlap and which functions in a basic way in inter-state relationships, influencing the manner in which these relationships are conducted. The location and role of this strategically over-arching and central massif spanning the weakest seams of the lowland-centric states and dominated by China would call to question the actual northern limits of "Southeast Asia".

Furthermore, policies which invoke the need for total exclusion or contrived limitation of the PRC from the political and security affairs of Southeast Asia need to be examined in the light of what are basically unequal geo-power configurations obtaining in the interiors of mainland Southeast Asia which affect the entire region and which have consequences reaching far beyond.

Bibliography

Adams, Nina S. and Alfred W. McCoy, eds. *Laos: War and Revolution*. New York: Harper and Row, 1970.
Ali Mazrui. "Ethnic Stratification and the Military Argrarian Complex: The Uganda Case", in *Ethnicity: Theory and Experience*, ed. Nathan Glazer and Daniel P. Moynihan, pp. 420–549. Cambridge: Harvard University Press, 1975.
Ambruster, Frank F. et al., eds. *Can We Win in Vietnam?* New York: Praeger, 1968.
Ancel, Jacques. *La Géographie des Frontières*. Paris: Gallimard, 1938.
Anderson, Benedict. *Imagined Communities: Reflections on the Origin and Spread of Nationalism*. London: Verso, 1980.
Armacost, Michael. "Comments on Robert W. Schwabb III, 'America's Golden Triangle' ". *Journal of Contemporary Asia* 8, no. 4 (1978): 584–94.
Aung Kin. "Burma 1979: Socialism with Foreign Aid and Strict Neutrality". In *Southeast Asian Affairs 1980*, pp. 93–120. Singapore: Institute of Southeast Asian Studies, 1980.
Badgley, John H. "Burma's China Crisis: The Choices Ahead". *Asian Survey* 7, no. 11 (November 1967).
Beaufre, Andre. *Strategy for Tomorrow*. London: McDonald James, 1974.
Bell, R. et al., eds. *Political Power: A Reader in Theory and Research*. New York: The Free Press, 1969.
Bernatzik, Hugo Adolf. *Akha and Miao: Problems of Applied Ethnography in Further India*. Translated from German by Alois Nagler. Conn., New Haven: Human Relations Area Files, 1970.
Blau, Peter. "Differentiation of Power". In *Political Power: A Reader in*

Theory and Research, edited by R. Bell et al. New York: The Free Press, 1969.
Buchan, Alastair. *Change Without War*. London: Chatto and Windus, 1974.
Burling, Robbins. *Hill Farms and Padi Fields: Life in Mainland Southeast Asia*. Englewood Cliffs, N.J.: Parentice Hall, 1965.
Burnett, Alain and Peter J. Taylor, eds. *Political Studies from Spatial Perspectives: Anglo American Essays on Political Geography*. Chichester: John Wiley & Sons, 1981.
Cady, John F. *A History of Modern Burma*. Ithaca: Cornell University Press, 1958.
_____. *The United States and Burma*. Cambridge, Mass.: Harvard University Press, 1976.
Calwell, C.E. *Small Wars: Their Principle and Practice*. London: His Majesty's Stationery Office, 1906.
Carey, Iskander. *Orang Asli: The Aboriginal Tribes of Malaysia*. Kuala Lumpur: OUP, 1976.
Cartwright, Dorwin, ed. *Studies in Social Power*. Ann Arbor: University of Michigan, 1959.
Chandler, David. "Kampuchea-Vietnam: The Roots of Strife". In *The Vietnam-Kampuchea-China Conflicts*, ed. Malcolm Salmon. Canberra: Australian National University, 1979.
Channarong Tacharracharkit. *China's Foreign Policy Toward Burma and Thailand*. Ann Arbor: University Microfilms, 1980.
Chen, King C., ed. *The Foreign Policy of China*. Seton Hall University Press, 1972.
Chi, Chao-ting. *Key Economic Areas in Chinese History*. First published London: George Allen and Unwin, 1936; reprint ed., New York: Paragon Book Reprint Corp., 1963.
Chia Lin Sien and Colin MacAndrews, eds. *Southeast Asian Seas: Frontiers for Development*. Singapore: McGraw-Hill, 1981.
Chong, Li-Choy. "International Development and International Dependence: A Study of Aid and Social Development". D. Soc. Sc. thesis, University of Bielefeld, 1977, University Microfilms International, Ann Arbor, 1977.
Cline, Ray S. *World Power Assessment: A Calculus of Strategic Drift*. Boulder, Col.: Westview Press, 1975.
Cohen, Saul B. *Geography and Politics in a Divided World*. London: Methuen, 1964.
Constitution of the People's Republic of China (PRC). *Documents of the First Session of the First National Congress of the PRC*. Beijing, 1955.

Cottrell, Alvin J. and R.M. Burrell. *The Indian Oceans: Its Political, Economic and Military Importance.* New York: Praeger, 1972.

Crane, Robert D. *The Role of Ethnic Nationalism in the Modernization and Stabilization of the Third World.* Discussion Paper. Hudson Institute, 13 December 1967.

De Vos, George and Lola Romanucci, eds. *Ethnic Identity.* Palo Alto: Mayfield, 1975.

Despres, Leo, ed. *Ethnicity and Resource Competition in Plural Societies.* The Hague: Mouton Publishers, 1976.

Dessaint, W.Y. and A.Y. "Economic Systems and Ethnic Relations in Northern Thailand". *Contributions to Southeast Asian Ethnography,* no. 1 (Singapore, September 1982).

Desschamps, H. and P. Chauvet. *Gallieni pacificateur* (Paris 1949).

Deutsch, Karl W. "The Growth of Nations: Some Recurrent Patterns of Political and Social Integration". *World Politics,* (1952–53): 168–95; also in *Southeast Asia: The Politics of National Integration,* ed. John T. McAlister, Jr., pp. 18–41. New York: Random House, 1973.

———. *The Analysis of International Relations.* Englewood Cliffs, N.J.: Prentice-Hall, 1968, p. 29.

Dommen, Arthur J. "Separatist Tendencies in Eastern India". *Asian Survey* 7, no. 10 (October 1967): 737.

———. *Conflicts in Laos: The Politics of Neutralization* New York: Praeger, 1971, footnote p. 342.

Dreyer, June Teufel. *China's Forty Millions.* Cambridge Mass.: Harvard University Press, 1976.

Duncanson, Dennis. "China's Vietnam War: New and Old Strategic Imperatives". *The World Today* 35, no. 6 (June 1979).

Earle, Edward Mead, ed. *Makers of Modern Strategy: Military Thought from Machiavelli to Hitler.* Princeton: Princeton University Press, 1948.

East, W.G., O.H.K. Spate, and C.A. Fisher. *The Changing Map of Asia.* London: Methuen, 1971.

Emerson, Rupert. "The Nature of the Nation". In *Southeast Asia: The Politics of National Integration,* ed. John McAlister, Jr. New York: Random House, 1973.

Enloe, Cythia H. *Ethnic Conflict and Political Development.* Boston: Little Brown, 1973.

———. *Ethnic Soldiers: State Security in a Divided Society.* Middlesex, England: Penguin, 1980.

Esman, Milton J. "Communal Conflict in Southeast Asia". In *Ethnicity: Theory and Experience,* ed. Nathan Glazer and Daniel P.

Moynihan. Cambridge, Mass.: Harvard University Press. 1975.
Fairbank, John K., ed. *The Chinese World Order*. Cambridge, Mass.: Harvard University Press, 1968, p. 8.
———. "China's Foreign Policy in Historical Perspective". *Foreign Affairs*, April 1969, p. 457.
Fall, Bernard B. *Street Without Joy*. Harrisburg, P.A.: Stackpole Co., 1961.
———. "The Pathet Lao; a 'Liberation' Party". In *The Communist Revolution in Asia: Tactics, Goals and Achievements*, ed. Robert A. Scalapino. Englewood Cliffs, N.J.: Prentice-Hall, 1965.
———. *Last Reflections on a War*. Garden City, N.Y.: Doubleday, 1967.
Fei, Hsiao-Tung and Chih-I Chang. *Earthbound China: A Study of Rural Economy in Yunnan*. London: Routledge & Kegan Paul, 1948, pp. 282–83.
Feingold, David. "Opium and Politics in Laos". In *Laos: War and Revolution*, ed. Nina S. Adams and Alfred W. McCoy. New York: Harper and Row, 1970.
Fforde, Adam. "Problems of Agricultural Development in North Vietnam". Paper presented to seminar on "Vietnam, Indochina and Southeast Asia", Institute of Social Studies, The Hague, Netherlands, Sept/Oct 1980.
Fifield, Russel Hunt. *Southeast Asia in United States Policy*. New York: Praeger, 1967.
———. *The Diplomacy of Southeast Asia: 1945–1958*. Hamden, Hamden, Conn.: Archon Books, 1968.
Fisher, Charles A., ed. *Essays in Political Geography*. London: Methuen, 1968.
Fitzgerald, C.P. *The Chinese View of their Place in the World*. London: Oxford University Press, 1969.
Fox, James C. "An Anthropologist's View". In *Southeast Asian Studies in China: A Report*, ed. Wang Gungwu et al. Canberra: Research School of Pacific Studies, Australian National University, 1981.
Franda, Marcus F. *Northeastern India in the Wake of Vietnam*. American Universities Fieldstaff Reports, South Asia Series 19, no. 13 (August 1975).
Fraser, Stewart E. "Vietnam's 1980 Census: Current Position and Future Outlook". *Contemporary Southeast Asia* 3, no. 3 (December 1981).
French, John R.P. and Bertram Raven. "The Bases of Social Power". In *Studies in Social Power*, ed. Dorwin Cartwright, pp. 150–67. Ann Arbor: University of Michigan, 1959.

Fryer, Donald W. *Emerging Southeast Asia*. 2nd ed. London: George Phillip and Son, 1979.
Gardner, Matthew M., Jr. "The Heritage of South Asian Borders". *SAIS Review* 13, no. 2 (Winter 1969).
Geertz, Clifford. "Primordial Sentiments and Civil Politics in New States: The Integrative Revolution". In *Southeast Asia: The Politics of National Integration*, ed. John T. McAlister, Jr. New York: Random House, 1973.
Girling, J.L.S. *People's War: Conditions and Consequences in China and South East Asia*. New York: Praeger, 1969.
Gittinger, J. Price. *Terminal Report of J. Price Gittinger*. U.S. Operations Mission to Vietnam, Saigon, 1957.
Glazer, Nathan and Daniel P. Moynihan, eds. *Ethnicity: Theory and Experience*. Cambridge: Harvard University Press, 1975.
Gottmann, Jean. "Bugeaud, Gallieni, Lyautey: The Development of French Colonial Warfare". In *Makers of Modern Strategy: Military Thought from Machiavelli to Hitler*, ed. Edward Mead Earle. Princeton: Princeton University Press, 1948.
─────. *The Significance of Territory*. Charlottesville: University Press of Virginia, 1973.
─────. "Organising and Reorganising Space". In *Centre and Periphery: Spatial Variation in Politics*, ed. Jean Gottman. Beverly Hills, London: Sage 1980.
Gottmann, Jean, ed. *Centre and Periphery: Spatial Variation in Politics*. Beverly Hills, London: Sage, 1980.
Gray, Jack, ed. *Modern China's Search for a Political Forum*. London: Oxford University Press, 1969.
Guyot, James F. "Ethnic Segmentation in Military Organisations: Burma and Malaysia". In *Political-Military Systems, Comparative Perspectives*, ed. Catherine McArdle Kelleher, pp. 27–37. Beverly Hills: Sage, 1974.
Hartshorne, Richard. "Morphology of the State Area: Significance of the State". In *Essays in Political Geography*, ed. Charles A. Fisher. London: Methuen, 1968.
Harvey, G.E. *British Rule in Burma*. London: Faber & Faber, 1946.
Heaton, William R. "China and Southeast Asian Communist Movements: The Decline of Dual Track Diplomacy". *Asian Survey* 22, no. 8 (August 1982).
Hewison, Kevin J. "Revolutionary Warfare in Thailand". *Australian Outlook* 34, no. 2 (August 1980).
Holmes, A. "China-Burma Relations Since the Rift". *Asian Survey* 12, no. 8 (August 1972).

Hong Lysa. *Thailand in the Nineteeth Century: Evolution of the Economy and Society*. Singapore: Institute of Southeast Asian Studies, 1984.

Huang, Yu-mei. "Guerrilla Veterans: Retire to a High Mountain Ranch". *Free China Review* 33, no. 1 (January 1983).

Huck, Arthur. *The Security of China: Chinese Approaches to Problems of War and Strategy*. London: Chatto and Windus for the Institute of Strategic Studies, 1971.

Huxley, Tim. *Indochina and Insurgency in the Asean States 1975–1981*. Working Paper no. 67. Canberra: The Strategic and Defence Studies Centre, Australian National University, January 1983.

Huynh Kim Khanh. *Vietnamese Communism 1925–1945*. Ithaca: Cornell University Press, 1982.

James, Preston E. "Some Fundamental Elements in the Analysis of the Viability of States." In *Essays in Political Geography*, ed. Charles A. Fisher. London: Methuen, 1968.

Johnson, G. "Terrain: Let's Not Just Add a Multiplier". *Military Review*, January 1982.

Kahin, George McT. "Minorities in the Democratic Republic of Vietnam". *Asian Survey* 12, no. 7 (July 1968).

Kahn, Herman. "On the Possibilities for Victory or Defeat". In *Can We Win in Vietnam?* ed. Frank E. Ambruster et al. New York: Praeger, 1968.

Kanok Wongtrangan. "The Revolutionary Strategy of the Communist Party of Thailand: Change and Persistence". In *Armed Communist Movements in Southeast Asia*, edited by Lim Joo-Jock and Vani S. Singapore: Institute of Southeast Studies, 1984.

Kautilya. *Arthashastra*. Translated by R. Shamasastry. 8th edition. Mysore: Sri Raghuveer Printing Press, 1951.

Kelleher, Catherine McArdle, ed. *Political-Military Systems, Comparative Perspectives*. Beverly Hills, London: Sage, 1974.

Keyes, Charles E., ed. *Ethnic Change*. Seattle: University of Washington Press, 1981.

Kirk, William. "The Inner Asian Frontiers of India". *Transactions*, XXXI (Institute of British Geographers, December 1962).

Komer, Robert W. "Maritime Strategy vs Coalition Defense". *Foreign Affairs*, Summer 1981.

Kundstadter, Peter. *Southeast Asian Tribes, Minorities and Nations*. Princeton: Princeton University Press, 1967.

_____. "Ethnic Group, Category and Identity: Karen in Northern Thailand". In *Ethnic Change*, ed. Charles E. Keyes. Seattle: University of Washington Press, 1981.

Kyaw Thet. "Burma: The Political Integration of Linguistic and Religious Minorities". In *Nationalism and Progress in Free Asia*. Baltimore: Johns Hopkins Press, 1965.

Lamb, Alistair. Asian *Frontiers*. New York: Praeger, 1968.

Lattimore, Owen. "Yunnan, Pivot of Southeast Asia". *Foreign Affairs*, April 1943.

———. *Inner Asian Frontiers of China*. American Geographical Society of New York, 1951.

———. "The Periphery as a Locus of Innovation". In *Centre and Periphery: Spatial Variation in Politics*, ed. Jean Gottmann. Beverly Hills, London: Sage, 1980.

Leach, E.R. *Political Systems of Highland Burma*. Boston: Beacon Press, 1968.

———. "The Frontiers of 'Burma' ". In *Southeast Asia: The Politics of National Integration*, ed. John T. McAlister Jr., p. 330. New York: Random House, 1973. This article was originally published in *Comparative Studies in Society and History* (Cambridge: Cambridge University Press, 1960).

LeBar, Frank M. and Adrienne Suddard, eds. *Laos: Its People, Its Society, Its Culture*. Conn., New Haven: Human Relations Area Files, 1960.

LeBar, Frank M., Gerald C. Hickey, and John K. Musgrave, eds. *Ethnic Groups of Mainland Southeast Asia*. Conn., New Haven: Human Relations Area Files Press, 1964.

Lebra, Joyce C. *Japanese Trained Armies in Southeast Asia*. Hong Kong: Heinemann, 1979.

Lee, Yong Leng. *The Razor's Edge: Boundaries and Boundary Disputes in Southeast Asia*. Singapore: Institute of Southeast Asian Studies, 1980.

Lehman, F.K. "Ethnic Categories in Burma and the Theory of Social Systems". In *Southeast Asian Tribes, Minorities and Nations*, ed. Peter Kunstadter. Vol. 1. Princeton: Princeton University Press, 1967.

———. *The Structure of Chin Society*. Urbana: University of Illinois Press, 1963.

Leifer, Michael. *The Foreign Relations of New States*. Camberwell, Victoria: Longman, 1974.

———. *Nationalism, Revolution and Evolution in South-East Asia*. Zug, Interdocumentation Co., 1970.

———. "Post Mortem on the Third Indochina War". *The World Today* 35, no. 6 (June 1975).

———. *Conflict and Regional Order in Southeast Asia*. Adelphi Paper no. 162. London: International Institute for Strategic Studies, 1980.

Lim Joo-Jock. *Geo-Strategy and the South China Sea Basin: Regional Balance, Maritime Issues, Future Patterns*. Singapore: Singapore University Press, 1979.

_____. "The South China Sea: Changing Strategic Perspectives". In *Southeast Asian Seas: Frontiers for Development*, ed. Chia Lin Sien and Colin MacAndrews. Singapore: McGraw-Hill, 1981.

Lim Joo-Jock and Vani S., eds. *Armed Communist Movements in Southeast Asia*. Singapore: Institute of Southeast Asian Studies, 1984.

Lim Joo-Jock and Vani S., eds. *Armed Separatism in Southeast Asia*. Singapore: Institute of Southeast Asia Studies, 1984.

Lintner, Bertil. "The Shans and the Shan State of Burma". *Contemporary Southeast Asia* 5, no. 4 (March 1984): 405–50.

Liss, Howard. *The Mighty Mekong*. New York: Hawthorn, 1967.

Liu Po-ch'eng. "Looking Back on the Long March". In *The Long March: Eyewitness Accounts*. Beijing: Foreign Languages Press, 1959.

Lyon, Peter. *War and Peace in South-East Asia*. London: OUP, 1969.

Machiavelli. *The Art of War*. Book 4.

Mackie, J.A.C. "China Report". In *Southeast Asian Studies in China: A Report*, ed. Wang Gungwu et al. Canberra: Research School of Pacific Studies, Australian National University, 1981.

Mahan, Alfred Thayer. *The Influence of Sea Power Upon History*. London: Sampson Low, Martan & Co., 1982.

Mao Tse-tung. *On Protracted War*. 3rd ed. Beijing: Foreign Languages Press, 1967.

Maran La Raw. "Toward a Basis for Understanding the Minorities in Burma: The Kachin Example". In *Southeast Asia: The Politics of National Integration* ed. John T. McAlister Jr., p. 345. New York: Random House, 1973.

Marr, David G. *Vietnamese Anticolonialism 1885–1925*. Berkeley: University of California Press, 1971.

Martin, L.W. *The Sea in Modern Strategy*. London: Chatto and Windus, 1967.

Marwah, O. and J.D. Pollack, eds. *Military Power and Policy in Asian States*. Boulder, Colorado: Westview Press, 1980.

Maxwell, Neville. *India's China War*. London: Cape, 1971.

McAlister, John T. Jr. "Mountain Minorities and the Vietminh: A Key to the Indochina War". In *Southeast Asian Tribes, Minorities and Nations*, ed. Peter Kunstadter. New Jersey: Princeton University Press, 1967.

―――, ed. *Southeast Asia: The Politics of National Integration*. New York: Random House, 1973.

McCoy, Alfred W., Cathleen B. Read, and Leonard P. Adams II. *The Politics of Heroin in Southeast Asia*. New York: Harper and Row, 1972.

McVey, Ruth T., ed. *Southeast Asian Transitions: Approaches Through Social History*. New Haven: Yale University Press, 1968.

―――. "Separatism and the Paradox of the Nation-State in Perspective". In *Armed Separatism in Southeast Asia*, ed. Lim Joo-Jock and Vani S. Singapore: Institute of Southeast Asia Studies, 1984.

Means, Gordon P. "Cease Fire Politics in Nagaland". *Asian Survey* 19 (October-November 1971).

Morell, David and Chai-Anan Samudavanija. *Political Conflict in Thailand: Reform, Reaction, Revolution*. Cambridge, Mass.: Oelgeschlager, Gunn & Hain, 1981.

Morley, James William, ed. *The Fateful Choice: Japan's Advance into Southeast Asia, 1939-1941*. New York: Columbia University Press, 1980.

Moseley, George V.H. III. *The Consolidation of the South China Frontier*. Berkeley: University of California Press, 1973.

Mote, F.W. "The Rural Haw of Northern Thailand". In *Southeast Asian Tribes, Minorities and Nations*, ed. P. Kunstadter, pp. 487-524. Princeton: Princeton University Press, 1967.

Mozingo, David. "Communist China: Its Southern Border Lands". *SAIS Review* 12, no. 2 (Winter 1968): 43-54.

Nguyen Khac Vien, ed. *Mountain Regions and National Minorities in the D.R. of Vietnam*. Vietnamese Studies no. 15. Hanoi, 1968.

Nishihara, Masashi. "The Sino-Vietnamese War of 1979: Only the First Round?". In *Southeast Asian Affairs 1980*. Singapore: Institute of Southeast Asian Studies, 1980.

Noone, Richard. *Rape of the Dream People*. London: Hutchinson, 1972.

Northedge, F.S., ed. *The Use of Force in International Relations*. London: Faber & Faber, 1974.

Nusit Chindarsi. *The Religion of the H'mong Njua*. Bangkok: The Siam Society, 1976.

O'Ballance, Edgar. *The Wars in Vietnam 1954-1973*. New York: Hippocrene Books, 1975.

O'Neill, Robert. "Insurgency and Sub-National Violence". In *New Directions in Strategic Thinking*, ed. Robert O'Neill and D.M. Horner. London: George Allen and Unwin, 1981.

O'Neill, Robert and D.M. Horner, eds. *New Directions in Strategic*

Thinking. London: George Allen & Unwin, 1981.
Odaka, Kunio. *Economic Organization of the Li Tribes of Hainan Island*. Ann Arbor: University Microfilms, c. 1950.
Parsons, Talcott. "On the Concept of Political Power". In *Political Power: A Reader in Theory and Research*, ed. R. Bell et al., p. 251. New York: The Free Press, 1969.
Pauker, Guy J. "Indonesian Perspectives on the Indian Ocean". In *The Indian Ocean: Its Political, Economic and Military Importance*, ed. Alvin J. Cottrell and R.M. Burrell. New York: Praeger, 1972.
Pauker, Guy J., Frank H. Golay and Cynthia H. Enloe. *Diversity and Development in Southeast Asia: The Coming Decade*. New York: McGraw-Hill, 1977.
Pearn, B.R., ed. *Military Operations in Burma, 1890–1892: Letters from Lieutenant J.K. Watson, K.R.R.C.*. Data Paper no. 64, Southeast Asia Program. Ithaca, New York: Cornell University, 1967.
Pollack, Jonathan D. "China as a Military Power". In *Military Power and Policy in Asian States*, ed. O. Marwah and J.D. Pollack. Boulder, Colorado: Westview Press, 1980.
_____. "The Evolution of Chinese Strategic Thought". In *New Directions in Strategic Thinking*, ed. Robert O'Neill and D.M. Horner. London: George Allen and Unwin, 1981.
Pounds, Norman J.G. *Political Geography*. New York: McGraw-Hill, 1963.
Pounds, Norman J.G. and Sue Simonds Ball. "Core Areas and the Development of the European State System". *Annals of the Association of American Geographers* 54 (1964).
Powell, Geoffrey. *The Kandyan Wars: The British Army in Ceylon 1803–1818*. London: Leo Cooper and Kandy: K.V.G. de Silva and Sons, 1973.
Preeda Chantagul. "Forest Village: A Vehicle for Reforestation and Rural Development". Paper delivered at the CCSEAS-ISEAS Joint International Conference, Singapore, June 1982.
Prescott, J.R.V. *Map of Mainland Asia by Treaty*. Clayton: Melbourne University Press, 1975.
Quang Canh. "Economic Transformation of the Highlands". In *Mountain Regions and National Minorities in the D.R. of Vietnam*, ed. Nguyen Khac Vien. Vietnamese Studies no. 15. 1968.
Quinn-Judge, Sophie, translator. "The Family and Family Relationships of the Tay and Nung People". *Journal of Ethnology*, no. 2 (Hanoi, 1979); the article was reproduced in "Southeast Asia Ethnicity and Development Newsletter" 5, no. 2 (Singapore, 1981).

Race, Jeffrey. "The War in Northern Thailand". *Modern Asian Studies* 8, no. 1 (January 1974).
Ratzel, Friedrich. *Politische Geographie*. (Munich: R. Oldenbourg, 1897) and "Die Geztz des raumlichen Wachstums der Staaten". In *Petermanns Mitteilungen* (1896).
Rokkan, S. "Dimensions of State Formation and Nation-Building: a possible paradigm for research in variations within Europe". In *The Formation of Nation States in Western Europe*, ed. C. Tilley, pp. 318–65. New Jersey: Princeton University Press, 1975.
――――. "Territories, Centres and Peripheries: toward a geoethnic-geoeconomic-geopolitical model of differentiation within Western Europe". In *Centre and Periphery: Spatial Variation in Politics*, ed. Jean Gottmann, pp. 163–204. Beverly Hills, London: Sage, 1980.
Rona, Thomas P. *Our Changing Geopolitical Premises*. New Brunswick: Transaction Books, 1982.
Roy, Jules. *The Battle of Dienbienphu*. Translated by Robert Baldick. Introduction by Neil Shoehan. London: Faber and Faber, 1965.
Sack, Robert D. "Territorial Bases of Power". In *Political Studies from Spatial Perspectives: Anglo American Essays on Political Geography*, ed. Alain D. Burnett and Peter J. Taylor. Chichester: John Wiley and Sons, 1981.
Salmon, Malcolm, ed. *The Vietnam-Kampuchean-China Conflicts*. Canberra: Australian National University, 1979.
Sao Saimong Mangrai. *The Shan States and the British Annexation*. Data Paper no. 57, Southeast Asia Program. Ithaca: Cornell University, 1965.
Sarasin Viraphol. *Tribute and Profit: Sino-Siamese Trade 1952–1853*. Harvard: Council of East Asian Studies, 1977.
Scalapino, Robert A. *The Communist Revolution in Asia: Tactics, Goals & Achievements*. Englewood Cliffs, N.J.: Prentice-Hall, 1965.
Schier, Pieter and Manola Schier Oum in collaboration with Waldtraut Jarke. *Prince Sihanouk on Cambodia: Interviews and Talks with Prince Norodom Sihanouk*. Hamburg: Mitteilungen des Instituts für Asienkunde, 1980.
Schram, Stuart. *Mao Tse Tung*. Middlesex: Penguin, 1967. Quoting Liu Po-ch'eng, "Looking Back on the Long March". In *The Long March: Eyewitness Accounts*. Peking: Foreign Languages Press, 1959.
Schweinfurth, Ulrich, "The Problem of Nagaland". In *Essays in Political Geography*, ed. Charles A. Fisher. London: Methuen, 1968.
Scoffer, A. "The Wars of Israel in Sinai". *Military Reviews*, April 1982.

Silverstein, Josef. "Politics in the Shan State". *Journal of Asian Studies* 18, no. 1 (1958).
──────. *Burmese Politics: the Dilemma of National Unity*. New Brunswick, N.J.: Rutgers University Press, 1980.
──────. *Burma: Military Rule and the Politics of Stagnation*. Ithaca: Cornell University Press, 1977.
Sivard, Ruth Leger. *World Military and Social Expenditures 1982*. Leasburg, Virginia: World Priorities, 1982.
Skinner, Elliot P. "Competition within Ethnic Systems in Africa". In *Ethnicity and Resource Competition in Plural Societies*, ed. Leo Despres, pp. 131 – 57. The Hague: Mouton Publishers, 1975.
Smith, Charles B., Jr. *The Burmese Communist Party in the 1980s*. Singapore: Institute of Southeast Asian Studies, 1984.
Snow, Edgar. *Red Star Over China*. Introduction by John K. Fairbank. New York: Grove Press, 1961.
──────. *The Other Side of the River*. London: Victor Gollancz, 1966.
Solomon, Robert L. "Boundary Concepts and Practices in Southeast Asia". *World Politics* 23, no. 1 (October 1970): 1 – 16.
Steinberg, David I. "Burma: Ne Win After Two Decades". *Current History* 79, no. 461 (December 1980).
──────. *Burma's Road Toward Development: Growth and Ideology under Military Rule*. Boulder, Col.: Westview Press, 1981.
──────. *Burma: Profile of a Socialist Southeast Asian Nation*. Boulder, Col.: Westview Press, 1982.
──────. "Constitutional and Political Bases of Minority Insurrections in Burma". In *Armed Separatism in Southeast Asia*, ed. Lim Joo-Jock and Vani S. Singapore: Institute of Southeast Asian Studies, 1984.
Stetler, Russel, ed. *Selected Writings of the Military Art of People's War*. New York: Monthly Review Press, 1970.
Stuart-Fox, Martin. "Tension within the Thai Insurgency". *Australian Outlook* 33, no. 2 (August 1979): 182 – 97.
──────. "Laos: The Vietnamese Connection". In *Southeast Asian Affairs 1980*. Singapore: Institute of Southeast Asian Studies, 1980.
──────. "Laos in China's Anti-Vietnam Strategy". *Asia Pacific Community*, no. 11 (Winter 1982), pp. 83 – 104.
Sukhumbhand Paribatra, M.R. "The H'mongs of Ban Vinai; A Future Factor in Thailand's Security Equation?" *ISIS Bulletin* 1, no. 1 (Faculty of Political Science, Chulalongkorn University, Bangkok, July 1982): 3 – 9.
Schwabb, Robert W., III. "America's Golden Triangle". *Journal of*

Contemporary Asia 8, no. 4 (1979): 584–94.
Tanham, George K. *Communist Revolutionary Warfare: The Vietminh in Indochina*. New York: Praeger, 1961.
Taylor, Robert H. "Burma's National Unity Problem and the 1974 Constitution". *Contemporary Southeast Asia* 1, no. 3 (Singapore, December 1979).
———. "Perceptions of Ethnicity in the Politics of Burma". *Southeast Asian Journal of Social Science* (Singapore), 10 January 1982.
Thakin Ba Thein Tin, Chairman. "The Entire Party! Unite and March to Achieve Victory". Political Report of the Politburo of the Central Committee of the Burma Communist Party. Submitted to the Central Committee Meeting, November 1981. Text broadcast by the Voice of the People of Burma (VOPB), 27 November 1979 to 29 January 1980 and monitored by the Foreign Broadcast Information Service (FBIS).
Thompson, Robert. *Defeating Communist Insurgency: Experiences from Malaya and Vietnam*. London: Chatto and Windos, 1966.
Tilley, C., ed. *The Formation of Nation States in Western Europe*. New Jersey: Princeton University Press, 1975.
Tilman, Robert O., ed. *Man, State and Society in Contemporary Southeast Asia*. London: Pall Mall Press, 1969.
Trager, Frank N. ed. *Marxism in Southeast Asia: A Study of Four Countries*. Stanford: Stanford University Press, 1965.
Trager, Frank N., comp. *Burma: A Selected and Annotated Bibliography*. New Haven: Human Relations Area Files Press, 1973.
Tyson, Geoffrey. *Forgotten Frontier*. Calcutta: W.H. Target & Co., 1945.
U.S. Army Special Warfare School. *The Montagnard Tribal Groups of the Republic of South Vietnam*. Fort Bragg, North Carolina, 1964.
Van der Kroef, Justus M. "Communism in Burma: Its Development and Prospects". In *Issues and Studies*. Taipei: Institute of International Relations, March 1979.
———. *Communism in South-East Asia*. London: Macmillan, 1981.
Van der Meer, Cornelis Lodewijk Johannes. *Rural Development in Northern Thailand: An Interpretation and Analysis*. Groningen: Rijsuniversiteit te Groningen, 1981.
Van Dyke, Jon M. *North Vietnam's Strategy for Survival*. Palo Alto, California: Pacific Books, 1972.
Viet Chung. "National Minorities and National Policy in the DRV". In *Mountain Regions and National Minorities in the D.R. of Vietnam*, Vietnamese Studies no. 15. Hanoi, 1968.
Vo Nguyen Giap. *Selected Writings of the Military Art of People's War*,

ed. Russel Stetler. New York: Monthly Review Press, 1970.
Vo Nguyen Giap and Van Tien Dung. *How We Won the War*. Ypsilanti, Mich.: Recon Publications, 1977.
Von der Mehden, Fred R. "The Growth and Development of the Religio-Nationalist Movement". In *Southeast Asia: The Politics of National Integration*, ed. John T. McAlister, Jr. New York: Random House, 1973.
Walker, Anthony R. "Highlanders and Government in Northern Thailand". *Folk* 21-22 (Copenhagen, 1979/80).
_____. "The Lahu of the Yunnan-Indochina Borderlands: Ethnic Groups and Village Community". D. Phil. thesis, Oxford University, 1972.
_____. "The Production and Use of Opium in the Northern Thai Uplands: An Introduction". *Contemporary Southeast Asia* 2, no. 2 (September 1980).
_____. "In Mountain and Ulu: A Comparative History of the Development Strategies for Ethnic Minority People in Thailand and Malaysia". *Contemporary Southeast Asia* 4, no. 4 (1983).
Wang Gungwu et al., eds. *Southeast Asian Studies in China: A Report*. Research School of Pacific Studies, Australian National University, 1981.
_____. "China-Vietnam: Nostalgia for, Rejection of, the Past". In *Vietnam-Kampuchea-China Conflicts: Motivations, Background Signifance*, ed. Malcolm Salmon. ANU Working Paper no. 1. Canberra: March 1979.
Watson, Burton. *Records of the Grand Historian of China translated from the Shih chi of Ssu-ma Ch'ien*. Vol. 1. Introduction to Vol. 1. New York: Columbia University Press, 1961.
Weatherbee, Donald. "The Indigenisation of ASEAN Communist Parties". In typescript.
_____. "The USSR-PRC-DRV Triangle in Southeast Asia". In *Strategies, Alliances and Military Power: Changing Roles*. Studies in U.S. National Security no. 1. Leyden: A.W. Sijthoff for the U.S Army War College, 1977.
Wekkin, Gary D. "Tribal Politics in Indochina: The Role of Highland Tribes in the Internationalization of Internal Wars". In *Conflict and Stability in Southeast Asia*, ed. Mark W. Zacher and R. Stephen Milne. N.Y.: Anchor Books, 1974.
Whittlesey, Derwent. *The Earth and the State*. New York: Henry Holt & Co., 1939.
Wiant, Jon A. "Burma: Loosening Up the Tiger's Trail". *Asian Survey* 13 (February 1973): 179-86.

_____. "Insurgency in the Shan State". In *Armed Separatism in Southeast Asia*, ed. Lim Joo-Jock and Vani S. Singapore: Institute of Southeast Asian Studies, 1984.
Wiant, Jon A. and Charles B. Smith. "Burma". In *Yearbook on International Communist Affairs 1981*. Stanford: The Hoover Institution, 1981.
Wiens, Herold J. *China's March Toward the Tropics*. Hamden, Conn.: Shoe String Press, 1954.
Woodman, Dorothy. *The Making of Burma*. London: Cresset Press, 1962.
Yahuda, Michael. *Towards the End of Isolationism: China's Foreign Policy After Mao*. London: Macmillan, 1983.
Yegar, M. "The Panthay (Chinese Muslims) of Burma and Yunnan". *Journal of South-East Asian History* 7, no. 1 (March 1966): 73–85.
Young, Gordon. "The Haw". In *The Hill Tribes of Northern Thailand*. Bangkok: The Siam Society, 1966.
Zasloff, Joseph J. *The Pathet Lao: Leadership and Organization*. Lexington. Mass.: Lexington Books, 1973.
Zasloff, Joseph J. and MacAlister Brown. "Laos: Coping with Confinement". In *Southeast Asian Affairs 1982*. Singapore: Institute of Southeast Asian Studies, 1982.
_____. *Communist Indochina and U.S. Foreign Policy: Postwar Realities*. Boulder, Colorado: Westview Press, 1978.
Zacher, Mark W. and R. Stephen Milne, eds. *Conflict and Stability in Southeast Asia*. New York: Anchor Books, 1974.

Index

administration, as route to power, 101-102
Ai Lao Dinh, 24
Akha, 25, 94
Annamese, fear of highlands, 24
anti-Chinese riots, 132
Arakan, 29
Asal, 13
ASEAN, 195-196, 197, 205
Asian Highway, 178
Assam, 5, 18, 25. 153
Assam, secessionist tendency, 135
autonomous regions, PRC policy towards, 158-164; as strategic elements, 163-164; pattern of, in China, 159-160, 161-162; transfer of resources to, 161-162

Bamboo, 154
Battle of Route Coloniale Four, 10-11
Boundaries and national integration, 78-81
Boundaries and protective distance, 68
Boundaries and smuggling, 63-64
Boundaries and unequal treaties, 57-58
Boundaries and warfare, 60-61
Boundaries, "Asian" traditional concept of, 69-73, 75, 209

Boundaries, colonial practice, 67-68
Boundaries, control and stability, 74
Boundaries, European ideals, 72, 73, 75-76
Boundaries, function of 51-52
Boundaries, symbolism of, 82, 174
Boundaries, Sino-Vietnamese, 53-54, 55-57, 58-60; Indo-Burmese, 54, 61; Laotian-Burmese, 61; Sino-Burmese, 54; Sino-Laotian, 61; Thai-Burmese 54, 62; Vietnam-Laos, 62, 70
British Indian Civil Service, 101
British Land Settlement Reports, 101
British Revenue Reports, 101
Buddhism, 32-33
Burma Communist Party, 109, 132-133
Burma Road, 12, 163
Burma, neutrality of, 174-175, 178
Burman nationalism, 27-33
Burmese Army, 178

Cambodia, post-1975 military situation, 190-194

Cambodia, Vietnamese migration into, 192
caravan trade, 63, 64
Central Highlands of Vietnam, 15-16
Chettiars, 30
Chiengmai, vii, 94
Chin, 1, 25, 29, 31
China, as montane power, 47
China, pressure against Vietnam, 199-203
Chinese agricultural settlement, 39
Chinese attitudes to minorities, 35-37
Chinese civilization, 35-36
Chinese highland settlement, 37-40
Chinese imperial strategic priorities, 77
Chinese military settlement, 157
Chinese Shan States, 161
Chinese strategic thinking, 199
Chinese traders, 27
Chinese, squatters in Malaya, 14
Christians, 29
Chuang see Xhuang
coalition defence, 203
coercive power, 169-171, 179-180, 197, 211
coercive power and military force, 171
COMECON, 149
Communist Party of Thailand, 127-129
concentric peripherality, concept of, 76-77
Confucius, 3
core domains, expansion of, 116
core domains and strategy, 111-112, 121, 173
core power domain, definition of, 106-108
core power domain, quality of, 117-118

Deo Van Long, 18
development, 124-127
Dienbienphu, 3, 42, 182
dual track diplomacy, 132

Ethnic equality in Laos, 34-35
Ethnic military recruitment by British, 31; by Japanese, 31
Ethnic reliability, 89-90

Federated Shan States Council, 30
Forest replacement, 125-127
Frontier administration, 92

Gallieni, ethnic policy of, 18-19
geo-power, concept of, 184-185, 186, 214
geo-strategic orientation, China, 95
geo-strategic orientation, conception of, 92-95
geo-strategic orientation, Indonesia, 94
geo-strategic orientation, Japan, 94-95
geo-strategic orientation, Thailand, 93-94
geo-strategic region, 208
geo-strategy, definition of, xi
Golden Triangle, 144-145
grasslands as economic resource, 154-155
Great Wall of China, 105-106
green manure, 155
Guangxi, 1, 160, 176, 196
Guangxi, strategic value of, 196-197
Guizhou, 1, 6
Guomindang, 6, 7, 19, 71
Gurkha, 2

H'mong, 6, 11, 12, 18, 25, 27, 36, 37, 75, 94, 127, 128, 182
H'mong in the Vietminh War, 12
Hainan, 17, 151, 197
Hakka, vii, 152
Haw, 37-38
heroin, 143-144, 145
highland economy, products of, 150-153
highland resources, perceptions of, 148-149
highland resources, value to PRC, 152-153

highland resources, value to Vietnam, 153-154
highland utilization, 155-157
highlanders, as source of labour, 11-12, 17
highlanders' avoidance of authorities, 69
highlands, as compared to sea, 173
highlands, as source of power, 168-169, 171-175
highlands, Vietnamese migration into, 156-157, 159
Ho Chi Minh, 10
Ho Chi Minh Trail, 62

intermarriage, 35-36
intermontane basins, 41-42
intermontane basins, in Yunnan, 152

Kachin, 23, 25, 26, 29, 31, 42, 91, 161
Kachin resistance to British, 91
Kachin State, 23
Karen, 1, 23, 29, 31, 64, 93, 128
Kautilya, 77, 168
"Kha", 33, 34
Khmer Resistance, 188-194
Khmer Rouge, 8, 9, 188-191, 195
Khun Sa, 144, 146
Kinh, 35, 156, 157, 192
Kipling, Rudyard, xii
Kuomintang see Guomindang
Kwangsi see Guangxi
Kweichow see Guizhou

Ladai Garh, 104-106
Lahu, 27-28, 94, 161
landlocked mountain states, 45-46
Lao, 23
Lao Thong, 33-34
Lao Thong, as slaves, 34
Lao Thong, hatred of lowland Lao, 34
Laos, ethnic policy of, 34, 35
Laos, roads from Vietnam to, 182, 194-195
Ledo Road, 12
Li, 17

"liberated areas", 112-114
limited war, hostile action, 183-184
limited war, 179
Lisu, 94
Liu Bocheng, 6, 162
Luoluo, 6
livestock rearing, 154-155
Long March, 5-8

Machiavelli, 4
Malayan Communist Party, 12-15
Mao Tsetung see Mao Zedong
Mao Zedong, 5, 8, 213
maritime power, 206
maritime strategy, 204
McMahon Line, 58
medicinal plants, 152-153
Meo, see H'mong
Miao, see H'mong
military assistance, 178
military expenditure, 133
minority autonomy, role of Han population in, 160
minority autonomy, 158-164
minority, diversities, 24-25
minority, languages, 158
minority, languages, Chinese attitude to, 162
minority, languages, Vietnamese attitude to, 162
Montagnard, 16
morphine, 143-145
mountains, no barrier to movement, 64
mulberry, 153

Naga, 5, 19, 46, 64, 108
Nagas, defects of resistance, 19-20
Nanchao, vii, 70
nation building, 98, 109
nation state, 78, 80, 82, 109, 110, 112, 121
Ne Win, 134
Neo Lao Haksat, 34, 35
Nung, 11, 19, 37, 159

opium, 141-148, 164
opium and COMECON, 149

Index

opium and ethnic suppression, 150-151
opium and instability, 147-148
opium and the BCP, 145-146
opium in the PRC, 149
opium in Vietnam, 149
opium, as source of power, 145-146
opium, cash returns to growers, 144-145
opium, defiance of authority, 143
opium, high value of, 143
opium, method of cultivation, 141-142
opium, suitability to highland economy, 142-143
opium, transportation of, 142

Pathet Lao, 9, 180, 202
People's Liberation Army, 71, 196, 198
People's Liberation Army, awareness of people's war, 194
peripheral domains and strategies, 111-112, 210
peripheral domains, definition of, 106-109, 111-112
Phizo, A.Z., 46
Plain of Jars, 62
Pol Pot, 9
"political isobars", 103
power domains and nation states, 109-110
power domains and Ratzel's theory, 115-116
power domains, concept of, 87-88
power domains, 102-103
power isobars, 103-104, 210, 211
power permeation, 210
PRC, Constitution of, 159
primordialism, 80

Red Army, 5-7
"reliable rear areas", 212-213
"reward" power, 169-171, 174, 179
rubber growing, 151-152

"Sakai", see Asal
"Security map", 89
Sedang, 16-17
Senoi, aiding MCP, 12-15
sericulture, 153
Shan, 1, 6, 26, 29, 31, 42, 46
Shans in hypothetical independent state, 46
Sichuan, 1, 2, 7
Sihanouk, 8, 71
Singapore, 178
Sinicization, 36, 37
small unit operations, 177
smuggling, 63, 64
South China Sea, 211-212
Southeast Asia, regionality questioned, 208-214
"spreading oil patch", 113-114
squatters, 14
Strategic Hamlets, 114
"Strategy of Persuasion", 180-181
swiddening, 125-126, 140-141
Szechuan see Sichuan

Tai, 11, 18, 23, 36, 39, 93, 161, 182
tax collection, 101-102, 108-109
Tay see Tho
Tay Bac, autonomous region, 158
tea, 153
terrain, in military thought, 4-5
terrain, in relation to power, 3
territorial diplomacy, 71-73, 77, 82
territoriality, concept of, 95-98, 209
territory, in relation to power, 85-90
territory, size not indication of power, 185
Tho, 10, 11, 159, 162
Tho, and the Vietminh, 9-11
Three Kingdoms, unification of, 3
Tibet, 2, 7
topography in relation to war, 2-3

U.S. Army, 4, 15
U.S. Navy, 204

Viet Bac, autonomous region, 158
Vietnam, Chinese punitive campaign against, 196-197
Vietnam, Constitution of, 159
Vietnam, destabilization of highlands, 199-203
Vietnam, North, as food deficit area, 189
Vietnamese, as "indigenous Southeast Asians", 204
Vietnamese, Cambodian attitude to, 189-190
Vietnamese population movement, 156-157, 159

Vo Nguyen Giap, 62, 162

Wa, 131, 132, 161

Xhuang, 24, 42, 158, 160
Xhuang, autonomous region, 15, 160
Xishuangpanna, 23-24, 161

Yao, 11, 28, 36, 94, 162
Yunnan, 1, 6, 24, 152, 160, 162, 196, 202
Yunnan, strategic value of, 196-212
Yunnanese dialect, 26-27

Zhou Enlai, 212-213

The Author

LIM JOO-JOCK is Senior Fellow at the Institute of Southeast Asian Studies, Singapore, where among other duties, he is editor of *Contemporary Southeast Asia*, a quarterly, and *Southeast Asian Affairs*, an annual review. His main research interest is strategic studies, particularly in the uses of the concepts of spatial analysis to further the understanding of strategic issues.

This book deals with the topic of Southeast Asia in relation to its large northern neighbour, China. Instead of treating this relationship on a state-to-state basis, it studies the power relationships existing between mainland Southeast Asia and China from the perspective of what is seen as a focal geo-strategic region which lies astride the boundaries of China and the states to its south. Although the basis of interpretation is largely spatial, the analysis is to a considerable extent also inter-disciplinary. In doing this, the conceptual tools of *power isobars* and *territorial power domains* are enunciated and applied to gain insights into the power configurations existing in the region.

How valid is the current definition of "Southeast Asia" as a region in strategic analysis? Where are the actual limits of Southeast Asia? Can power be measured in terms of territorial size?; or conversely what is the linkage between national power and territorial size? What are the strategic implications of two sacrosanct ideals brought into the region by the Western powers in the course of their colonial advance — namely, territorial sovereignty as expressed in immutable boundary lines and the Western-style nation-state? This book seeks to answer these questions, among others. For example, it also examines the strategic implications of policies designed to contain the influence of the People's Republic of China.

In the conclusion, attention is drawn to the relevance of the regional strategic environment to a debate, discernible in the early 1980s, on the relative merits of coastal coalition defence and a purely maritime strategy as seen in the context of global superpower rivalries.

INSTITUTE OF SOUTHEAST ASIAN STUDIES
Heng Mui Keng Terrace
Pasir Panjang
Singapore 0511

ISBN 9971-902-89-3

RAYMOND H. FOGLER LIBRARY
DATE DUE

BOOKS ARE SUBJECT TO RECALL AFTER TWO WEEKS